RETHINKING LEARNING IN AN AGE OF DIGITAL FLUENCY

Digital connectivity is a phenomenon of the twenty-first century and while many have debated its impact on society, few have researched the relationship between the changes taking place and the actual impact on learning. *Rethinking Learning in an Age of Digital Fluency* examines what kind of impact an increasingly connected environment is having on learning and what kind of culture it is creating within learning settings.

Engaging with digital media and navigating through digital spaces are things that many young people appear to do with ease, although the tangible benefits of these activities are unclear. This book, therefore, will present an overview of current research and practice in the area of digital tethering, whilst examining how it could be used to harness new learning and engagement practices that are fit for the modern age. The book also addresses such questions as:

- Is being digitally tethered a new learning nexus?
- Are social networking sites spaces for co-production of knowledge and spaces of inclusive learning?
- Are students who are digitally tethered creating new learning maps and pedagogies?
- Does digital tethering enable students to use digital media to create new learning spaces?

This fascinating and at times controversial text engages with numerous aspects of digital learning amongst undergraduate students, including mobile learning, individual and collaborative learning, viral networking, self-publication and identity dissemination. It will be of enormous interest to researchers and students in education and educational psychology.

Maggi Savin-Baden is Professor of Education, University of Worcester, UK. She has researched and evaluated staff and student experience of learning in higher education for over 20 years.

Current Debates in Educational Psychology
Series editor: Kieron Sheehy

Rethinking Learning in an Age of Digital Fluency:
Is being digitally tethered a new learning nexus?
Maggi Savin-Baden

RETHINKING LEARNING IN AN AGE OF DIGITAL FLUENCY

Is being digitally tethered a new learning nexus?

Maggi Savin-Baden

Routledge
Taylor & Francis Group

LONDON AND NEW YORK

First published 2015
by Routledge
2 Park Square, Milton Park, Abingdon, Oxon OX14 4RN

and by Routledge
711 Third Avenue, New York, NY 10017

Routledge is an imprint of the Taylor & Francis Group, an informa business

© 2015 Maggi Savin-Baden

British Library Cataloguing in Publication Data
A catalogue record for this book is available from the British Library

Library of Congress Cataloging in Publication Data
Savin-Baden, Maggi, 1960–
    Rethinking learning in an age of digital fluency : is being digitally tethered a new learning nexus? / Maggi Savin-Baden.
        pages cm
    Includes bibliographical references and index.
    1. Education—Effect of technological innovations on.   2. Educational technology.   3. Educational innovations.   4. Information society.
    5. Educational psychology.   I. Title.
    LB1028.3.S298 2015
    371.33—dc23   2014037589

ISBN: 978-0-415-73817-0 (hbk)
ISBN: 978-0-415-73818-7 (pbk)
ISBN: 978-1-315-71891-0 (ebk)

Typeset in Bembo
by Keystroke, Station Road, Codsall, Wolverhampton

Printed and bound in Great Britain by
TJ International Ltd, Padstow, Cornwall

For my brilliant, bright and beautiful daughter Anna, whose digital tethering inspired both the title and the idea for this book

CONTENTS

Acknowledgements   *ix*

Introduction   1

  1 Useful tethering?   5

  2 The landscape of learning   16

  3 Piracy and pedagogies   32

  4 Learning on the move? Liquidity and meshwork   45

  5 Being digitally tethered   62

  6 Learning together alone   76

  7 Digital fluency   90

  8 Tethered identities?   103

  9 Digital surveillance and tethered integrity   115

 10 Wizards and brinkmanship   130

Glossary   *140*
References   *147*
Index   *167*

ACKNOWLEDGEMENTS

This book has been a challenge to create in these liquid times of moving technologies. I am grateful to colleagues and family for keeping me up to date and informed and to the initial reviewers of the proposal, including Ron Barnett and Kieron Sheehy, who were so positive about it as a project.

Particular thanks are due to Hamish MacLeod, Kieron Sheehy, Christine Sinclair and Gemma Tombs for being critical readers of this text who have pointed out areas for development whilst being very affirming.

Finally, thanks are due to my family: John Savin-Baden for being a sounding board, critic and proofreader all in one, as well as a great supporter of my triathlon endeavours; and Anna and Zak, my 'cool', 'sick' teenagers who assure me I am neither but remain willing to keep me up to date, and therefore necessarily ensure I am slightly less boring.

INTRODUCTION

This book emerged from my reflections whilst taking some time to think and read during a short sabbatical in New England in the fall of 2013. My time visiting interesting colleagues at the Massachusetts Institute of Technology and Harvard was punctuated by reading a range of literature in an attempt to re-energize my creative spirit. Despite periods of frustration and stuckness, of living with liminality and being unable to write the books and articles I desired, I also experienced irritation from reading negative perspectives about the relative value and impact of digital media on young people. The difficulty, it seemed to me, was that there was a lot of pontificating based on relatively little evidence. Whilst this is not entirely still the case, there remains confusion and a number of unjustified and strongly argued positions. Further, much of the currently referenced work (and probably still the most up to date) was based on research conducted in 2008 (e.g. Crook, 2008; Ito et al., 2010), but now, in 2015, it would appear things have moved on considerably. This text therefore reviews a diverse range of studies and opinions and seeks to shed light on a broader range of issues than those covered in other texts.

Digital tethering is defined here as the constant interaction and engagement with digital technology, the sense of being 'always on', 'always engaged', characterized by wearing a mobile device, texting at dinner, or driving illegally while 'Facebooking'. The argument of the text centres on the idea that while digital tethering might be challenging and troublesome, it might also be resulting in a different kind of networked society, and education systems that are creating new genres of learning and participation which are of value for staff, students, policy-makers and wider society. As yet, this still remains unrecognized. This book seeks to examine what kinds of impact an increasingly connected environment is having on learning and what kinds of cultures this is creating within learning settings.

Central to the idea of digital tethering is the recognition that online lives are extensions of offline lives. Some of the questions this book will seek to explore are:

- To what extent is being digitally tethered creating a new learning nexus?
- How and to what degree are social networking sites becoming spaces for coproduction of knowledge and spaces of inclusive learning?
- Are students who are digitally tethered creating new learning maps and pedagogies and hence becoming 'cartographers on tour' (Lammes, 2008)?
- To what extent is digital tethering enabling students to use digital media to create new learning spaces?

Thus, the book aims to explore the impact of digital tethering on learning in education and illustrate its benefits and distractions on student engagement. It also delineates strategies for managing digital tethering in ways which will enhance digital learning and digital fluency across the education sector. It will be argued that digital tethering is a phenomenon of the twenty-first century, and while many have debated its impact on society, few have researched its impact on learning. It will present an overview of current research and practice in this area thus far (e.g. Turkle, 2010; Ito et al., 2010; Buckingham, 2007).

The idea of exploring digital tethering in this text is to move beyond an exploration of what people are *doing*, and with whatever technology, in the realm of digital media, and instead examine what they are *learning*, where they are learning and from whom they are learning. To date, the focus has tended to be on what is being used rather than what is being learned, with relatively little acknowledgement that digital tethering could be harnessing new learning and engagement practices that are fit for the age of digital fluency (following Crook, 2012).

The book is divided into ten chapters which address various questions and issues. Chapter 1 explores how digital tethering could be seen as harnessing new learning and engagement practices that are fit for the age of digital fluency. It begins by setting out the argument of the book as a whole, and then presents different types of digital tethering, before examining contexts in which digital tethering is currently in evidence.

Chapter 2 begins by exploring digital tethering as something that offers choice, development and opportunities for becoming in the context of a behavioural learning culture. It argues for the need to shift away from the current (and even possible future) rhetoric about flexible pedagogies, student satisfaction and engagement and instead move towards new spaces where students' choices and responses are recognized as being central to the way learning is configured and structured. Digital tethering, it is suggested, is creating 'new spaces of response' and prompting pedagogies of the imagination.

Chapter 3 begins by reflecting on what are deemed or presented as pedagogies and examines the validity of the argument that these actually are pedagogies, rather than theories or methods. The chapter then advocates some reconceptualization of higher education, suggesting a need to revisit its purposes and values in the digital age. Finally, it presents a range of media that are being adopted and developed in higher education, but offers a critique of current practices, proposing that some are new whilst others are in fact reconfigurations of older methods and technologies adapted for the twenty-first century that may not have a sound fit.

Chapter 4 examines expanding theories surrounding new mobilities and geographies, proposing that we should be concerned not only with an exploration of polarities such as home/school and formal/informal learning, but also about the kinds of learning trajectories that digital tethering is prompting. Analysis is needed to determine whether this makes learning more or less effective than, or just different from, current practices, and whether it is different across diverse disciplinary contexts. This chapter will therefore explore learning and engagement and examine how universities could be more open, accessible and engaging.

Chapter 5 examines how students share learning, essays, learning resources and techniques, and how they learn both in collaborative learning spaces and across large, proliferating networks. Furthermore, this chapter will analyse the extent to which digital tethering is liminal in nature, since students seem to be working at the border of the real and the augmented, and across diverse digital media, with high degrees of fluency: they sift, shift, research, explore, critique, learn and question, moving through these spatial zones and landscapes with an ease that seems to deny complexity or troublesomeness. It would appear, then, that making digital tethering practice explicit is likely, at one level, to unsettle staff perspectives about when and where learning occurs (and with whom).

Chapter 6 explores what it means to learn in an age of digital fluency. It analyses a range of pedagogies and draws on earlier thinking in the area to examine current practices and suggest future pedagogies. This chapter also explores the contradictions in the presence and use of social media in the classroom, in terms of about when and how it is acceptable to use digital technology. These contradictions arise from the mixed messages circulating in the classroom, at home and in society in general about the usefulness of technology.

Chapter 7 presents the concept of digital fluency and explores its emergence as an idea and a way of viewing current practices. It also explores digital fluency in relation to other relatively recent concepts, such as digital literacy and electracy. The second section of the chapter argues that in the context of digital fluency, a new view of digital literacy is needed, which takes into account wider concerns and moves away from a focus on gaining and developing particular predefined skills. Instead, it is suggested that digital fluency needs to incorporate a wide array of practices, such as lifewide learning, moving knowledge, disruptive media learning and vectors of transformation. The new forms of digital fluency are defined and exemples are provided.

In the final chapters of the book, more recent developments are considered. In Chapter 8, tethered identities are examined from a number of angles, beginning with a short overview of earlier perceptions of identity and then analysing the notion of friendship identities. It then explores the impact of context collapse on identities and suggests that this has resulted in many of us becoming what Lammes

(2008) calls 'cartographers on tour'. The second part of the chapter examines some of the darker concerns around identity – such as security, secrets and suspicion – whilst the final section suggests that our tethered identities bear some relationships with Plato's metaxis and the notion of in-between-ness.

Chapter 9 examines the way in which surveillance and privacy are affected in online spaces, and analyses the research findings to date. It suggests that the concepts and practices associated with privacy have become increasingly complex and remain areas that many users of social networking sites still find troublesome. Furthermore, it introduces some questions about the ethics that need to be considered in relation to being digitally tethered. The chapter argues that, rather than focusing solely on surveillance, privacy and disclosure, it is perhaps more helpful to engage with the possibilities for creating and sustaining some forms of tethered integrity in order to cope with the shifts and changes that are occurring continually across cyberspace.

Finally, Chapter 10 identifies the levels of brinkmanship that occur across higher education and examines some of the worries, ideas, suggestions and agendas that are being promoted. It suggests that play and performativity, as well as improvisation, have rather been lost and that these need to be regained, whilst also proposing the idea of a university that has been mislaid. In the context of such losses and the marketization of learning, it is argued that it is perhaps the case that students have not lost their way; rather, that they have become capable users of digital technologies who are able to engage with the wider debates about power and politics.

Conclusion

The use of technology is already a culturally embedded practice, even if its impact on learning is not entirely understood. For example, there is a sense that participatory culture characterized by the use of Facebook and YouTube prompts or encourages the democratization of media production, bringing with it the suggestion that young people are not only central to the digital age but key players in its formulation and (re)creation. It seems important to understand how students live and learn across the many digital media available to them, what is new, changed or changing about how they live and learn today, and what evidence there is for these shifts.

1

USEFUL TETHERING?

Introduction

This book aims to explore the impact of digital tethering on learning in education, illustrate its benefits and distractions on student engagement, and delineate strategies for managing it to enhance digital learning and digital fluency across the education sector. It will be argued that digital connectivity is a phenomenon of the twenty-first century, and while many have debated its impact on society, few have researched its impact on learning. It will present an overview of current research and practice in this area thus far.

This chapter will begin by setting out the argument of the book as a whole, present different types of digital tethering and then examine contexts in which digital tethering is currently in evidence.

Digital tethering

This is defined as both a way of being and a set of practices that are associated with it. Being digitally tethered is generally associated with carrying, wearing or holding a device that enables one to be constantly and continually in touch with digital media of whatever kind. Practices associated with digital tethering include being 'always on', 'always engaged', texting at dinner, or driving illegally while 'Facebooking'.

It remains unclear as to whether digital tethering and (too much) digital influence are resulting in learning and engagement imbalances. Students might be spending too much time in virtual spaces or distracting each other via messaging in lectures. Alternatively, young people might be over-influenced by virtual realties and immersive virtual worlds. The difficulty with all of these concerns and interesting virtual spaces is that we are largely unsure of their impact: we do not know whether too much fuss is being made about them or whether digital media really are affecting students' engagement, learning and concentration. This chapter will explore how digital tethering could be seen as harnessing new learning and engagement practices that are fit for an age of digital fluency.

The argument . . .

With the increasing use of technology across home, work and school, most of us are digitally tethered. Across the media there has been considerable criticism about schoolchildren's use of mobile devices, along with anecdotes across education about students being continually distracted by technology. Nevertheless, it is unclear if this is all unnecessary worry and media hype, or if the notion of technological determinism really does have some currency. Thus, there are questions to be asked about the value and impact of digital tethering, and it is vital that university staff consider these issues.

There are still many university staff and schoolteachers who are concerned about technological determinism: the idea that those who have grown up in the digital age are necessarily different from their predecessors and that their persistent 'connectivity' is damaging them. Buckingham argues:

> From this perspective, technology is seen to emerge from a neutral process of scientific research and development rather than from the interplay of complex social, economic and political forces. Technology is then seen to have effects – to bring about social and psychological changes – irrespective of the way it is used, and of the social contexts and processes into which it enters ... [T]he computer is seen as an autonomous force that is somehow independent of human society, and acts upon it from outside.
>
> *(Buckingham, 2007: 17–18)*

Although there continue to be debates and discussion, more recent research suggests that young people (ages twelve to eighteen) and university students are aware of the impact and the dangers (as well as the value) of technology in their lives. Perhaps instead there needs to be an appreciation of 'useful tethering': tethering that can be harnessed for learning and engagement. This in turn will mean that staff will become new pedagogical designers who are 'wizards of brinkmanship' (Turkle, 2005: 21), creating and managing liquid and complex curricula for the twenty-first century.

Digital tethering would seem to offer students choices about how they use information, how they share it with others (or not), whether they learn together or apart, and how they support each other in ways that current classroom practices often prevent or discourage. Nevertheless, there is still negativity about digital tethering, despite research that defies this. This book argues that:

1. As yet, there is little research which enables us to understand the impact of being tethered both to technology and to people, educationally or sociologically.

2. Many of the opinions and arguments presented to date are unnecessarily negative and fail to examine the positive effects of being digitally tethered.

3. Although research has been undertaken into the impact of multitasking (including being interrupted by texting), it is unclear what kind of impact, if any, digital tethering is having on formal and informal learning.

4. There is little research or understanding about the extent to which capabilities developed through digital tethering are transferred to or have an impact on formal learning settings.

5. There is an absence of educational policy or institutional positioning about the value (or not) and impact of digital tethering.

6. There is little recognition that what young people do with digital media (text, audio, video and graphics that are electronically transmitted over the internet or computer networks) and digital knowledge (an informed understanding of the power and impact of digital media) will have a considerable impact on work, society and lifewide learning.

7. As yet, it is unclear why some young people are highly tethered whilst others are not tethered at all.

8. It is unclear whether digital tethering is a problem, or whether it just allows for different forms of interrogation: students choose which games to play and decide if the media, such as apps, are any good.

The story so far

Engaging with digital media and slipping through digital spaces with ease are things that many (young) people appear to do well, although the benefits of such proficiency are unclear. Using mobile phones for communication, searching and catching up with missed programmes or popular YouTube clips is commonplace, and Eynon (2009) has reported that 82 per cent of learners in the UK live in internet-connected homes (rising to 84 per cent in 2014).

Despite the widespread use of digital media, there remains a strong determinist stance that has been promoted and popularized by Prensky (2001) and affirmed further by Tapscott (2008), whereby it is argued that those who have grown up in a digital age are necessarily different and that 'connectivity' is damaging to students. Similarly, Turkle (2005: 14) has argued: 'The dramatic changes in computer education over the past decades leave us with serious questions about how we can teach our children to interrogate simulations in much the same spirit. The specific questions may be different, but the intent needs to be the same: to develop habits of readership appropriate to a culture of simulation.' Her argument remained much the same in 2011 (Turkle, 2011a, 2011b). Despite these opinions, Rideout et al. (2010) have found that engagement with digital media has increased significantly across *all* groups and that highly educated households are beginning to engage more heavily with 'popular' media. However, their findings also indicate that:

> The jump in media use that occurs when young people hit the 11- to 14-year-old age group is tremendous – an increase of more than three hours a day in time spent with media (total media use), and an increase of four hours a day in total media exposure ... Differences in media use in relation to race and ethnicity are even more pronounced, and they hold up after controlling for other demographic factors such as age, parent education, or whether the child is from a single- or two-parent family. For example, Hispanic and Black youth average about 13 hours of media exposure daily (13:00 for Hispanics and 12:59 for Blacks), compared to just over 8½ hours (8:36) among Whites.
>
> *(Rideout et al., 2010: 5)*

Furthermore, Ito et al. (2013) argue that the current literature suggests that young people who have sound learning support at home and are educationally privileged are the ones gaining the most from digital media in relation to career achievement and academic success. According to the EU Kids online study (Livingstone and Haddon, 2009), young people climb a relatively predictable 'ladder of opportunity' in terms of digital media use. Sefton-Green (2013) generated Figure 1.1 to provide a visual representation of these findings.

In terms of this ladder of opportunity, the work by Ito et al. (2010) suggests that young people require appropriate support in order to translate media engagements into academically oriented activities. It is also evident that there are class and race differences that have changed little over the past ten years. For example, Clark and Alters (2004) found that middle-class families believed that limiting access to television was a marker of good parenting. More recent surveys indicate that in lower-income households of African Americans and Latinos, children watch more television and play more video games than their middle-class, white and Asian counterparts (Rideout et al., 2010; Ferguson, 2006). Further, debates around young people's use of digital technology have been likened to academic 'moral panic', with the suggestion that those in opposition are out of touch (Bennett et al., 2008). What still seems to be occurring is an unhelpful dualism, promoted by experts and in the media, in the sense that managed and ordered technology is somehow good, while messy, unmediated, chaotic and liquid technology is bad. Nevertheless, it remains unclear what kind of impact an increasingly connected environment is having on learning, and what kinds of cultures this is creating within learning settings. This is because to date the challenges of digital tethering remain troublesome and the research remains disparate and inchoate. Furthermore, few authors have dealt in depth with the complexities of the ways in which students' identities are shifting and changing as digital media become more fluid and the users become more fluent. (This is discussed in detail in Chapter 7.)

Issues need to be explored, such as who is doing the tethering and harnessing and how much coercion is (or is not) involved. It is not clear whether digital tethering really is a problem, or whether it promotes and allows for a different

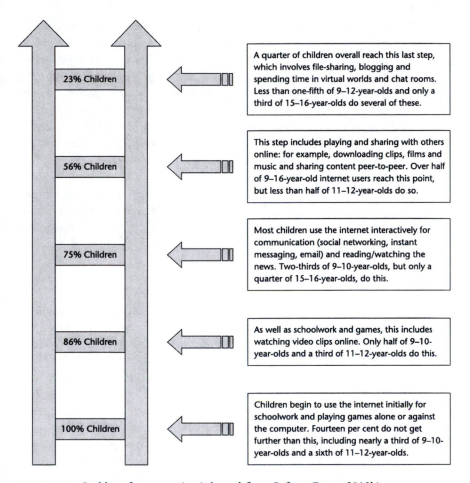

FIGURE 1.1 Ladder of opportunity (adapted from Sefton-Green, 2013b)

form of interrogation: students and young people are highly critical of games, apps and hardware. Perhaps we are dealing with different ways/forms of 'reading' and 'interrogating' that we have not yet come to understand. Questions need to be asked about the value of digital tethering, so that rather than returning to a position of technological determinism, a view of 'useful tethering' needs to be harnessed to support learning and improve engagement. Criticism of digital tethering by such authors as Turkle (2011a) seems to ignore the need for young people to learn through exploration and problem-solving in informal settings. This very 'messing around' seems to be important to the development of autonomy, self-direction and problem-solving in young people, but to date research findings have tended to focus on the time they expend online, rather than examine in depth the lifewide capabilities they are developing. For example:

The Kaiser Family Foundation study found that young Americans spend on average 6.5 hours with media per day: almost 4 hours a day with TV programming or recorded videos, approximately 1.75 hours per day listening to music or the radio, roughly one hour a day using the computer for nonschool purposes, and about 50 minutes a day playing video games (Rideout, Roberts, and Foehr 2005). Pew's 2007 survey found that daily 63 percent of teens go online, 36 percent send text messages, 35 percent talk on a mobile phone, 29 percent send IMs, and 23 percent send messages through social network sites … With respect to gender distinctions, the same Pew survey found that a significantly greater proportion of teenage girls than boys owned mobile phones and communicated daily via text messaging, talking on mobile phones, talking on landlines, sending IMs, and messaging through a social network site (Lenhart et al. 2008). The Kaiser survey found that girls spent significantly more time than boys listening to music and significantly less time than boys playing video games (Rideout, Roberts, and Foehr 2005).

(Ito et al., 2010: 32–33)

It would seem, then, that the challenge of understanding digital tethering and its impact on learning lies in an examination of what is really going on in these hidden spaces and in exploring the cost and value of digital tethering on student learning and engagement.

There has been increasing interest in learner identity and learner engagement over the last twenty years (as will be discussed further in Chapter 8), and Furlong and Davies (2012) argue that young people's engagement with new technologies is fundamentally bound up in their own identity. Identity play and exploration are evident not only through representations on social networking sites but also in the ways in which people accessorize themselves technologically, whether through Apple products, diamond-studded phone cases or personal microchip implants. Digital tethering is linked (or even central) to identity and to the way in which people operate in these diverse digital spaces. Further, Ito et al. (2010: 14–18) argue for the term 'genres of participation' to describe different and often diverse ways of engaging with new media. What they mean is that by shifting the focus away from the individual and towards broader networks of social relationships, it is possible to recognize, study and acknowledge that people learn in all contexts of activity, because they are members of shared cultural systems. Thus genres of participation within new media are delineated as a means of describing and analysing everyday learning and media engagement. What is important is that they make a distinction between friendship-driven and interest-driven genres of participation:

- Friendship-driven genres of participation are seen as those emerging from (largely) age-related friendship groups, so that the media practices within this category emerge from local, face-to-face friendships.
- Interest-driven genres are those that have developed from specific activities and therefore the interest is more important than the friendship.

Whilst this is an interesting distinction, it is perhaps a little dualistic, and it would seem there are other genres that could be usefully included: for example, school-driven, subject-driven or family-driven genres of participation. It is important to recognize that there are several different types of digital tethering, relating to identity, interests, engagement and participation in relation to people's contexts and cultural settings.

Types of digital tethering

Whilst digital tethering is defined broadly as the constant interaction and engagement with digital technology – the sense of being 'always on', 'always engaged' – it is also important to consider the ways in which such tethering manifests itself in diverse ways. Further, it is helpful to make distinctions between students' digital tethering as part of their formal educational process and when they do all manner of other things through digital tethering beyond their narrow role as students. Digital tethering, it may be said, is strongly located in students' lives informally; but now it is finding its way into formal educational settings, too. It is not yet clear to what extent students should be digitally tethered in formal settings, whether this is a distraction, or indeed whether it has any place in such settings at all (with many arguing that it does not).

Tethered to technology

In this type of tethering the focus is on the importance of the *technology* to the individual, the need always to be on, rather than on the necessity of being tethered to other people. Being tethered to technology is characterized by needing to be able to search for information, access websites and emails, and always having access to others who might be able to retrieve information, even if being connected to others is not the central focus of the tethering. Much of the focus here is on the ability to gain knowledge and research information through the media; to be continually tethered to knowledge and evidence. Not being connected often results in a sense of anxiety, a requirement to buy airtime in remote places, moving a phone or computer around to get the best signal, and becoming angry or frustrated about any lack of connection.

Tethered to people

The focus here is on the need always to be connected to *people*; the technology is merely the mechanism that enables that connection. This is usually achieved through social networking sites or messaging systems, such as Kik and Whatsapp. People who are constantly tethered to others engage in: maintaining contact with family and friends; casual entertainment that they watch or share with friends (often on the move); arranging meetings; sharing photos; and accessing web-based information for use within their friendship groups or to find activities that are undertaken with others. However, being tethered to other people is often about more than maintaining friendships and sharing; it also important for the digitally tethered to know what is going on in other people's lives and always to be in touch with them, moment by moment. Not being tethered means not knowing what other people are doing, not being able to share oneself and one's activities, and feeling anxious that something unknown and unshared is occurring. This kind of tethering generates a sense that there is a right to share and a right to know everything about everyone, all the time, which introduces questions about when sharing is appropriate, and when it is inappropriate.

Tethered to both

Being tethered to both means that individuals are constantly, actively participating in distributed social networks, to both invisible and known audiences. This can be through blogs and social networking, often involving keeping in contact and sharing personal information, and through ostentatious knowledge-sharing of information gained through constant tethering to technology. What occurs in these spaces often involves identity exploration and experimentation, so that being tethered to both is about examining how to represent oneself, how best to use knowledge that has been gained, and how to explore which identities work best in diverse online contexts and spaces.

Digital debates

Much of education still tends to organize learning as if it were a hierarchical root system rather than something *rhizomatic* – spreading in all directions with no real hierarchy of importance. In many disciplines learning is still seen as linear and knowledge is perceived largely as the covering of solid content. In the early 1990s there was a shift towards infotainment. With the advent of the web, most learners now learn in ways that are liquid and rhizomatic. Thus, they see learning and evaluating information as a process of *ways of connecting*, between nodes of information and knowledges, on the one hand, and social interactions that occur via links provided through search engines, peers or even parents' links, on the other.

Thurlow (2006, 2007) found that adult debates about young people's use of new communication technologies are consistently negative. Such negative stances indicate the underlying presence of traditional views about how time should be spent – so that reading a book is seen as more valuable than reading a blog – yet tend to overlook the meaningful and creative use of technologies. It might also be that traditional academic practices erode or prevent creative learning practices in young people by failing to acknowledge the playful practices involved in the use of new technologies. For example, young people often use Facebook to create informal study groups to help each other with homework. Thus, despite the current culture of being always on, many schools and universities still control and patrol what counts as acceptable knowledge and websites. For example, young people are told not to use Wikipedia for research and schools block particular websites, even though many young people can access anything they like on their phones or at home.

It would also appear that digital capabilities remain contested and troublesome. 'Digital capabilities' are defined here as the abilities and skills that equip people for learning and working effectively in the digital age. Yet currently in education there is little clarity about what constitutes digital capability and who decides. It therefore seems timely to consider digital tethering and how young people use social media to support/get help with/get through learning and life. Further, the increasing demand for education that is customized to each student's unique needs is driving the development of new technologies that provide more learner choice and control. It has become clear that one-size-fits-all teaching methods are neither effective nor acceptable for today's diverse students; indeed, they never were.

Digital media continues to rise in importance as a key skill in every discipline and profession, but most academics are not using new and compelling technologies for learning and teaching (Johnson et al., 2012). Further, institutional barriers continue to present an array of challenges whenever academics attempt to introduce emerging technologies. Despite this, most young people today learn much (and possibly most) while they are digitally tethered. Central to the idea of digital tethering is a recognition that online lives are extensions of offline lives.

Digital media on the move

The research into digital media to date ranges from studies that have examined texting (Wood et al., 2011a, 2011b) to those that have examined innovations such as Fablab (Blikstein, 2013) and virtual labs (Gustavsson et al., 2011).

Texting is invariably seen as problematic and damaging to children's literacy. However, in 2008, Crystal argued:

> Children could not be good at texting if they had not already developed considerable literacy awareness ... Some people dislike texting. Some are bemused by it. But it is merely the latest manifestation of the human ability to be linguistically creative and to adapt language to suit the demands of diverse settings.
>
> *(Crystal, 2008)*

This opinion was confirmed by Plester et al. (2009). In their study of eighty-eight British 10–12-year-olds, the researchers explored the children's knowledge of 'textisms' and how this related to their school literacy. They found that the ratio of textisms to total words used was positively associated with word reading, vocabulary and phonological awareness measures, and that the children's textism use predicted word-reading ability.

Whilst mobile phone use/texting is largely chosen and controlled by the young people, there are also opportunities for them to learn in supported spaces, such as fablabs. In these their attendance is obviously optional, but studies seem to indicate that learning and exploring in these informal environments is something that young people value. A fablab is a low-cost digital workshop equipped with laser-cutters, routers, 3D scanners, 3D milling machines and programming tools, where you can 'make almost anything'. The use of virtual labs for school science teaching is exemplified in the VISIR Open Lab Platform, an architecture that opens existing types of hands-on laboratories for remote access, thereby giving students a feeling of being within the hands-on laboratory (Gustavsson et al., 2011). Thus, a VISIR laboratory is more or less a replica of a hands-on one. Replication means that the experiments can be created and conducted in the same way as in a hands-on laboratory, albeit that the equipment located on campus is computer mediated and the student's fingers are replaced by their mouse cursor.

The use of technology is already a culturally embedded practice and digital practices are evolving and new uses of technology continue to be discovered. For example, there is a sense that participatory culture characterized by the use of Facebook and YouTube prompts or encourages the democratization of media production, bringing with it the suggestion that young people are not only central to the digital age, but key players in its formulation and (re)creation. Furlong and Davies (2012) argue that young people's engagement with new technologies is fundamentally bound up in their own identity: for example, how they choose to use technology to engage with others, represent themselves and manage their worlds. Katz (2006) also found that students use their phones as symbols in social relationships: for example, pretending to have a mobile phone conversation to avoid talking face-to-face, or pretending to get a call to avoid an embarrassing social situation. Katz (2006: 11) argues that 'there is a large world of communication usage having little to do with those who are distant or virtual and everything to do with those who are colocated, socially and physically with the user'. However, there are disjunctions in the minds of students and young people about the presence and use of social media in the classroom, because there are contradictions about when and how it is acceptable to use digital technology.

It is important to understand how students and young people live and learn across the many digital media available to them, what is new, changed, or changing about how they live and learn today, and what evidence there is for these shifts. boyd (2010) has explored social media in the context of young people's friendships. She suggests that learning to socialize and make friends 'is a key component of growing up as a competent social being, and that young people need to be immersed in peer cultures from an early age' (boyd 2010: 83). She has also found that social media are not seen as separate from the rest of young people's lives, but rather are another way to connect with peers 'that feels seamless with their everyday lives' (boyd 2010: 105).

It remains unclear whether digital tethering and (too much) digital influence are resulting in learning and engagement imbalance. Such imbalance can occur when too much time is spent in virtual spaces, when students are distracted by messaging in lectures, or when virtual lives become overlaid and confused with real lives. Further, Tomlinson (2007: 74) suggests that we now live in a culture of instantaneity – a culture accustomed to rapid delivery, ubiquitous availability and the instant gratification of desires. Yet digital tethering seems to be liminal in nature, at least in the way that young people operate: they sift, shift, research, explore, critique, learn and question, seemingly moving through these spatial zones and landscapes with an ease that denies complexity or troublesomeness.

Digital tethering now seems to be a central practice in our learning society, but it is not yet clear what its benefits and drawbacks are. These need to be examined in depth, in particular because:

- Personalization, choice and control in teaching and learning are high on students' agendas, and digital tethering appears to offer students opportunities. It is not known whether this improves or impairs student engagement.
- Digital tethering appears to be affecting learning practice. It is unclear whether it affects teaching practice, and whether a mismatch between the two will affect student engagement adversely. It seems likely that digital tethering might help peer-to-peer learning, although as yet there is no concrete evidence to support this theory, partly because many people still refer to the use of social media as 'informal' learning, resulting in the segregation of (unseen) digital learning from the perceived formality of institutional learning.
- Digital tethering might bring together useful, innovative learning opportunities for students. However, as yet it is unclear how these new practices and opportunities might be harnessed to generate improved learning.

Conclusion

Digital tethering needs to be understood as a concept, a practice and a complex societal issue, because it seems to be changing the nature of social interaction and affecting learning practices in different environments. Much of this is a quiet, creeping change, and not nearly as fast or as pernicious as some media scare stories imply. It is important to remember that digital media, of whatever sort, is not responsible for undermining formal learning or family life. Digital media in the twenty-first century is a component of society which underpins everything from education to entertainment. In order to appreciate digital tethering and its impact on lives and learning, it is important to locate and understand it in the broader context of learning approaches and theories in the wider landscape of education.

2

THE LANDSCAPE OF LEARNING

Introduction

This chapter begins by exploring digital tethering as something that offers choice, development and opportunities for becoming in the context of a behavioural learning culture. It suggests the need to shift away from the current (and possibly future) rhetoric about flexible pedagogies, student satisfaction and engagement, and instead move towards new spaces, where students' choices and responses are recognized as being central to the way learning is configured and structured. It suggests that digital tethering is creating 'new spaces of response' and prompting pedagogies of the imagination.

The learning landscape

Many of the theories about learning that are used to inform discipline-based pedagogies remain disparate, even within those disciplines that study it, such as education and psychology. Furthermore, much of the current research that transcends pedagogy, technology, education studies and computer science remains disconnected, with the result that although we know students adapt to the cultures of school and university, their learning preferences and practices in the twenty-first century continue to be under-researched. However, some research does suggest that students use technology in one way in formal learning settings and in a different way in their everyday interactions with family and friends. For example, Salaway et al. (2007) found students preferred social networking to remain private, as they did not want it to get in the way of their face-to-face interactions with tutors.

There has, and continues to be, a long-term reliance on the deep and surface approaches in learning research, and the more recent innovative literature on threshold concepts helps us to understand how students get stuck in learning. There have been studies by Crook (2008) and Ito et al. (2013), but relatively little that addresses this complex issue of learning and digital tethering. Pedagogy – the art and science of teaching and learning – encompasses a range of theorists and the continuing debates about the nature and process of learning have created a minefield of overlapping concepts, with few clear frameworks for understanding the relationship between the context and the experience of the learner.

Traditionally, learning theories have been grouped into categories – from the behavioural traditions through to the critical awareness theorists – but with full acknowledgement that one may overlap with another. Those in the field of critical awareness have argued that theirs is not simply another perspective on adult learning, but rather a shift in ideology. The ideals of this tradition stem largely from theorists such as Freire (1972, 1974), who argued that social and historical forces shape the processes through which people come to know themselves and develop their view of the world. Learning is therefore seen to occur in a social and cultural context and this necessarily influences what and how people learn. Learners must therefore seek to transcend the constraints that their world places upon them in order to liberate themselves and become critically aware.

The developmental theorists offer us models that in many ways seem to take account of cognition and development. Perry's classic study of men at Harvard presents an interesting challenge when considering both digital tethering and the development of knowledge and understanding across the (higher) education landscape. Perry devised nine positions that described how students' conceptions of the nature and origins of knowledge evolved (Perry, 1970, 1988). In this description of the attainment of intellectual and emotional maturity, the student moves from an authoritarian, polarized view of the world, through stages of uncertainty and accepting uncertainty, and finally to an understanding of the implications of managing this uncertainty. The student then accepts the need for orientation by a commitment to values and eventually gains a distinct identity through a thoughtful and constantly developing commitment to a set of values. Belenky et al. (1986) were stimulated by Perry's work to explore diverse women's perspectives: they identified five categories of 'ways of knowing' and from this drew conclusions about the way women see truth, knowledge and authority. For example, women began from a position of silence where they saw themselves as mindless and voiceless and subject to the whims of external authority. In later stages they constructed knowledge; this was when the women viewed all knowledge as relating to the context in which it occurred, and experienced themselves as creators of knowledge.

Yet, in the context of digital tethering, it would seem to be the humanistic field (Rogers, 1983) that offers the most theoretical purchase for understanding learning in, with and through digital media. Those in the humanistic field contend that significant learning is obtained only within situations that are defined by, and under the control of, the learner. Here the aims of education are based on self-development and the development of a fully functioning person. The prior experience of the learner is acknowledged and it is also recognized that students may be constrained by their own negative experiences of learning. The teacher (termed the 'facilitator' in this tradition) helps to provide a supportive environment in which learners are enabled to recognize and explore their needs. Learning is seen as involving the whole person, not just the intellect, so humanistic educators aim to liberate learners and allow them the freedom to learn.

The promoters of the cognitive tradition (Ausubel et al., 1978) argued that new information has to be interpreted in terms of both prior knowledge and shared perspectives. Thus the existing cognitive structure is the principal factor influencing meaningful learning. In practice this means that meaningful material can be learned only in relation to a previously learned background of relevant concepts.

The literature on threshold concepts to some extent builds on the theories of the cognitive tradition. Threshold concepts are discipline-related concepts essential for understanding and creating knowledge in a discipline, while conceptual thresholds are moments of enlightenment and learning leaps in the learning journey, the development of learning, often referred to as 'aha!' moments. The literature concerning threshold concepts (Meyer and Land, 2006) concentrates on the identification of discipline-specific concepts which are in a sense essential in the acquisition of the thinking, learning and communication of understanding within specific subject learning: for example, to think like a mathematician, or to think, learn and express oneself like an economist. It is argued that developing understanding and use of these concepts is crucial for student learning and knowledge construction. The threshold literature is both fascinating and helpful, but Davies (2006) and Meyer and Land (2006) argue that threshold concepts are generalizable concepts that can necessarily be embedded in a curriculum structure. Yet to argue for such a position immediately implies that threshold concepts are dislocated from learner identities. However, it is the overemphasis on the cognitive dimensions of threshold concepts, as delineated by Entwistle (2006), where this seems to be most apparent. For example, Entwistle argues that engaging with threshold concepts is related to *conceptual* change and relates his argument to Perry's (1970) conceptions of knowledge and Säljö's (1979) conception of learning. Thus, there would seem to be too much emphasis on conception and cognition and not enough on identity. For example, work carried out with postgraduate students in terms of their development of conceptual-level thinking, engagement with the question and the interdisciplinary disciplines – the disciplinary mix in their writing of theses – has identified moments of 'learning leaps' (Wisker et al., 2006; Kiley and Wisker, 2009; Wisker and Kiley, 2008). Learning leaps are where students perceptibly and audibly cross conceptual thresholds to raise the level of their critical thinking and expression. Conceptual threshold crossings are moments when students make the learning leaps start to work at this higher, more conceptual, critical and creative level, and it is perhaps on learning leaps that we need to focus in order to engage staff in understanding students being digitally tethered and digital tethering practices; and to enable students to recognize that digital tethering can be both useful and disruptive (in both positive and negative ways).

Flexible pedagogies?

Despite moves, in the UK at least, towards flexible pedagogies, considerable resistance remains. The focus seems to be on shoring up the disciplines and using outcomes, benchmarking and standards to pin down knowledge and quality, rather than open them up. There is something inherently troublesome about a wish to operate a behavioural framework whilst expecting pedagogical flexibility to be both possible and viable. Such intransigence is seen in the need to hold on to both a focus on outcomes and a misplaced notion of 'the discipline'. Disciplines are seen to be vital, but there appears to be little in-depth questioning of disciplines in the twenty-first century, although Trowler (2014) has begun to discuss this issue. He argues that previous research has employed a strong essentialist approach, which has exaggerated the homogeneity of specific disciplinary features. Instead, he suggests there should be a more sophisticated conceptualization of disciplines that applies Wittgenstein's notion of family resemblances to the task of depicting disciplines. Disciplines comprise bodies of knowledge, traditions, values and discourses, yet these transcend, change and overlap with other disciplines and discourses. It is not clear whether (and which) disciplines need to be preserved, and if they do, why this is the case. It seems questionable for a student of physics or psychology to be inducted into particular disciplinary norms and values if they are to be of relatively little use in the digital age.

There have been suggestions that there is a pedagogicalization of everything, following what Bernstein argued for in 2001 – the pedagogicalization of society (Bernstein, 2001). The argument is that pedagogy is integrated into all spheres of life, which is seen as problematic. Further, such a position seems to suggest that seeing everything as a learning opportunity is unhelpful. What perhaps does need consideration is what counts as learning at different stages. What is higher learning as opposed to further learning? Quality, credit transfer and standards are all tightly bound within the current system and held on to by tenacious academics. Meanwhile, students have, in the main, moved beyond such performative practices and bounded systems and instead use whatever apps, forums and sites enable them to gain, create, recreate and repurpose knowledge.

The difficulties in attempting to introduce flexible pedagogies appear to be:

- Funding regimes that fail to support different types and lengths of degree.
- Quality, standards and professional bodies that are risk averse and behaviourally driven.
- Academics who are overly focused on the maintenance of disciplinary norms and learning outcomes.
- Institutions that will engage only with managed risk, are concerned about their student retention and contentment, and are worried about being lambasted by the local competition (the university up the road). At the same time, they are afraid of the quality agencies and funders and as a result have become increasingly managed by bureaucratic administrators, who insist on courses being run in particular, and invariably inflexible, ways (for example, insisting

that a UK-based horticulture diploma begins in September rather than March, even though it needs to coincide with the growing season).

Barnett (2014) has argued for fifteen conditions of flexibility:

> In moving towards greater flexibility in higher education, and to safeguard educational integrity, programmes should:
>
> 1. lead to a qualification that contributes to major awards (such as degrees or their equivalent);
> 2. offer all students access to suitable materials and appropriate cognitive and practical experiences;
> 3. offer academic interaction with other students;
> 4. offer access to tutors, in real-time interaction;
> 5. offer prompt and informative (formative) feedback from tutors;
> 6. offer access to other academic services (such as counselling, academic and careers advice);
> 7. offer financial services (appropriate to the cost to students in financing their studies);
> 8. enable students to offer feedback on their total experience;
> 9. provide a pedagogical openness;
> 10. be academically and educationally structured;
> 11. offer ladder(s) of progression;
> 12. be suitably robust and reliable (with built-in safeguards appropriate to the risk);
> 13. be cost-effective;
> 14. have sufficient structure so as to enable student completion to be a likely outcome;
> 15. contain sufficient challenge that students are likely to be cognitively and experientially stretched and to be informed by a spirit of criticality appropriate to each stage of a programme of studies (so as fully to realise the promise of a higher education).
>
> Flexible provision has the potential to enhance student learning, widen opportunities for participation in higher education, and develop graduates who are well-equipped to contribute to a fast-changing world. This report shows how these conditions of flexibility provide the foundations for the implementation of robust, well-informed and thought-through structures and strategies that will lead the sector into the future.
>
> *(Barnett, 2014: 10)*

Conditions of flexibility is an interesting idea, particularly amidst claims by many academics that students remain entrenched and still want to attend lectures and write essays (despite little reflection from those academics about how students might have become quite so entrenched in the first place). Further, whilst some universities in the UK are moving away from strongly bounded modular systems, it seems that it is actually the academics wedded to disciplinarity and the systems within institutions that are inflexible.

Although Barnett introduces some fruitful notions, the idea of profiling universities for flexibility seems misplaced. This in turn could result in conditions of flexibility becoming the focus of staff development and student engagement in bounded and performative ways. However, it might be that Barnett's report prompts quality assurance agencies across the globe to rethink their priorities and helps to promote the development of curricula that are daring and imaginative (Barnett, 2014: 73).

Some of the questions that need to be asked in the context of a desire for flexible pedagogies in the context of digital tethering are:

- Why are objectives still useful?
- What are the boundaries and borders of a discipline and who decides?
- What is – and what is not – a discipline?
- What is valuable about a three-year degree?
- To what extent does credit transfer and modularity result in flexibility?
- What are the most effective ways of ensuring quality?

If flexible pedagogies that focus on human beings are to be adopted, as Barnett (2014) suggests, then the overly accepted behavioural norms that are the central planks of education worldwide need to be rejected in favour of something better. The ideals of Stenhouse (1975) and his important argument for learning intentions rather than objectives remain buried, yet they seem to be much more appropriate, not only for flexible pedagogies but also, and perhaps more importantly, for the digital age.

So what is a course or a curriculum? Who decides and why do they get to make the decision? Can we really live without outcomes and objectives? It seems we are not ready for flexible pedagogies, and nor are we really prepared to implement them unless they sit safely within a behavioural framework.

Barnett (2014) has suggested pedagogical flexibility mediated by institutional and national contexts, yet this is unrealistic with the shift towards MOOCs (massive open online courses), open media, disruptive media and the increasing digital fluency of those in/beside our systems of higher education. What kinds of learning spaces do we really need to enable and enhance flexible pedagogies? Perhaps we already have the flexible human beings Barnett identifies but do not recognize them. Is hacking the school computer flexible pedagogy? Or perhaps we place our learners in inflexible spaces.

Digital tethering creating 'spaces of response'

As I suggested earlier in this book, being digitally tethered is invariably seen in negative ways as being a central concern in an 'always on' culture. However, digital tethering offers different freedoms and wider choices, characteristics that seem to be largely lost or ignored in present educational systems and institutions. Being digitally tethered provides students with different spaces to explore that are neither narrow nor predefined by teachers. Thus, rather than seeing it as something unhelpful that continually obstructs learning, it might be celebrated as a 'pedagogy of the imagination' (Calvino, 1995: 92) that shifts students away from rules, completion, outcomes and stipulations. It offers students spaces of exploration and curiosity, as well as opportunities to consider their stance.

The notion of 'learning ecologies' has been suggested as a means of offering creativity, freedom and choice, and stimulating curiosity. This notion stipulates that:

- individuals are simultaneously involved in many settings;
- individuals create learning contexts for themselves within and across settings;
- the boundaries among settings can be permeable; and
- interest-driven activities can span contextual boundaries and be self-sustaining given adequate time, freedom and resources (Barron, 2006: 199–201).

Thus, what students learn outside university, college and school shapes what they learn within those institutional settings. Barron (2004, 2006) suggests that learning can manifest itself across settings, and that informal or formal crossing of boundaries might enhance learning. However, I suggest that it is not learning ecologies that are needed, but 'spaces of response' that offer flexibility, attention to learners' perspectives and motivation, and a means of transcending and transmuting institutional forms of learning.

Being digitally tethered then offers spaces of response that include:

- choosing speeds of operation;
- living curiously;
- valuing error;
- recognizing silences;
- valuing relational learning;
- learning on the move; and
- liquid learning.

Choosing speeds of operation

The issue of fast time, living with speed and a perceived need for more slow time continues to be an area of controversy. For example, Whelan (2008) has argued for a notion of metaxis for the modern age, claiming that 'we humans are suspended on a web of polarities – the one and the many, eternity and time, freedom and fate, instinct and intellect, risk and safety, love and hate, to name but a few'. Yet, at the same time, there is an almost inherent stress that appears to be associated not just with fast time (Eriksen, 2001) but with 'continuous telepresence'. Such an unrelenting sense of immediacy might at one level be linked to a sense of constant busyness, but it also appears to result in reduced time for thinking, a feeling that time is being taken away by others, and a means of avoidance of activities that are central to learning spaces, such as reflection, reflexivity and critical thought. Indeed, Virilio (1997: 80) suggests: 'The paradoxes of acceleration are indeed numerous and disconcerting, in particular the foremost among them: getting closer to the "distant" takes you away proportionally from the "near" (and dear).'

We are in a world in which we are, as Virilio predicted, universally telepresent without moving our physical bodies. Thus, there is often a sense that we arrive and depart from spaces and encounters without actually doing so. The question, then, is whether we are victims or beneficiaries (or both) of this 'chronic telepresence'. For example, Clayson and Haley (2012) undertook a literature review and found that young people spend 15 per cent of their time texting and that women text more often than men (Ling and Pederson, 2005). Despite a ban on mobile devices in classrooms, one study found 58 per cent of students still sent text messages from these classes (Vecchione, 2010). Clayson and Haley's (2012) study shows results for staff noticing texting in class, and whilst the authors note that a number of articles reported staff's attempts to control texting, most of these were ineffective. Clayson and Haley (2012) therefore investigated texting in a marketing class and found that this did not appear to affect students' overall grade averages, even though much of the metacognitive literature to date has suggested that it should hinder learning. It is perhaps important to consider that learning and passing graded assessments are two very different activities. Thus, whilst texting may not affect grade point averages, it may affect effective learning. However, surveys have also discovered that young people like texting because it offers unparalleled freedom to communicate on their own terms, irrespective of place and time.

It is easy to assume that digital tethering results in always living in fast time. Yet the opportunity to use technology at all times can bring with it a sense of safety and choice, and perhaps even balance, rather than a sense of urgency. In education, staff and students invariably expect fast response times and assume everyone is busy all of the time. Nevertheless, the skill is in recognizing that it is helpful to be fast when this makes sense, but that response is a choice and so recognizing the value of being slow for considered or strategic reasons is also important. Fast time and slow time are not polarities but choices, spaces to decide on our response to what is put before us. Thus, managing slowness requires discipline and a recognition of our need for balance and space, of walking to a different drum.

Living curiously

Much has been made of student engagement (Trowler and Trowler, 2010) and of 'a will' to learn (Barnett, 2007). More recently, strong arguments by Selwyn (2013, 2014) have suggested that neutral forms of educational technology have resulted in educational provision and practices with neo-liberal values. This, he believes, has changed the nature of education, moving it away from a public good and towards the individualistic tendencies of twenty-first-century capitalism. It therefore seems that curiosity has disappeared from the lexicon of higher education whilst remaining in the purview of the young, often the very young.

In terms of living curiously, it may be that Barnett is our only hope. He argues that there is an extraordinary but largely unnoticed phenomenon in higher education: by and large, students keep going with their studies. What Barnett suggests is that, as a student begins her studies, she is plunged into a state of uncertainty with complex problems and loose connections; the infinity of learning results in anxiety and further uncertainty. Barnett questions why students persist, and suggests that this persistence or will to learn is something that staff in higher education really need to understand, since it is fragile. In fact, he believes that the *primary* responsibility of teachers in higher education is to sustain and develop the student's will to learn. To me, this appears to be the beginning of recognizing, supporting and believing in the importance of curiosity, unlike studies and policies on student engagement, which, in the main, seem to miss the point. However, other authors, such as Juul (2013), rather than suggesting that student engagement is a straightforward practice, argue for 'the art of failure' – the idea of turning failure into curiosity – and this has some resonance with stuckness, troublesome knowledge and the valuing of error.

The literature on student engagement encompasses selected non-academic and social as well as academic aspects of student experiences. In their reviews of this literature, Kuh et al. (2007) and Krause and Coates (2008) consider student engagement in terms of the extent to which students engage in activities that contribute towards desired (high-quality) learning outcomes. The definitions promote a predominantly institutional focus centred on outcomes (such as retention, success rates and acknowledging diversity). Zepke and Leach (2010) also focus on 'high quality learning', but broaden their accepted definition to include a focus on the student's cognitive investment, active participation and emotional commitment to learning. This latter review highlights that responsibility for engagement is shared; some students experience engagement negatively; and engagement requires successful transition. Some studies have considered what institutions and educators can do to improve engagement (and retention), including: the roles of institutional structures and cultures (Porter, 2006); a focus on learning design and how educators practise and relate to their students (Haug, 2006); how student agency and motivation are recognized (Hockings et al., 2008); and the impact of environmental factors, such as family, relationships and economic status (Miliszewska and Horwood, 2004). Much of the research and focus on student engagement is about students' degree experience rather than what and how they learn. Mawer (personal communication) suggests that some of the focus on structural arrangements is due to the assumption that the ways in which students learn are accepted and settled. He explains:

> How students learn is a relatively well-settled question and structural changes
> in higher education (including fees, private providers . . .) should be treated as
> a market economics issue (how do you make the 'consumers' happy with the

market?) rather than an educational theory issue (how do you make the system do what it is supposed to do?) . . . The pressure from academic league tables – which don't measure learning (unless learning = graduate employability) – also seems to distort topics about educational theory and practice through the lens of satisfaction and engagement, and of course the league tables are pretty poorly regarded and attract a lot of discussion in educational research and media, so this creates a double distortion: either a distortion through the lens of satisfaction and engagement, or a response to that distortion which still doesn't really address the issues being distorted . . . Even when the focus is not overt – and there is some limited basis for it in the evidence presented – there is still a tendency to look toward structural issues of institutional setup and student expectations and to cast aside both discussion and projects related to student learning. [More detailed perspectives on these issues can be found in Kandiko and Mawer, 2013.]

Thus, it would seem that there is still considerable emphasis on teaching and institutional practice, and relatively little on student learning and practices. Boughey (2006) questioned the extent to which engagement is an autonomous skill, since the rules of engagement are formulated by academic expectations and traditions, which students need to learn in order to participate in academic dialogues, processes and practices. Thus, the way in which staff present a text to students locates their position in terms of the values and purpose they accord to it. In the new student satisfaction arena one of the troublesome challenges is to understand the relationship between quality, learning and engagement. Furthermore, quality appears to be continually equated with satisfaction, while learning and engagement are often confused with one another and used interchangeably, which leads to misplaced assumptions, such as effective engagement being seen as a predictor of satisfaction.

Perhaps it is important to remember that students do have a will to learn, that they are curious and seek to explore, yet schooling and university – and indeed the disciplines – often box in their thinking and questioning. Freire (1997: 31) argued that 'only an education of questions can trigger, motivate and reinforce curiosity'. Students need to be encouraged towards a pedagogy of imagination that focuses on encouraging critical questioning and prompting curiosity.

Valuing error

In earlier texts I have stressed the value of disjunction, stuckness and failure as a central part of learning. Many staff have described disjunction as being a little like hitting a brick wall: there is an overwhelming sense of 'stuckness' and they have then used various strategies to try to deal with it. This is similar to the conceptually difficult knowledge that Perkins (1999) describes as 'troublesome knowledge'. This is knowledge that appears, for example, counter-intuitive, alien (emanating from another culture or discourse), or incoherent (discrete aspects are unproblematic but there is no organizing principle). Disjunction, then, is not only a form of troublesome knowledge but also a 'space' or 'position' reached through the realization that the knowledge is troublesome. Disjunction might therefore be seen as a 'troublesome learning space' that emerges from smooth learning spaces. Indeed, Deleuze and Guattari (1988: 551) have argued:

> Of course, smooth spaces are not in themselves liberatory. But the struggle is changed or displaced in them, and life reconstitutes its stakes, confronts new obstacles, invents new paces, switches adversaries. Never believe that a smooth space will suffice to save us.

In the current system of education, failure remains deeply problematic. It is not seen as a valuable component of the development of learner identity, nor as coming into oneself as a human being, nor as discovering how we learn, how we learn best and what we want to learn. The value of making mistakes, committing errors of judgement or getting stuck is either generally passed over or referred to in hushed tones. As Leggo (2011: 76) remarks, 'we are not kind towards failure'. Current institutional education appears to be more about getting over hurdles than about working out why we trip over them. Yet our failures help us to become who we are; we learn the most when we fall over. Hanh (2003: 67) notes that *tuteur* (French for 'mentor') derives from the stake used to support a sapling. This is the role that staff in the digital age need to adopt in order to support students: each tutor should be someone for students to lean against after a failure and in times of weakness, and someone with whom they can learn curiosity.

Recognizing silences

Many of us struggle with silence and seek to fill it with some kind of noise. Whilst silence varies in different contexts, it is perhaps helpful to consider that language and silences are intertwined and that both silence and stuckness are central components in learning. Many forms of silence are recognized in education, but they are invariably disregarded or cast aside. In the context of digital tethering we need to attend to silences, because often they are different. Some of the more obvious silences include students feeling they are 'being silenced' or 'rendered voiceless' (Belenky et al., 1986). Silence as disengagement in the classroom, whether face to face or online, is also recognized, as is the behaviour of lurking in online space – both of which are generally seen as negative forms of silence, although this may not be the case. However, silence to hear others and yourself and then reflect upon this is a form of disregarded knowledge in education. Mezirow (1991) suggested that learning occurs as a result of reflecting upon experience. Thus, content reflection is an examination of the content or description of a problem, process reflection involves checking on problem-solving strategies that are being used, and premise reflection leads the learner to a transformation of meaning perspectives. Silence taken for thinking space, before responding verbally or to an email, is silence as wisdom in social networking. Being digitally tethered means that fast responses can often be unwise responses, and the valuing of silence in digital spaces needs to be (re)captured. Online spaces can also seem to be very noisy places, with many people 'talking' at once and using a language that may be alien, at least in part. Further, as Land (2006: 108) has noted, rather poignantly:

> The Web, for example, remains unruly, risky and troublesome, an implacable aspect of the supercomplexity and intractability of the post-modern condition. An intriguing irony is that though current commercial virtual learning environments (themselves global corporations) might be seen as spaces that dis-place older collegial spaces, symbolised by the quadrangle, they nonetheless still attempt to wall in their own 'onscreen real estate', to fend off, perhaps, the post-modern wildness of the Web ... Like many modernist practices and spaces, they are singularly rectangular.

Further, Phipps (2007) has discussed the notion of 'sound/s' in academia and argues that changes in sounds are having a somewhat unhelpful impact on the quality of academic life experiences. For example, she suggests that sound knowledge has been taken over by management speak, that new sounds are emerging (such as 'consumers', 'joined up thinking', and 'strategic realignment') while other sounds (such as music from practice rooms) are vanishing, since the practice room itself has disappeared. These silences and sounds need to be recognized and re-engaged with, and central to understanding them is relational learning.

Valuing relational learning

Some months ago a journalist in the *Daily Telegraph* newspaper wrote dismissively that collaborative learning was just students sitting about chatting. My first reaction was flippant – wondering what her educational qualifications were – until I realized I had a much deeper concern: that her assumption that just sitting about chatting was not necessarily learning.

Years of research have indicated that learning is more effective if it is interactional and relational. Dialogue is central to learning (as is silence). It is through the relational nature of learning that students are transformed through one another, as well as through the knowledges and challenges set before them by teachers. Relational learning captures the idea that students can learn with and through others in ways that help them to make connections amongst their lives, with other subjects, disciplines and personal concerns, thereby offering them particular kinds of learning opportunities. For example, while students may learn in lectures or in groups, they may also learn through discussion in common rooms and as they debate the material with which they have just been presented while walking between lectures.

Mezirow (1985) argued for the notion of dialogic learning; learning that occurs when insights and understandings emerge through dialogue in a learning environment. This is a form of learning where staff and students draw upon their own experiences to explain the concepts and ideas with which they are presented, and then use those experiences to make sense for themselves and also to explore further issues. Interacting with others in a learning situation becomes a key component of relational learning, since it is through dialogue within a given context that students begin to make sense of concepts for themselves. Working and learning with others offers students opportunities to explore their own perspectives as well as those of their peers. In particular, working in groups can help students to become effective researchers of information, who work in teams to learn to explore and critique material together.

Barnett (1994) has suggested that higher education is necessarily a process of becoming, and has argued for a process of education in which the student can be 'released into herself'. Barnett sees this 'being released' not in terms of empowerment, self-realization or emancipation, but in terms of constructing 'their own voice'. Essentially, Barnett seems to be arguing for the development of a learner identity through which the learner is able not only to construct (and presumably deconstruct) and articulate her own perspective in her own way, but also defend this perspective before her peers and authorities.

Learning on the move

Whilst there have been countless studies about mobile learning (e.g. Traxler, 2011; Sharples et al., 2005) and discussion about what counts as learning on the move, more recent studies have examined how learning is played out as people move around. A study by Squire and Dikkers (2012), for example, studied the ways in which young people used mobile media devices inside and outside school in the US. Squire (2009) argued that current media activities create a multiplicity of place, so that people can involve themselves in virtual communities and access content throughout the day in order to deepen their understanding. However, these authors suggest that whilst the affordances of such media have been investigated, the ways in which users adapt the media in their contexts and the particular features of the technology that they value have not been explored. For example, they suggest that 'mobile media devices ... have been constructed as entertainment, in *opposition* to learning and schooling' (Squire and Dikkers 2012: 447; original emphasis). Thus, they examined the ways in which users construct and adopt digital media. Ten diverse students were given mobile phones and data were collected through observation, interviews and document analysis of journals kept by the students. Although this was a small-scale study, the findings offer some useful notions of mobile media learning as creating different forms of amplification.

Amplification of self

Participants in the study found that possessing and using mobile devices promoted their feeling of empowerment and of being useful because they were able to access and use information easily.

Amplification of social networks

Whilst the assumption is often that the use of media devices will be disruptive in a negative way at home and school, the researchers found that this was not the case. A somewhat unexpected advantage was that it helped young people to transcend face-to-face awkwardness with other teenagers. They also used phones to share and learn together.

Amplification of interest

Young people used phones for searching and researching information to support their interests. However, they also used them explicitly to support personal interests, such as taking photographs and for help with songwriting.

Amplification of learning

Participants found learning was quick and easy through the use of mobile devices as they found access to and retrieval of information straightforward. Further, they used mobile phones to access and retrieve books. One of the pertinent findings of Squire and Dikkers' study (and one which seems to remain relatively under-explored) was the way in which mobile phones were used for 'filler time', for example while waiting for the bus or to be picked up by parents. The phone was used to fill gaps in the day with things that interested the young people and enabled them to develop their own personal curricula. For the majority of participants in the study, the devices did not change their schedules; rather, they enhanced them.

Squire and Dikkers (2012) argue for the notion of mobile devices creating a multiplicity of place, but this is mistaken. Instead, the use of mobile devices creates a sense of travelling through diverse spaces, whilst either in one physical place or moving across places, such as when travelling. However, increasingly these physical and temporal uses of space and place are meshed together. An example of this would be the Eye Shakespeare app, created by the Shakespeare Birthplace Trust and Coventry University's Serious Games Institute, which features items that were previously unavailable to the public, such as images of a lock of Shakespeare's hair and his birth and death records. A further example is the virtual geography field trip developed by Minocha. It was developed in order to carry out a range of practical scientific enquiries using three-dimensional models on a virtual field trip, through which students learn to assemble apparatus and instruments and then control them, compare results and share good practice (Minocha, 2013).

Liquid learning

Bauman (2000) has argued that we are living in an era of 'liquid modernity' that is characterized by the social and technological changes that have occurred since the 1960s, embodied by the sense of living with constant change, ambivalence and uncertainty. Liquid modernity is thus a chaotic continuation of modernity, yet until the rise of social networking the solidity of technology initially seemed to overlay this notion of liquidity. Liquid curricula are defined here as curricula that focus on students' and tutors' stances and personal identities, and provide opportunities to design modules and lessons in open and flexible ways. In practice this means that universities need to stretch beyond open courseware and closed virtual learning environments. Instead, learning would need to be created around a constellation of uncertainties, such as negotiated assessment, and open and flexible learning intentions. Liquid learning spaces are open, flexible and contested, spaces where both learning and learners are always on the move. Movement in such curricula is not towards a given trajectory. Instead, there is a sense of displacement of notions of time and place, so that curricula are delineated with and through the staff and students, and they are defined by the creators of the space(s).

Connected mobile media technologies are currently transforming the experience and expectations of students' engagement with knowledges, learning and technologies, and universities are facing this shift in the form of students tethered to their mobiles. Learning at university is now just one of many sources of information and learning with which students engage on a daily basis, so we have to compete for their attention. This means that traditional modes of teaching (broadcasting) educational content via the lecture/seminar/tutorial model are no longer adequate. Liquid learning and disruptive media (networked/connected/digital) enable and indeed encourage collaboration and the co-creation of content, which breach the walls of the classroom but remain relatively untapped. They could be used in ways that would be transformative for academics and students alike.

Such curricula are risky since they prompt consideration of what counts as legitimate knowledge. Students are encouraged to examine the underlying structures and belief systems implicit within what is being learned in order to understand both the disciplinary area and its credence. What is important in the creation of these disruptive spaces is the position of disregarded knowledge as a central space, in which uncertainty and gaps are recognized, along with the realization of the relative importance of gaps between different knowledge and different knowledge hierarchies. For example, disregarded forms of knowledge (Cockburn, 1998) include knowing when to keep your mouth shut and the virtues of tact. These are forms of knowing that are required in many professions, but they are not made explicit in the academy.

Conclusion

It is unclear how new models of education, precipitated by technological change, are likely to be shaped by and shape student learning in the future. We need explorations into how students are responding to and creating new learning spaces, how pedagogies and technologies are informing each other, and the impact of the learning and learning theories that are used in these new learning landscapes. However, the current state of play is troublesome, since it is argued that many diverse approaches to learning are useful, yet it is unclear if this is truly the case. Furthermore, in terms of pedagogy, the academy seems to have lost its focus. It is both confused and confusing, as is explored in Chapter 3.

3

PIRACY AND PEDAGOGIES

Introduction

Higher education worldwide is experiencing rapid change in the ways that it is perceived externally, although the underlying university systems and procedures per se are not the root cause of this. Driving this change are the high expectations of students, in terms of what higher education will provide, whether face to face or online.

This chapter begins by reflecting on what are deemed or presented as pedagogies and examines the validity of the argument for these being pedagogies, rather than theories or methods. It then suggests that some reconceptualization of higher education needs to be done, highlighting the need to revisit its purposes and values in the digital age. It then presents a range of media that are being adopted and developed in higher education, and offers a critique of current practices, suggesting that, whilst some are new, others are in fact reconfigurations of older methods and technologies that have been adapted for the twenty-first century – and they may not have a sound fit.

Piracy and pedagogies

In the various *Pirates of the Caribbean* films (2003–2007) there are numerous references to the 'pirate code'. Yet, in practice, the pirates argue that 'the code is more what you'd call "guidelines" than actual rules'. Today, what passes for pedagogy often seems more like methods and guidelines than any kind of reasoned pedagogy. Originally, the pirate code was a code of conduct used for governing pirates and each pirate crew tended to have its own code for discipline and the division of stolen goods. However, I suggest that we need to re-examine the 'code' because it appears to me that there is currently rather more piracy than pedagogy.

The growing instantiations of 'pedagogy' illustrate the value placed on this in higher education. Pedagogy is defined here as the arts and science of education, but it is increasingly confused with the practices of teaching, so that pedagogy and teaching methods have become confused. This section suggests that a number of developments have occurred that have resulted in confusion and difficulty for many teachers in primary, secondary and higher education. These areas are problematic because they result in rigid thinking and the imposition of structures that close down rather than open up learning spaces.

Disciplinarity

'Disciplinarity' is used here to describe all that is seen as central to a given discipline: its pedagogy, values, beliefs, rhetorics and expected norms that are embodied by the academics who guard it. The challenge for higher education when facing disciplinarity is 'how?' How should learning and teaching be redesigned? How can we create learning environments, opportunities and contexts that help students to be critical of both themselves and the discipline?

The examples in this section have been used to illustrate that disciplinarity and being locked in to subject knowledge are troublesome in the digital age. What is needed is an ability to be critical about how much value there is in disciplinary boundaries and entrenched views about pedagogical content knowledge. I suggest that disciplines are no longer needed and their very existence builds walls around knowledges that are unhelpful for education and learning in the digital age.

In order to illustrate the difficulty with disciplinarity I will draw on a particular area of engineering that, whilst discrete, helps to map some generic challenges. It is a story that illustrates the broader issues rather than provides a direct critique of this discipline. As Okri (1997: 120) argues:

> It is easy to forget how mysterious and mighty stories are. They do their work in silence, invisibly. They become part of you while changing you. Beware of the stories you read or tell: subtly, at night, beneath the waters of consciousness, they are altering your world.

To explain: a group of academics have been developing virtual and remote engineering laboratories across the globe and sharing their practices at annual conferences for over eleven years. However, they are faced with three difficulties:

1. They wish to make virtual and remote labs interesting, but they have based their teaching on current disciplinary norms and prior experience, rather than on educational theory that may enhance their teaching.
2. Although they are developing learning in digital spaces, much of what is designed is decontextualized, so that students are provided with an experiment to undertake which would be more challenging and interesting if it were located in a real-life science scenario. Furthermore, much of the teaching that

occurs in these labs does not appear to take account of the digital capabilities most students bring to the classroom.

3. There is sometimes a tendency to impose personal norms and values on teaching, whilst failing to recognize that 'different' might also be a useful place to stand. For example, at a recent engineering conference I remarked that many of us are digitally tethered and surrounded by knowledge; so our students could access and check the information we were supplying to them during a lecture. A response from the audience was: 'They are surrounded by information, not knowledge.' This comment prompted later discussion over dinner as a group of us debated how it might be possible to delineate the parameters of information versus knowledge, who might make such a decision, and what the trajectory might be between the end of information and the beginning of knowledge. Despite this somewhat tongue-in-cheek debate, the conversation showed how problematic it still is for many teachers, in whatever discipline, to have their expertise and power over knowledge questioned by students.

We need to see things differently. Instead of offering judgement, we should be surprised by and appreciative of a different stance, a new view. To take such a position does not ignore the past, but builds on it and sees things as not necessarily worse, just different. Thus, it would seem that there are some missing questions in all of this. How should learning and teaching be redesigned? How can we move towards an interest of study rather than a discipline, a focus on *Ersiehung*, which shifts towards an interest in emancipation of the person? How can we create learning that has impact and helps students to be critical learners?

One example of this is Circuit Warz, an immersive game that engages students and teaches electrical and electronic theory and principles. The way in which the game has been designed helps students to think critically, and its immersive nature makes it both fun and challenging. In turn, this interrupts assumptions about learning this subject. Circuit Warz can be downloaded freely and played on PCs, tablets and phones (Callaghan et al., 2014).

Multimodality theory

Multimodality theory has been widely accepted in higher education with what would seem to be relatively little criticality. In reality, different modes of communication and expression change the ways in which we see and think about the world, and there is nothing fundamentally new offered through this theory. The original argument posited by Kress and van Leeuwen (2001) was that there has been a recent shift away from monomodality (text based versus image) and towards multimodality (text and image). They argued that the past dominance of and preference for text began to shift towards multimodality when the screen rather than the book became the most common form of representation. Multimodal media are those that incorporate both text and visual artefacts, such as web pages, blogs, and social media sites and spaces. Moreover, many traditionally text-based formats, such as books and newsletters, are now incorporating additional visual elements and thus might be classified as multimodal. Kress (2003: 65) subsequently argued, 'what is fundamental is that the screen is the site of the image, and the logic of the image dominates the semiotic organisation of the screen'. However, Bazalgette and Buckingham (2013) argue that the increasingly popular (and somewhat simplistic) use of this theory merely reinforces an unhelpful distinction between print and non-print texts, thereby neglecting moving image media.

It is clear that there is a good deal of confusion, because multimodal theory is increasingly seen as something to do with bringing digital media into the classroom. Bazalgette and Buckingham (2013) suggest that this has resulted in a continuing distinction between 'proper' texts (i.e. books) and other texts (digital, visual or other media). The main difficulties they suggest are:

- Multimodality theorists suggest that their approach brings together theory and tools for meaning making across disparate modes of communication. Yet art history and film studies have been using diverse modes for decades, and multimodality offers little beyond a recognition that there are different modes.
- There is an assumption that the changing balance between text and image is resulting in a different form of learning, but with little substantial research to support this. For example, Bazalgette and Buckingham (2013: 98) note that Kress et al. (2005) assert that:

  > in the classroom, the use of typewritten rather than handwritten text, or video clips rather than spoken text, *in itself* transforms the relationships of authority between teachers and learners. The mode apparently 'shapes both *what* is to be learnt (e.g. the curriculum) and *how* it is to be learnt (the pedagogic practices involved)' (Jewitt and Kress, 2010, p. 349, emphasis in original).

- There is an assumption in multimodality theory that meaning making is somehow systematic rather than haphazard and the rigid approach to analysis that is adopted tends to ignore issues of context, production and audience.
- It appears to provide little insight into how people use text in their everyday lives and also neglects the fact that print-based texts are multimodal.

It should be noted that research indicates that critical engagement by children in media such as film interrupts notions of 'ability' and illustrates that children as young as six can discuss complex questions about production, circulation and the use of media texts such as news and celebrity images (Buckingham et al., 2014). Such media have a strong impact on students outside school, but they tend largely to be ignored in primary education. Bazalgette and Buckingham (2013) suggest that it is important to recognize the need for 7–11-year-olds, who traditionally learn about how meanings are constructed, also to focus on how assumptions and ideologies are conveyed and sustained. I suggest that they are probably doing this already, in peer groups and online spaces, but not in school.

New literacies

In the main, the notion of 'new literacies' refers to the idea that new forms of literacy have both emerged and developed through digital technology. The definition is open, contested and problematic, and a range of terms have been adopted, which adds further confusion: for example, 'digital literacies', 'new media literacies', 'multiliteracies' and 'information literacy'. I suggest that 'new literacies' is a misplaced term and concept. Much of what is described as new literacies is merely based on general literacy capabilities, or just on skills and abilities within students' current repertoires that have been adapted or recognized from other contexts: for example, collaboration, responsibility and ethical behaviour. For instance, Simsek and Simsek (2013: 128) argue:

> Gilster (1997) defined basic skills for digital literacies as assembling knowledge, evaluating information, searching, and navigating in non-linear routes. Hobbs (2008) underlined the importance of ethical responsibilities and self-confidence for new literacies. In addition to some skills and ethics, digital literacy also covers knowledge and creative products in the digital environments (Calvani, Cartelli, Fini, & Ranieri, 2008; Jewitt, 2008) … Generally speaking, the concept of digital literacy may be considered the sum of all these literacies (Lankshear & Knobel, 2003).

Nevertheless, if we unpack this list, it is possible to see that none of these capabilities is necessarily related to 'the digital'. There is also a common assumption that young people are always texting and gaming, to the extent that other use of media (books) and the ability to take a critical stance have been driven out. Furthermore, the concept of media literacy is problematic, since it is defined as 'the ability to access, analyze, evaluate and communicate messages in a variety of forms' (Pathak-Shelat, 2014: 2058), which suggests little more than the need to take a critical stance and having the ability to interpret subtext. Notions of digital literacy are misplaced. Children and young people have just adapted capabilities for contexts and spaces in which they play and learn. Ito et al.'s notion of 'messing around and geeking out' is more useful than delineations and typologies of literacies (Ito et al., 2010).

Design for learning

Design for learning has gained popularity since about 2007, when a number of authors believed that it was important to see design as a central component of teachers' work. The phrase was developed by Beetham and Sharpe in that year (see Beetham and Sharpe 2013: 7) and was coined to describe the process – formerly known as curriculum design (Cox et al., 1981) – by which teachers and others planned and structured learning. They argued that it involved:

- Investigation: locating the users and relevant principles and theories.
- Application: considering how the principles should be applied.
- Representation or modelling: working out what solution will work best.
- Iteration: examining how useful it is in practice and exploring what changes are required.

Beetham and Sharpe (2013: 8) suggest that this model is intentional, creative and responsive, since learners and learning situations are unpredictable. This is laudable and in many ways refreshingly helpful. However, despite helpful arguments and theorizing around this approach (e.g. Goodyear and Dimitriadis, 2013), much of what is presented remains pedagogically dislocated and appears to be just decontextualized curriculum design.

Behavioural theories, such as the classical conditioning model proposed by Watson (1924) and the operant condition proposed by Skinner (1953), seem to run contrary to design for learning, but do seem to be dominant instructional design models. Hull's work and his notion of drive reduction theory (Hull, 1935), which asserts that behaviour is determined in part by learner motivation, promotes a key aspect of design for learning, which asserts that students should be motivated as stakeholders attempting to solve an important problem.

In contrast to the behavioural theories, cognitive theories are directly concerned with mental processes (which include insight, information processing, memory and perception) rather than products (behaviour), which some would suggest is more in keeping with the process approach of design for learning. Cognitive theorists seek to understand how individuals learn and what goes on inside the mind when learning occurs. This kind of education focuses on cognitive structuring, which is essential for developing capacity and skills for better learning, or to learn how to learn. Thus, perhaps the cognitive development theorists provide the best fit in providing an underlying pedagogy for design for learning: cognitive development theories offer us models that take account of cognition and development. The teacher's concern here is to enable students to develop both understandings of the nature of knowledge and ways of handling different conceptions of the world, so that knowledge acquisition is seen as an active process.

A number of innovative studies have arisen from this field. Piaget's cognitive development theories (Piaget, 1929), for example, rely on the notion of cognitive structures. Like Vygotsky, Piaget believed that the activities learners could complete matched their cognitive stage or readiness, although it should be noted that they did have differing views as to what counted as readiness. Later, Perry (1970, 1988) extended this concept in his qualitative study of men at Harvard, and devised nine positions that described how students' conceptions of the nature and origins of knowledge evolved. Whilst Beetham and Sharpe do not suggest this is a pedagogy, it is being increasingly adopted. Moreover, as Goodyear and Dimitriadis (2013: 1) suggest:

> research and development in the field of design for learning is producing some useful insights, tools and methods. Before these become too engrained, it is worth considering whether the fundamental conceptions underpinning this practical work are strong enough for the growing loads being placed upon them. In short, it is time to check whether work is moving in the right direction, and with a sufficiently comprehensive idea of the challenges that need to be addressed.

Those adopting the notion of design for learning should also consider including reasoning components more explicitly. Mercer et al. (2004) investigated the claims that students' learning of science is a discursive process so that ways of reasoning are learned through practical enquiry and social interaction. The results obtained indicated that children can be helped to use talk more effectively as a tool for reasoning and that talk-based activities can support the development of reasoning and scientific understanding.

It is perhaps within such cognitive developmental theories and reasoning research that design for learning can be best located. These also link to the idea of communities of practice.

Communities of practice

Community of practice has come to be seen as a pedagogy (although it was not seen as such by the original authors), but I suggest this work focuses more on participation and collaboration than on roundly created learning theory.

The concept of a community of practice (Lave and Wenger, 1991) refers to the process of social learning that occurs when people who have a common interest in some subject or problem collaborate over an extended period to share ideas, find solutions and build innovations. The focus here is thus more on the relationship between the individual and the community, and the way in which they learn the practices of that community. Much of what occurs in the community of practice literature concerns group work and team endeavours – which may be just as much about teamwork or research projects as it is about induction into a profession. Many of these short-term communities have the hallmarks of activity theory, too. However, like design for learning, many of the arguments for engagement in communities of practice focus on the learning and undemanding nature of communities, rather than provide pedagogical theories that might help to position it.

Actor network theory and activity theory

Actor network theory is a means of exploring the relational ties within a network, although it is more of a method than a theory. It was originally created by

Callon (1986) and Latour (1987) in an attempt to understand processes of techno-logical innovation and scientific knowledge creation. It does not typically attempt to explain why networks exist, but rather how they are formed and why they fail. Thus, it is not a pedagogy or a theory, or indeed a research methodology; so, in terms of its utility in exploring learning, networks and online environments, it is deeply problematic. This is because it decontextualizes action and experiences, and those using it tend to adopt post-positivist stances, when much of what occurs in these spaces is constructionist and should be examined as such. Constructionists believe that hidden or private phenomena, such as emotions, gain their meaning through social settings and practice, and are therefore socially constructed. Reality is therefore not entirely external and independent of individual conceptions of the world, and thus signs and systems play important roles in the social construction of reality as individuals make and experience meaning together (Savin-Baden and Major, 2013).

Activity theory is also not a pedagogy, but rather a conceptual framework. The underlying idea of the framework is purposeful activity, and the framework is used to examine the interactions between actors (subjects) and the world (objects). The original formulation of activity theory was developed by Leontiev (1947/1981), and was later developed and popularized by Engeström (1987). Both forms of activity theory are widely used in education and psychology, and more recently in professional learning (e.g. Markauskaite and Goodyear, 2014). Those who adopt such actor network theory and activity theory suggest their work is built on a constructivist stance. This seems a more utopian stance than a reality, since constructivism is the notion that knowledge lies in the minds of individuals, who construct what they know on the basis of their own experiences. It suggests that the process of knowledge construction is active rather than passive. Researchers who adopt this approach believe that research involves an attempt to understand individual construction of knowledge and that it is their role to understand the ways in which individuals construct meaning, since knowledge, truth and reality are created rather than constructed.

In practice, actor network theory operates with the hallmarks of post-positivism, as exemplified in the work of Karl Popper. He explored the relationship between scientific belief and the guarantees for such beliefs, and argued that the essence of science was the extent to which it could be refuted. Actor network theory could also be located in cognitive theories that are directly concerned with mental processes (which include insight, information processing, memory and perception) rather than products (behaviour). Cognitive theorists seek to understand how individuals learn and what goes on inside the mind when learning occurs. This kind of education focuses on cognitive structuring, which is essential for developing capacity and skills for better learning, or learning how to learn.

Goodyear and Carvalho (2014) argue that activity is central but emergent – that activities are designed to resource and guide learner activity – suggesting that activity looks different when it begins with goal-directed action rather than embodied cognition. The framework has been developed for analysing learning networks to show how knowledge, human interaction and physical and digital resources combine in the operation of productive learning networks (Carvalho and Goodyear, 2014).

It is important that ideas such as actor network theory are not used in behavioural ways separating learner, learning methods, learner identity and learning context. The danger with many of the current instantiations of design for learning, communities of practice, actor network theory and activity theory is that they can be oversimplified and/or misused, resulting in pedagogical piracy, as discussed further in the conclusion to this chapter.

Commodification of learning?

Learning has been commodified through both the commercialization of learning technologies in universities and schools and the increasing standardization of learning through government policies and European directives, along with the development of the edutainment market. The way in which technology is employed in many universities is resulting in the sense of an institutional panopticon, where visibility and calculability are not seen as problematic. Yet, such 'exteriorisation' (Land, 2006: 101) is largely ignored by both staff and students.

In 1993 Ritzer suggested that society, and higher education in particular, was becoming commodified, and expressed this in terms of 'McDonaldization'. His argument was that the principles of the fast-food industry had come to dominate all parts of American society and the rest of the world. The central argument is that everything has become homogenized in terms of *efficiency*, so that achieving a task in minimal time is a key focus, as is *calculability* – the manufacture of high-quality products at minimum cost. Workers are judged by how fast they operate, instead of the quality of the work they do. *Predictability* is essential, so that no matter where or who the customer is, they will receive the same service and product every time. Finally, *control* is vital: employees are standardized and uniform. Ritzer argued that as these processes extended across society new social and cultural characteristics were created and hybridization occurred.

Ten years later, Barnett (2003) argued that ideologies had entered and taken a grip on universities in ways that were both virtuous and pernicious, and that it was impossible to remove such ideologies. He advocated the development of positive ideologies – which he termed 'idealogies' – to prevent the corrosion of positive ideologies and embrace and promote universities' ideals: 'Amid the ideologies that threaten to overwhelm it, the university can find itself again through virtuous *idealogies*. Such *idealogies* call for a leadership that can stand apart from the rhythms of the age and can forge alternative sources of *being* in the university' (Barnett, 2003: 131; original emphasis). Barnett therefore argued for qualities such as reasonableness and willingness to learn that will enable universities to operate within and with a flexible structure in the context of a fluid world.

In order to shift from ideology to idealogy, it is important to recognize the increasing number of performative practices that pervade the lives of students and academics. These focus on narrow categories, such as Bloom's taxonomy (Bloom, 1956), behavioural learning approaches, lesson plans and learning outcomes. They are mechanisms that regulate and delimit learning spaces. Just as the focus on outcomes pedagogy has created a particular type of curriculum, this pedagogy has also occluded academics' visions about possible alternatives. We still have behavioural objectives, but there is a need to shift the focus and create rewritable learning intentions: we need to intend that learning should occur, rather than expect our teaching objectives to be met. Curricula designed using behavioural objectives rather than learning intentions close down opportunities for creative and innovative forms of learning, and in turn occlude the vision to create smooth learning spaces. Pernicious performativity pervades judgement, and academics see themselves as being required to replicate the same narrow practices in their own learning spaces.

It could be argued that digital media has made the situation worse and that propriety software for learning exemplifies this. For example, both commodification and containment of knowledge are particularly evident in virtual learning environments (VLEs), such as Blackboard, that structure and manage learning; for some academics, there is a sense that the technology disables rather than enables the pedagogy. In other arenas, the pedagogy is missing or it is unclear who the learning audience actually is. For example, many of the recent Open Science projects (www.open.ac.uk/researchprojects/open-science/about-openscience-laboratory) use technology in innovative ways but seem unsure about the identity of their audience. The result is that the citizen science projects are often deemed unreliable and need to be checked by experts, which seems to negate the very idea of 'openness' itself.

Language, with a subtext of control, is evident in many VLEs, not only through semiotics, symbols and terminology, but also in the way learning is ordered in ways that suggest how teaching and learning should be. The fact that VLEs continue to be fraught with images is deeply problematic and such structure and safety suggests stability and control. Further, all these systems encourage students to manage knowledge and their discussions, and possibly even to think and learn in linear ways. There are further difficulties with the language of online learning. The notion of 'moderating' clearly locates the control with the lecturers. The notion of 'lurking' implies that silence and watching are inherently bad, and simultaneously raises questions about what counts as presence in digital spaces – and who decides.

Massively open online courses (MOOCs) are also increasingly commercializing and commodifying learning. Whilst the rhetoric for MOOCs is to provide open and flexible learning that is 'free', the presence of companies who are in the market for selling knowledge through them indicates that it is far from free. For example, in 2012 Udacity announced plans for students to pay eighty dollars to take exams at testing centres operated by Pearson, an education company. As *The Economist* pointed out in July 2013:

> The MOOCs themselves may be free, but those behind them think there will be plenty of revenue opportunities. Coursera has started charging to provide

certificates for those who complete its courses and want proof, perhaps for a future employer. It is also starting to license course materials to universities that want to beef up their existing offering ... For Udacity, in contrast, working with companies to train existing and future employees is now the heart of its business model. It has tie-ups with several firms, including Google. It recently formed a partnership with AT&T, along with Georgia Tech, to offer a master's degree in computer science. Course materials will be free, but students will pay around $7,000 for tuition. EdX is taking yet another tack, selling its MOOC technology to universities like Stanford, both to create their own MOOC offerings and to make physically attending university more attractive, by augmenting existing teaching.

Many MOOCs are indeed open, but often if you want to do more, you have to pay. Certainly, in many cases, if they are to have any value or credit through assessment, students are required to pay. As Matt Mawer (personal communication) reflects:

> It seems the major discourse of MOOCs (as tech du jour) is, for all the bluster about democratizing HE access, about re-colonializing education by allowing universities or whoever to teach kids in the Nairobi slums (rather than help enhance and develop locally led provision) and about creating a marketable product for big player HEIs to sell abroad.

It is particularly interesting that there has been a relative lack of criticality across the higher education sector about MOOCs; they are generally seen as a good thing and they are designed in ways that business companies expect learning to be designed. Currently there is a lack of a critical focus on pedagogy, with little or no realization that these commercial forms of education will have an impact on the values of higher education. This somewhat arbitrary acceptance of MOOCs appears to indicate that there is increasingly a sense among universities themselves that what academics have to offer is valued less, if at all. It seems that the idea of higher education providing education centred on values, ethics and civic engagement, within which students wrestle with important issues through study and criticality, is starting to be lost in the mists of time. Instead, MOOCs are offering a system of collecting chunks of knowledge through random modules.

Institutions such as the Open University appear to be very naïve about MOOCs. This extract seems particularly telling:

> Pedagogies that could benefit such learners are missing from much of the first wave of massive courses. These pedagogies include materials designed to provide an integrated learning experience, feedback that is customized to meet learner needs, and direct mentoring of learners in difficulties. Some of these are hard to supply in a cost-free model ... The issue of where MOOCs are going is perhaps less important in the short term than how they are

shaping expectations from individuals, organizations and governments that they should meet the growing need for education and learning.

In that case they clearly do have a role.

(Sharples et al., 2013: 10)

There is a sense that pedagogy somehow equates to materials that meet learner needs, yet there have been some interesting developments in the area of MOOCs, which will be discussed in Chapter 4.

Much of current practice appears to be about training rather than education. Stenhouse (1975) argued that training is seen as the acquisition of skills, with the result that successful training is deemed to be the capacity for performance. In fact, higher education should be about the introduction of someone into the thought system of the culture of knowledges, and here successful induction would be characterized by that person's ability to develop relationships and judgements in relation to that culture. If we continue to engage with performative enterprise practices and fail to recreate spaces and voices, universities will soon become sites of closure, where criticality and questioning are submerged in the quest for fast money and solid learning. Universities need to rethink their interpretive repertoire, since much of higher education still locates itself with the values about how teaching and research should operate. Certainly, at the higher management levels of universities, the focus is on how large sums of money might be gained to sustain the institution, rather than on the nature or value of teaching.

Yet students are engaged in forms of social learning and networking that transgress these spaces and values. There have been arguments that higher education needs to be reclaimed. For example, Giroux and Giroux (2004: 120) write:

> In opposition to the commodification, privatization and commercialization of everything educational, educators need to define higher education as a resource vital to the democratic and civic life of the nation. The challenge is thus for academics, cultural workers, students and labour organizers to join together and oppose the transformation of higher education into a commercial sphere.

We need a reconstitution of what learning and teaching *might be* in light of what a university *might be for.* At the same time, it is important to question the ways in which media, practices and learning designs are shaped through the digital world, not merely in terms of their impact on learning, but *if* they contribute to learning and, if so, *how.* Livingstone (2010b) has argued:

> Instead of celebrating young people's creativity or sophistication – though undoubtedly this is significant – we ought to be observing when and how young people lack the skills required to bend technologies to their own ends or struggle to protect their privacy from intrusive others – both because this also exists and because only in this way can research argue for the provision

of resources for children and young people. If they truly were 'digital natives', they could get on perfectly well by themselves.

Conclusion

Criminal profit-seeking is undesirable, yet in the case of piracy the practice of pirate slavery ultimately led to progressive racial practices (Leeson, 2009). Whilst I suggest that pedagogical piracy has many undesirable outcomes, some of the theories and methods presented here offer a means of reconsidering how higher education has positioned itself. It also prompts consideration of its values and an exploration of what really counts as pedagogy in the context of a liquid digital age, as Ingold (2012: 435) has suggested:

> In the act of production, the artisan couples his own movements and gestures
> – indeed, his very life – with the becoming of his materials, joining with and
> following the forces and flows that bring his work to fruition. Crucially, these
> paths of movement and lines of flow do not connect: they are not between
> one pre-existing entity and another but perpetually on the threshold of
> emergence. They are the lines along which materials flow and bodies move.
> Together, these entangled lines, of bodily movement and material flow,
> compose what I have elsewhere called the meshwork . . . And this meshwork
> . . . is nothing other than the web of life itself.

Narrow conceptual frameworks that lock down and distinguish discrete parameters between subject and object are not useful in the digital age. Digital tethering is a way of acting and a way of being whereby people's lives and learning are entangled and perpetually on the threshold of emergence.

New approaches to learning and new designs and methods are diverse, complex and tend to interrupt what many members of staff in higher education might see as straightforward teaching and learning. Yet changes in these areas continue apace. What is seemingly disruptive now will probably not be so in six months' to a year's time. Thus, it is important for staff and students to be prepared to manage the disruption and change, as well as to embrace it as part of the increasingly liquid terrain of higher education in the twenty-first century.

4
LEARNING ON THE MOVE?

Liquidity and meshwork

Introduction

It would seem that making digital tethering practice explicit is likely, at one level, to unsettle staff perspectives about when and where learning occurs (and with whom), while at another level it will enable the creation and mapping of learning theories and practices that will be sufficiently expansive to encompass the new learning mobilities and geographies we are starting to see in students' lives. These expanding theories surrounding new mobilities and geographies should be concerned with exploring polarities such as home/school and formal/informal learning, and with the kinds of learning trajectories that digital tethering is prompting. Analysis is needed to determine whether this makes learning more or less effective than, or just different from, current practices, and whether it is different across diverse disciplinary contexts. This chapter will therefore explore some of the newer developments in, and conceptions of, learning.

Learning

Whilst theories of learning have never been static, the distinction between and across the approaches – behavioural, cognitive, developmental and critical pedagogy – continues to erode. There is increasing focus on what and how students learn and on ways of creating learning environments to ensure that they learn effectively – although much of this remains contested ground. Models and theories of learning have emerged and older ones have been re-evaluated over the last two decades which inform the concept of curriculum spaces. For example, the work of Trigwell et al. (1999) on teachers' conceptions of learning offers useful insights into the impact such conceptions have on student learning, as does earlier work that has gained recent popularity, such as Vygotsky's (1978) zone of current and proximal development. By contrast, the work of Meyer and Land (2006), Haggis (2004), and

Meyer and Eley (2006) has been critical of studies into conceptions of teaching and approaches to learning.

This recent body of work, along with shifts away from the certainty of learning styles and towards more holistic conceptions of learner approaches, is important in developing the debate away from generalizations and cognitive foci and towards an understanding of learner and teacher identities. Much recent work indicates that learning is located in identity and that developmental learning is more profoundly influential than other forms. Yet the Lancaster studies on deep and surface approaches to learning (Entwistle and Ramsden, 1983) continue to remain popular.

The notion of approaches to learning is rooted in the cognitive tradition, emerging from the work of Marton and Säljö (1976a, 1976b), who distinguished two different approaches to learning: those learners who concentrate on memorizing (surface approaches to learning); and those who put meaning in their own terms (deep approaches to learning). Entwistle (1981) then extended the work of Marton and Säljö in what are known as the Lancaster studies, which were first undertaken to identify the factors associated with academic success and failure at university. He also built upon the work of Pask (1976), who had claimed that two general categories of learning strategy can be identified in cognitive tasks: those of holists – students who identify the main parameters of a system and then fill in the details; and those of serialists – who progressively work through details to build up the complete picture as they go. More recently, Baeten et al. (2010) undertook a review that examined encouraging and discouraging factors in stimulating the adoption of deep approaches to learning in student-centred learning environments. The results indicate that students in different disciplines use different approaches to learning, with those in human sciences generally showing the deepest approaches. Of particular note in this research was the impact of teachers: for example, if teachers supported and encouraged students to change their learning approaches, the students were more likely to adopt a deep approach. Mature students and students who were conscientious, self-confident and self-efficacious preferred teaching methods that enhanced understanding.

One of the central issues to emerge from the Lancaster studies tradition was that of the 'learning context', which has shifted and changed with the advent of digital media. The acknowledgement of the importance of the learning context has thus begun to raise concerns about student learning per se, whilst also highlighting the importance of the learner as a person whose experience is often somewhat marginalized in studies about the ways and new contexts in which students learn. For example, Ito et al. (2010: 17) argue:

> Examining learning as changes in genres of participation is an alternative to the notion of 'transfer', where the mechanism is located in a process of individual internalization of content or skills. In a participatory frame, it is not that kids transfer new media skills or social skills to different domains, but rather they begin to identify with and participate in different social networks and sets of cultural referents through certain transitional social and cultural

mechanisms. It is not sufficient to internalize or identify with certain modes of participation; there also needs to be a supporting social and cultural world.

The issue of learning context is more fluid now than it was in the 1970s and 1980s, when learning was predominantly seen as being based in schools and universities. Today, the notion of learning context transcends institutions and it is seen as mobile and liquid. Perhaps that means it is now redundant and ripe for replacement with a term such as 'learning habitus'. Mauss's (1934) use of habitus is the best fit here, since he defined it in terms of facets of culture that are anchored in the practices of individuals, groups, societies and nations – things that, as it were, go without saying and operate at a level of subtext. Thus, a learning habitus would include learned habits, skills, styles, tastes and other forms of knowledge that are necessarily located within and across culture and agency. The idea of a learning habitus is valuable because it shifts the notion of learning away from specific contexts, institutions or practices and locates it as a more liquid genre that travels with the learner across spaces, places and temporalities. Using the concept of habitus captures the idea that learning is not located in a physical place or space; instead, it is located in daily practices, choices, styles and experiences.

The following approaches perhaps recognize liquidity and meshwork in ways that might be transformative for digitally tethered students:

- multimedia assessment feedback;
- pedagogical agents;
- massively open online courses;
- serious and epistemic games;
- problem-based simulations;
- flipped learning;
- virtual and remote labs; and
- liquid books.

Multimedia assessment feedback

Although much of the literature on multimedia assignment feedback refers to the research into assessment feedback, it draws on it to only a limited degree. To date, there has been relatively little research into the value or impact of podcasting for learning, as much of the literature centres on practice rather than pedagogy (see, e.g., Salmon and Edirisingha, 2008). Although studies in the use of audio feedback have been in existence since the 1980s (see, e.g., Rust, 2001), much of the recent practice and research into multimedia assignment feedback is based on an isolated group of studies (Gibbs and Simpson, 2005; Nicol and Macfarlane-Dick, 2006). These studies may be grouped into those that used multimedia assignment feedback for formative assessment, those that used it for summative assessment, and those that used it for both. The difficulty with the early teacher-led models of feedback is a sense that assessment feedback is a one-way process, from staff to students. Such teacher-led approaches result in a kind of 'assessment monologism'.

Student engagement with assessment feedback (Hounsell, 2003) remains a source of frustration for both students and tutors. What is needed is the transformation and reshaping of feedback practice: students should be involved in the execution of the research, rather than simply the subjects of it. For example, better practice could include students in designing the feedback on their work using audio and video technologies. This would entail working with them to understand what works best for them, with the likely result that it would improve student engagement and learning in the future.

Effective multimedia assessment feedback therefore needs to be student-centred, so that students believe it to be better than current feedback practices in their discipline. Using multimedia feedback makes it possible to focus on the student work itself, rather than on the mark or grade, because the tutor speaks directly to the student, and the work is visible and can be annotated as the student watches the video. The student then becomes part of an ongoing conversation and dialogic space, instead of being in a position of responding to feedback that remains, predominantly, a monologue. Multimedia assignment feedback should:

- foster the delivery of high-quality feedback that helps students self-correct;
- enable staff to explain to students what counts as good performance; and
- encourage staff–student dialogue about assessment expectations and practices.

Pedagogical agents

Pedagogical agents have a long history of use, beginning with the work of Turing (1950), who developed one of the first evaluation methods for pedagogical agents. It is still applied today. The popularity of pedagogical agents is perhaps best represented by the Loebner Prize, awarded each year since 1991 to the agent deemed most successful in answering Turing-like tests that assess realistic interactions. The understanding of these technologies is inchoate and often untheorized, influenced by factors such as individuals' willingness to trust technologies, the aesthetic appearance of an agent and individuals' technical literacy. Integration of pedagogical agents into educational settings is more recent, but publications over the past five years suggest an increase in interest in the ways in which they might be adopted and adapted for teaching and learning (Heidig and Clarebout, 2011).

Daily activities, such as socializing and learning, are increasingly mediated through cyberspace environments. These environments can be predominantly textual two-dimensional websites, such as forums or commercial websites, or three-dimensional graphical environments, such as virtual worlds. However, whilst they vary considerably in nature, certain similarities can be identified. One such pattern is the increasing presence of the agents in commercial, industrial and educational settings.

The use of pedagogical agents in both commercial and educational settings has the potential to disrupt the ways in which we interact in online settings, as 'robots [become] part of our relational futures' (Turkle, 2010: 4). Kerly et al. (2007: 128) argue:

> Pedagogical agents are autonomous agents that occupy computer learning environments and facilitate learning by interacting with students or other agents. They may act as peers, co-learners, competitors, helpers or instructors. For effective pedagogy, agents should be able to ask and respond to questions, give hints and explanations, monitor students and provide feedback.

The technology to deliver pedagogical agents as dynamic and speaking avatars (e.g. Flash) is now in mass-market use, making pedagogical agents a far richer and more engaging experience than lines of text on a screen. Furthermore, the integration of web services into pedagogical agents means that they can access live services to provide up-to-date information in their responses, and prevent the need to store all knowledge in the agent. Innovative and disruptive learning using pedagogical agents with problem-based learning could encourage students to develop high-level digital fluency, since this example combines a critical pedagogy with technology that personalizes learning and is interactive. The use of pedagogical agents might disrupt the ways in which interaction in online settings occurs, but there is a greater need to understand the ways in which individuals relate and disclose information to pedagogical agents. As pedagogical agent technologies are increasingly integrated into commercial and educational arenas, it seems likely that they will transfer to mobile as well as blended learning settings. These technologies also seem particularly relevant when considering the increasingly popular massive online open courses (MOOCs) and their potential influence upon the future of education.

Massive open online courses

Massive open online courses (MOOCs) are founded on the theory of connectivism and an open pedagogy based on networked learning. Connectivism was devised by Downes (2006) and Siemens (2008a) as a learning theory for the digital age. The central idea is that learning occurs through connections within networks and the model uses the concept of a network with nodes and connections to define learning.

MOOCs are large, open-access courses that are normally free, have no entry requirements and are usually run two to three times each year. The original authors never intended for them to become the large commercial ventures they are now, hence the critique provided below. Invariably, they are led by world-class academics and supported by teaching assistants, and they are self-directed, meaning students follow the course materials, complete the readings and assessments, and get help from a large community of fellow learners through online forums.

MOOCs have evolved into two distinct types: those that emphasize the connectivist philosophy; and those that resemble more traditional courses. To distinguish between the two, Downes (2012) developed the terms cMOOC and xMOOC. The first MOOCs were cMOOCs, which are associated with the notion of connectivism, a view that sees learning as a network comprising nodes and ties.

cMOOCs

The central premise of connectivism is that learning takes place with and through networked information and resources. This means that learning is seen as accessing and evaluating relevant information, and relating it between different forms of knowledge. Thus, Siemens (2008a, 2008b) argues that learning takes place through the connections that students make between knowledge, opinions, resources and views accessed via search engines and online sources. Connectivist pedagogy suggests the need to ensure:

1. Learning and knowledge rest in a diversity of opinions.
2. Learning is a process of connecting specialized nodes or information sources.
3. Learning may reside in non-human appliances.
4. The capacity to know more than is currently known is most critical.
5. Nurturing and maintaining connections are needed to facilitate continual learning.
6. The ability to see connections between fields, ideas and concepts is a core skill.
7. Currency (accurate, up-to-date knowledge) is the intent of all connectivist learning activities.
8. Decision-making is itself a learning process. Choosing what to learn and the meaning of incoming information are seen through the lens of a shifting reality.

cMOOCs are characterized by connections, openness and autonomy so that students learn though debate. They share characteristics with problem-based learning (PBL), because in both approaches the focus is on the students' ability to make connections between the forms of knowledge they encounter. Nevertheless, those who have adopted PBL can learn from connectivism the need to begin to ask, whatever instantiation is being adopted, the following questions suggested by Siemens (2009):

> How are connections formed? What does a particular constellation of connections represent? How important is technology in enabling connections? What, if anything, is transferred during an interaction between two, three, or more learners? What would learning look like if we developed it from the world view of connections?

xMOOCs

At the core of the xMOOC course is the instructor-guided lesson, although xMOOCs may also include discussion forums and allow people to bounce ideas around and discuss learning together. Each student's trajectory through the course is linear and based on the absorption and understanding of fixed competencies. Learning is seen as something that can be tested and certified.

xMOOCs were derived largely from the work of Thrun and Norvig, who developed an artificial intelligence course in which over 160,000 students enrolled. Currently the three leading providers of xMOOCs are: EdX, a non-profit company formed by the University of California at Berkeley, MIT, Harvard and the University of Texas; Coursera, a for-profit company originating from the University of Stanford, and now with many other university partners (largely US Ivy League institutions); and UDACITY, another for-profit company with University of Stanford roots but with no university affiliations. Early xMOOCs were similar in pedagogy to early Open University courses, in that they focused on watching lectures and clips and undertaking online assessments.

Gamified MOOCs

The notion of G-MOOCs (gamified MOOCs) may extend the current state of the art and improve retention and optimize benefits. Such MOOCs capitalize on the existing pedagogy-driven game development approach and game-based learning (GBL), but they are still very much in development (Arnab et al., 2014).

MOOLs

Following the growth of MOOCs, Lowe (2014) has considered the development of MOOLs – massive open online laboratories – and examined the ways in which it might be possible to support remote laboratory experimentation in massive-scale courses. Lowe notes that there is a wide variability in the capacity needed to support remote laboratory experimentation for large-scale courses, and also suggests research is needed into students' experiences of using such MOOLs.

Serious games and epistemic games

There has been much debate about the relationships between games, learning games and serious games. Serious games are seen as simulations of real-world events or processes designed for the purpose of solving a problem. Thus, their main purpose is to educate users: they have a clear educational purpose and are not intended to be played primarily for amusement. Epistemic games were developed by Collins and Ferguson (1993), who categorized them into structural analysis games, functional analysis games and process analysis games. The idea is that each type presents increasing levels of challenge, so that structural analysis games are the easiest and process analysis games the most difficult. In short:

- Structural analysis games determine the components or elements of a system. Examples include: making a list, creating a timeline, drawing a map and filling in a matrix.
- Functional analysis games show how the elements in a system are related to each other. Examples include: creating a hierarchical chart, deriving an equation and making a causal chain diagram.
- Process analysis games describe how a system behaves. Examples include: drawing a flowchart, creating a graph to show change in a system over time and creating a spreadsheet to project business profits.

Shaffer (2006), who built on this work, argued that epistemic games are simulations that link knowing and doing. His work focused on their use in professional practice, suggesting that reflective practice is an important component. Thus, for Shaffer, epistemic games should develop the values, skills, ethics and epistemology that professions use to think in innovative ways. This stance links to work on signature pedagogies, discipline-based pedagogies and threshold concepts as well as to the importance of disjunction in learning. To date, these concepts have often been disregarded in games design and development.

Newman (2004) has argued that the world of computer games is messy and complex. He suggests that seven 'types' can be delineated:

- action and adventure;
- driving and racing;
- first-person shooter;
- platform and puzzle;
- role-playing, strategy and simulation;
- sports; and
- beat-'em-ups.

However, he also asserts that such categorization takes little account of the diversity and complexity of games, game designers and the notion of games. As he suggests, such delineation is rather nebulous and in recent years there has been a shift away from game typologies towards the purposes and complexities of games design.

Arnab et al. (2014) argue for the importance of a model of games-based learning. They propose the learning mechanics–game mechanics (LM–GM) model, which locates pre-defined game mechanics and pedagogical elements to be used in a game. Whilst this complex model is a very useful starting point, it tends to draw on older theories and models of learning that have been superseded by more sophisticated ones that take into greater account the ways in which young people and students learn in the twenty-first century. If it were to be developed by focusing on threshold concepts and instantiations of problem-based learning that centre on critical pedagogy, rather than on the outdated Bloom's taxonomy, it could help to shift games-based learning away from linear, solid and content-driven models of learning and towards one that focuses on supercomplexity and liquid learning. Further, Waern (2013) has suggested that game analysis might be seen as a signature pedagogy of game studies. This is based on the work of Shulman (1986, 1987, 2005, 2006), who has argued for a framework for understanding teacher knowledge in which he describes several layers that include both subject knowledge and pedagogical knowledge, which he terms 'signature pedagogies'. Subject or content knowledge comprises the theories, principles and concepts of a particular discipline. In addition to this, general pedagogical knowledge or knowledge about teaching itself is an important aspect of teacher knowledge. Somewhere between subject-matter knowledge and pedagogical knowledge lies pedagogical-content knowledge.

Whilst Waern (2013) provides an interesting argument in her study, as well as links between game studies and game analysis, there is little reference as to how discipline-based and signature pedagogies might be linked with game design to support and enable twenty-first-century learners. It is vital to see games (serious and epistemic) through both their structure and the way in which modes of knowledge are located in the curriculum. By doing this, it will be possible to create games that increasingly move away from outcome-based models and instead provoke disjunction and uncertainty in learning. Yet, as Žižek (1998) notes, gaming can also be deeply troublesome:

> The mystification operative in the perverse 'just gaming' of cyberspace is thus double: not only are the games we are playing in it more serious than we tend to assume … but the opposite also holds, i.e., the much celebrated playing with multiple, shifting personas (freely constructed identities) tends to obfuscate (and thus falsely liberate us from) the constraints of social space in which our existence is caught.

Sherwood (1991) argues that games helped children to engage in 'fundamental elements' of the 'new curriculum': namely, enquiry, creative expression, social interaction and cooperative effort. These would seem to be fundamental to learning, whether at school or in higher education. Yet, as Hämäläinen et al. (2006) suggest, there has been little research into collaborative learning games. Ravenscroft and Matheson (2002) discuss the importance of dialogue facilitation games in improving students' conceptual understanding through dialogue, rather than through competition. There have also been few, if any, problem-based learning games that link strongly with models and theories of PBL. Further, there seems to be a lack of understanding about the difference between problem-based learning and problem-solving, which makes the landscape of problem-based learning and digital games-based learning rather murky. For example, Kiili (2005: 17) illustrates this:

> Generally, games provide a meaningful environment for problem-based learning. The ability to solve problems is one of the most important features

of human skills (Holyoak, 1991). Thus, one goal of education is to groom students to encounter novel situations (Bruer, 1993). Problem solving can be regarded as striving toward a goal which is not immediately attainable. Games provide a meaningful framework for offering problems to students. In fact, a game itself is a big problem that is composed of smaller causally linked problems. The nature of challenges that constitute the problem can vary greatly. Generally, a problem can be anything that somehow restricts a player's progress in the game world.

What is also interesting about Kiili's argument is the importance of 'flow' in game play. He suggests, 'Bad usability decreases the likelihood of experiencing task based flow because the player has to sacrifice attention and other cognitive resources to inappropriate activity' (Kiili, 2005: 15). Yet there is little sense throughout his article that experiencing disjunction is an important part of learning – about the game, oneself as a game player, and understanding, though not necessarily achieving, the objectives of the game.

Recently, Markauskaite and Goodyear (2014) provided a comprehensive overview of games for knowledge action, which is perhaps one of the most useful conceptualizations of epistemic games:

> *Situated problem-solving games* are played during the investigation and solution of specific professional problems, such as conducting reviews of medications used by patients with multiple diseases in order to identify possible issues, with an aim of proposing better medication plans (pharmacy), or designing lessons for classroom teaching (education).

> *Meta-professional discourse* games are usually played with other professionals within a broader professional field, in order to evaluate various professional products, actions or events. They involve various deconstructions, evaluations and reflections, such as analyses of new medications, evaluations of teaching resources, and reflections on one's practices.

> *Translational public discourse games* are played by professionals when they engage in interactions with people who broadly could be described as 'clients'.

> *Weaving games* are played in dynamic action and involve continuous intertwining of meaning-making, social interaction and skilled performance. They range from very specialised games that can require fine-tuned physical skill – such as strategies for capturing all the spelling mistakes in a literacy test – to quite generic games that require complex coordination of various general and specialised strategies and skills.

This kind of classification of games is helpful in ensuring strong pedagogical foundations, and also indicates the game types which need to be created to compel players to work together; because, when individuals become stuck, they are more likely to work collaboratively, as is the case in both well-designed problem-based games and in problem-based learning as a whole.

Problem-based simulations

In problem-based learning the focus is in organizing the curricular content around problem scenarios rather than subjects or disciplines. Students work in groups or teams to solve or manage these situations but they are not expected to acquire a predetermined series of 'right answers'. Instead, they are expected to engage with the complex situation presented to them and decide what information they need to learn and what skills they need to gain in order to manage the situation effectively. There are many different ways of implementing problem-based learning but the underlying philosophies associated with it as an approach are broadly more student-centred than those underpinning problem-solving learning.

The Inspiring Science Education Demonstrator is an example of a problem-based simulation that brings together existing technological solutions and customizes and integrates them appropriately, so as to create an integrated educational environment that will facilitate orchestration of eLearning tools from the Inspiring Science Education inventory. Work by Lameras et al. (2014) is innovative in its use of problem-based learning in providing a consistent experience to students while accessing the available eLearning tools and resources and also creating templates for the development of educational scenarios for staff.

Simulations have been used in real-world settings for many years for learning and practising skills. Perhaps the most notable and complex are those used for aviation and space programmes. Growth in the use of simulations occurred in the 1980s particularly in the areas of medicine and healthcare with increasing use of skills labs. More recently, other high-quality simulations have been developed, such as those provided by Medical Education Technologies Inc. Simulations are very effective for trial-and-error learning – the idea that skills can be gained through practice – but one of the difficulties is that any learned skill needs to have been practised across contexts for it to be effective. For example, Eva et al. (1998) have suggested that the problem-solving theories concerning ways in which students transfer knowledge from one context to another fall into two broad areas: abstract induction and conservative induction. Abstract induction presumes that students learn principles or concepts from exposure to multiple problems by abstracting a general rule, thus it is independent of context. Conservative induction assumes that the rule is not separated from the problem context, but rather that expertise emerges from having the same principle available in multiple problem contexts. What is important then is that practice occurs across different types of context.

Studies in both psychology and medical education have found that transfer from one context to another is less frequent and more difficult than is generally believed. Schoenfeld (1989) showed that students trained on a geometry problem did not transfer their knowledge to solving construction problems, because they believed that these latter problems should be solved using trial and error. Eva et al. (1998)

suggest that the transfer of knowledge between problems of the same domain (such as chest pain) is much more likely when the context has changed. This means that we can give students the opportunity to practise solving similar problems in the virtual worlds; in this case, an example would be different clients with various types of chest pain.

Research on virtual reality and simulations would seem to suggest that transfer is more likely from virtual situations to real-life situations than early work on transfer across different real-world settings had previously implied. Additionally, immersion provides a high level of motivation to learn. Dede (1995) argues that the capacity to shape and interact with the environment is highly motivating and sharply focuses attention. Similarly Warburton (2009) indicates that the immersive nature of virtual worlds can provide a compelling educational experience, particularly in relation to simulation and role-playing activities.

It is important to recognize that there are three dimensions in the design of a simulation in Second Life:

- The context of the activity or task: this needs to be realistic and something to which students relate.
- The content: the domain of knowledge that relates to the area of the discipline being studied.
- The schema or deep structure: the 'underlying game'.

For example, it would seem that in the learning process many students fail to locate what Perkins (2006) refers to as the 'episteme', or underlying game (what it is that is required by the tutor). Staff attempts to communicate the underlying game have taken a number of forms. For example, Kinchin et al. (2010) suggest that providing information in chains is unhelpful to students as these are merely procedural sequences. They argue that teaching students within a linear lecture structure fails to help students to link together different knowledges. Instead, they suggest we should teach networks of understanding, illustrating how knowledges and practices are connected so that knowledge is integrated and holistic. The advantages of using simulations in Second Life are:

- Through them it is possible to create a sense of reality and immersion.
- Once they have been designed, they are easy to set up and play again. This means if they are designed well, students can practise skills at any time. Indeed, paramedic students on the PREVIEW project (Savin-Baden et al., 2011) valued the opportunity to use the scenarios to practise for examinations.
- It is possible to practise skills and undertake experiments that would be too dangerous or complex in real life.
- Students can be placed in situations that are impossible in reality, such as deep space or within an illness: for example, they can experience a psychotic episode.
- Once simulations have been created, they are inexpensive to adapt and reuse.

- By using holodeck technology – changeable environments where the scene changes at the touch of button – it is possible to cater for different and easily changeable simulations.

These forms of media have and are prompting transformations in learning, teaching and notions of knowledge. For example, Upton has created a humanitarian engineering project in Second Life for second-year university students (see box).

The humanitarian engineering project is about providing experience for students about to embark on international work placements. In essence, developing world culture and environment are different from those of the developed world, and developed world perspectives may be inappropriate in the working situations in which students find themselves.

The project takes a group of students, divides them into three groups, and asks them to answer a question: 'Should we support the building of a dam?' Each group of students discusses the issues and creates a short presentation while immersed in a developing world environment. These environments are quite different from each other, and they expose different views on dam-building issues. There is an economic and social environment, exposing students to the population who will be displaced by the lake created by the dam. There is a technological environment, exposing students to the benefits and infrastructure gains that building a dam will bring. Finally, there is a history environment, exposing students to the archaeological losses dam flooding will bring.

After discussion, all of the students are immersed in the developed world environment of a City of London financial office, where each group presents their case. The juxtaposition of environments and viewpoints is designed to make the students think and question. There are no right answers.

The final section of the experience asks students to 'vote with their feet' – they have to stand their avatars in a 'build', a 'do not build' or an 'undecided' space. The students are then encouraged to convince those with different views to join them in their space by entering into personal discussion.

This project worked hard to address issues that are often faced when using virtual worlds in the classroom. The avatars provided were pre-configured, so that students could allocate their own name to them, instilling a sense of ownership and professionalism.

The environment stripped back the skills needed to a minimum, and used voice, not chat, for communication.

Sources: http://vimeo.com/55523534 (short video) and http://vimeo.com/55521132 (long video)

Flipped learning

Flipped learning is a form of blended learning in which students learn new content online by watching video lectures, usually at home. What used to be homework (assigned problems) is now done in class, with teachers offering more personalized guidance and interaction with students, instead of lecturing. This is also known as a backwards classroom, reverse instruction, flipping the classroom, reverse teaching or flipped teaching.

Flipped learning began in US education in 2007, when staff began to realize that there was an increasing need for flexible approaches to classroom learning. Bergmann and Sams (2012) reported that after implanting this approach students interacted more in class and the flexible approach enabled staff to provide more individual attention to students. The Flipped Learning Network™ was launched in 2012 – a not-for-profit organization to provide resources for educators wanting to implement flipped classrooms. Hamdan et al. (2013: 4) argue that 'In the Flipped Learning model, teachers shift direct learning out of the large group learning space and move it into the individual learning space, with the help of one of several technologies.' They also suggest that there are four pillars of flipped learning:

1. Flexible environments: where the teaching space can be adapted and students can learn when and how they wish. A variety of teaching modes are adopted, which range from small group work to performance; and staff expectations about students' learning and assessment are flexible.
2. A shift in learning culture: there is a move away from teacher-centred classrooms to a student-centred approach. In practice, this means that students explore the material before class and use class time to explore topics in greater depth.
3. The use of intentional content: staff decide which material students explore first on their own and which material needs to be taught directly through lectures. They also decide on the modes of teaching and learning, so that they may use lectures, peer instruction, problem-based learning, or Socratic methods.
4. Professional educators: skilled professional educators are needed to decide what and how material should be taught and when information should be taught as lectures, in small group learning or in peer-to-peer instruction.

Whilst the flipped learning model is a helpful pedagogic shift, it has many similarities with peer group learning, action learning and some constellations of problem-based learning (Savin-Baden, 2014). To date, there has been relatively little research into the value, effect and impact of this kind of learning. The research that has been conducted suggests that students work faster, more effectively and in more depth than in lecture-based approaches (Papadapoulos and Roman, 2010). However, Strayer (2012) found that students who were undertaking introductory courses felt less satisfied than with lecture-based courses and less prepared for the work they were expected to undertake in class. Further, Johnson and Renner (2012) found no significant differences in mean test scores between those who learned in flipped classrooms and those who did not.

Virtual and remote labs

Many academic institutions have created virtual experimentations and a variety of laboratories supporting remotely operated physical experimentations. Usually, they are accessible 24/7. Virtual experimentations are simulations based on software that can be local and/or remote. There are currently a large number of European research and development funded initiatives related to remote and virtual labs. Unfortunately, these funding initiatives currently lack the broader integration and sharing of resources with similar facilities across the world, with minor exceptions being PeTEX (Terkowsky et al., 2011) and the LiLa portal (Richter et al., 2011), which provide a number of virtual experimentations and remote experiments.

Traditionally, in schools and universities, students perform (individually or in pairs) a number of hands-on physical experiments during a lab session that takes place in an instructional laboratory. The experiments, which are specified in a manual, are supervised by an instructor who prevents the students from performing dangerous experiments that might harm them or damage the equipment. The laboratories are open for students only when an instructor is present. Remote laboratories, by contrast, are operated remotely, via the internet; the actual experiments take place in the room where the experimental equipment is located. An example is VISIR (Virtual Instrument Systems In Reality), which is designed for university-level students, although it has also been used successfully in secondary schools. The VISIR Open Lab Platform is a model architecture for opening existing types of hands-on laboratories for remote access (Gustavsson et al., 2011). A unique interface gives students a feeling of being in the hands-on laboratory and they are able to create and perform experiments within the limits set by a virtual instructor. In such an online VISIR laboratory, teachers will be able to compose laboratory sessions in the same way as they can in a hands-on laboratory on campus. However, many of the explorations and experimentations with the use of virtual and remote labs tend to focus on the technology rather than the pedagogy. This results in little in-depth discussion about learning design, problem typologies or types of learning scenarios. The focus is also on use in secondary schools, yet this work would bear extending to primary schools.

Liquid books

The initial idea for liquid books (Hall, 2009) was to collect texts by theorists and publish them online as open source rather than print them as inked text. Hall explained the use of the term 'liquid' was borrowed from Kelly (2006), who argued:

Once digitized, books can be unravelled into single pages or be reduced further, into snippets of a page. These snippets will be remixed into reordered books and virtual bookshelves. Just as the music audience now juggles and reorders songs into new albums (or 'playlists', as they are called in iTunes), the universal library will encourage the creation of virtual 'bookshelves' – a collection of texts, some as short as a paragraph, others as long as entire books, that form a library shelf's worth of specialized information. And as with music playlists, once created, these 'bookshelves' will be published and swapped in the public commons.

Since 2006, playlists, vidding and mash-ups have become common practice for many, but liquid books remain uncommon, although the concept of liquid publishing can been seen in blogs, wikis and some open source documents. Hall (2009) suggests liquid books might be created to:

- challenge the limitations of a traditional printed, edited book;
- include diverse media, such as excerpts from books, podcasts and tags;
- explore the limits and possibilities of publication and dissemination online;
- break down the barriers between the developed and developing worlds by providing open access and making texts freely available to anyone;
- allow books to be openly edited, annotated, remixed and reformatted by diverse users, so that liquid books can be (re)produced by a range of collaborators worldwide.

There has been considerable discussion about liquid books' knowledge use and value in the light of practice such as the UK Research Excellence framework, as Hall (2009: 35) points out:

One issue that still remains to be addressed . . . concerns the extent to which the ability of users to annotate, link, tag, remix, reversion, and reinvent such liquid books actually renders untenable any attempt to impose a limit and a unity on them as 'works'. And what in turn are the potential consequences of such 'liquidity' for those of our ideas that depend on the concept of the 'work' for their effectivity: those concerning individualized attribution, citation, copyright, intellectual property, fair use, academic success, promotion, and so on?

Some interesting assumptions are also being made about not just liquid books but open access, since it is still, in the main, perceived as more environmentally friendly. Yet the internet footprint continues to grow, seemingly unnoticed by most.

Conclusion

The shift to liquid learning and the use of disruptive media for learning introduce some important questions. For example, are these new ways of learning just adaptations of old knowledge and practices moved into new formats? Or do they merely deal with new knowledges and new practices? This in turn raises queries about whether new knowledge and learning should be assessed in new ways. Amidst all this it is important to consider how we are equipping (or not) students to be digitally fluent in order to manage new requirements and expectations as they learn together and alone.

5

BEING DIGITALLY TETHERED

Introduction

This chapter will examine how students live and learn across the many digital media available to them, what is new, changed, or changing about how they live and learn today, and what evidence there is for these shifts. It is important to move beyond an exploration of what people are *doing* and with what in the realm of digital media, and instead examine what they are *learning*, where they are learning, with whom and from whom they are learning it. I shall also explore how students share learning, essays, learning resources and techniques, and how they learn both in collaborative learning spaces and across large proliferating networks. Finally, the extent to which digital tethering is liminal in nature will be examined, since students seem to be working at the border of the real and the augmented, and across diverse digital media, with high degrees of fluency: they sift, shift, research, explore, critique, learn and question, seemingly moving through these spatial zones and landscapes with an ease that appears to deny complexity or troublesomeness.

Being tethered

Despite considerable media publicity that positions youth culture *with* digital technology, it is important to remember that digital tethering applies across generations. It might be that some young people become well known through blogging or YouTube videos, but it is not just the so-called digital youth who are affected by the onslaught of digital media. Furthermore, it is important to take a realistic stance towards narratives about empowerment, collaboration, net-savinesss and digital fluency that both present unresearched rhetoric and trivialize the complexity of media consumption. As Burwell (2010: 385) notes:

There must also be a recognition of the culturally constituted desire to participate. Rather than falling into the trap of regarding digital participation as the outcome of technological innovation, we must relocate it within the realm of social desires, desires that create a demand for, shape, and recreate interactive technologies and practices (Cover 2006).

Although digital tethering is embedded in cultural practice, it is important to understand how this is having an impact on learning, whilst also examining the many and varied media claims. boyd (2010: 5) has explored social media in the context of young people's friendship, suggesting that learning to socialize and make friends 'is a key component of growing up as a competent social being, and that young people need to be immersed in peer cultures from an early age'. She also found that social media were not seen as separate from the rest of young people's lives but were another way to connect with peers 'that feels seamless with their everyday lives'. Furthermore, Fisher (2010) undertook a study to understand why some social media sites were more viral than others, and found that giving users high control over co-production and their own self-identity was more likely to stimulate viral growth than the particular attributes of the site per se.

Thus, amidst the many arguments about the negative impact of technology (Selwyn, 2013) and suggestions that we may be dupes of cognitive capitalism, it is not enough just to say that digital media and the assorted related corporations are undermining education and society. Consumer choice and agency still appear to have some effect on the way products are accepted, used and shared. Perhaps, therefore, it is important to examine both what is enabling learning and change, and how current systems need to be changed further to facilitate effective learning and communication for this digital age. It is also important to acknowledge, as Burwell (2010: 396) argues, that:

> Processes such as centralization, commodification, and the exploitation of free labor coexist and intersect with the appropriation of dominant narratives, the organization of alternative economies, and the imagination of alternative worlds. Such intersections complicate the popular rhetoric about online participation, demonstrating that opportunities to participate are variously seized, taken, created, managed, constrained, controlled, sold, and profited from. They also complicate one-dimensional representations of youth as either empowered or exploited by digital technology, instead suggesting that young people's creative responses to popular culture are neither solely resistant nor simply reproductive. Instead, they may be both simultaneously and, more than that, are always transformative in some way, creating new cultural ground that must constantly be renegotiated (Willis 2003).

Hence, some of the central questions that need to be considered are:

- How are devices worn and held?
- Where are they placed and shown?

- How are they referred to?
- How are they used?
- How are they part of everyday life?
- How are they used for personal representation?
- How, when and where are they used for communication?

Stald (2008) undertook a study into youth mobile phone use and found that, for most people, the mobile was always on, near by and used as a means of self-expression, creating and sustaining networks and sharing views. Young people experience 'a kind of symbiosis with their mobiles, in which the physical devices come to be understood as a representation of personal meanings and identities' (Stald, 2008: 158).

The impact of digital tethering would seem to be on connecting with others, using it for creative purposes (such as vidding), supporting interpersonal needs and reworking language and learning. As Thurlow and Bell (2009: 1040) have argued:

> It seems that, when 'grownups' take up new communication technologies, this is something to be celebrated. When young people do the same thing, however, their practices are reduced to 'hieroglyphics', 'gobbledegook', 'technobabble', 'cryptic chat', 'hodgepodge communication', 'jumble', 'ramblings', 'cryptic symbols', 'gibberish' and 'argle-bargle' to quote some of the media's terms of preference (Thurlow, 2006).

It seems that digital tethering is resulting in translocality, social support for marginalized groups and the development of different but effective forms of literacy. For example, Leppanen et al. (2009) present four studies that explain the particularities of the linguistic, social and cultural action of young Finns in translocal new media spaces. Translocality describes the use of media for hybrid identity formation and in practice occurs through the mixing of language registers, genres and styles. It enabled young girls to present themselves in a virtual social group whilst developing their values and self-image through a range of media.

Other work has illustrated the importance of digital media in diverse arenas, such as the provision of social support for low-income youth (Greenhow and Robelia, 2009) and digital access at school for disadvantaged young Latinos (Trip and Herr-Stephenson, 2009). A further example is Wood et al.'s (2011a, 2011b) research into the improvement in literacy skills due to text messaging.

One of the key areas of difficulty is that, in the main, universities and schools still only see the web as being useful to supplement learning through informational retrieval, despite students' creative abilities in knowledge management, reuse and effective organization of media away from formal learning settings. To counteract this, learning needs to be unbundled.

Unbundling learning

In the context of new technologies, distinctions have been made between schooling and education: namely, education is viewed as a lifewide enterprise whilst schooling generally spans anywhere between the ages of four and twenty-one. Collins and Halverson (2009: 43–47) suggest that there are a number of challenges that bear unpacking. These are summarized and built upon below:

- *Uniform learning versus customization.* The expectation that in schools all students need to learn the same knowledge and capabilities at the same time, whereas computers can enable the customization of learning, so that learning can be focused on the particular needs and interests of the individual student.

- *Teacher as expert versus diverse knowledge sources.* Schooling is largely built on the assumption that knowledge is fixed; thus, the role of the teacher is to present this to students. As experts, teachers generally dislike having their authority challenged by students who ask questions beyond their expertise. Yet information technologies provide access to diverse sources, opinions and forums.

- *Standardized assessment versus specialization.* Although in some systems, notably in the US, there is a tendency to use only standardized testing to provide objective scoring, this is no longer the case worldwide. However, many schools worldwide use formal testing and common examinations at given ages. The result is that the young are largely expected to learn the same thing. Yet digital media, such as gaming, performance-based assessments and problem-based assessment, can be integrated into learning environments to customize learning and assessment.

- *Knowledge in the head versus reliance on outside resources.* Learning is often seen by teachers and parents as something that must be memorized, retained and then repeated (often verbatim). The result is that in examinations students are rarely allowed to use books, articles or calculators, never mind the web. With digital media, the focus is on knowing how to find and use information, or, if you are unable to find it, knowing who to ask or which sites to access.

- *Coverage versus the knowledge explosion.* Both at school and university there is still a strong focus on covering content, and this is also invariably equated with learning. With an increasing amount of knowledge available, staff attempt to squeeze more content into the curriculum, instead of changing their approach to become more student-centred and use problem-based methods. Using the internet effectively means students are prompted to consider what they need to know, what constitutes quality knowledge and sound research, and how they might best use it. Students need to be able to ask effective questions in order to find the information and resources they need.

- *Learning by absorption versus learning by doing.* Learning a large body of knowledge is deeply embedded in the culture of schooling. However, information technologies should (although they appear unable to) push staff towards a learner-oriented understanding of knowledge acquisition and learning by doing, rather than the absorption of knowledge and disciplinary norms – which is the view of education that permeates schooling and universities.

The practices documented below are either anecdotal or seen in the literature (e.g. Ito et al., 2010; Buckingham, 2007; Jenkins, 2006). They appear to support the need to move away from traditional practices.

- *Subverting school practices:* typically texting in the toilet or under the desk during class. This may be friendship driven, but in class it is often to share and discuss learning and check answers. Thus, when students want to undertake peer-to-peer support, the school disallows it.
- *Mentorship:* using mobile devices to keep in touch with parents or other significant adults in order to get advice, feel supported or use as a sounding board. This can be achieved through Whatsapp or Facebook messaging, which can be kept relatively private and covert (important when peers deem it uncool to do this type of checking).
- *Gaming:* alone and together to share, teach, learn, offer advice, negotiate, and give and receive hints, tips and solutions.
- *Cooperative learning:* supporting and guiding each other about homework, assignments, exam revision; this can occur on the bus or on Facebook.
- *Collaborative learning:* using friendship groups to collaborate over homework (where the more experienced or confident help those who are struggling), or just to share ideas and critiques concerning the work set.
- *Teaching technology:* sharing and teaching each other about apps, new devices and helpful sites.
- *Emotional learning:* using digital media for peer-to-peer support to manage personal challenges and difficulties, and to receive advice.
- *Playful learning:* trying things out and fiddling around, in order to experiment and discover.
- *Co-production:* creating presentations together, making and sharing cybercreations, creating posters, mash-ups and vidding.

In relation to these practices it is important both to unpack the differences between government requirements and people's actual learning activities and also to create a new vocabulary to describe and delineate the kinds of activities that take place across home, schooling, education and other social and virtual spaces. We need to see learning as unbundled, as something that no longer takes place largely within educational institutions. The activities presented above centre on the idea of participatory cultures, where students create and share ideas and materials with each other. Activities are peer-based, non-hierarchical and not guided by institutions. Importantly, as Jenkins (2006) notes, the participatory norms and networks occurring through social media socialization are being transferred to the optical realm. Leander et al. (2010: 385) have pointed out:

> While children are experiencing new and rapid movements and new opportunities to learn, they are not simply caught up in an idealized version of global life that includes rapid and unfettered travel, continual technologies of instantaneity, and the compression of space by time. Rather, their learning lives are located, positioned, and emplaced in relations of power, politics, and culture. However, the locations of children, in and through which they learn, are not simple containers, are not bounded, and will not hold still.

We must recognise that schools and universities need to focus more than they do at present on what students bring to the learning context, and how their capabilities can be harnessed so they become both more digitally fluent and effective critical managers of knowledge. Furlong and Davies (2012: 54) suggest that 'new learning practices' might need to be delineated. These would be under the control of the learner and beyond the notion of new literacies, which also draw on the classification and framing of knowledge and skills (Bernstein, 1971). They suggest the following are informal learning practices:

Resources for learning

a) Digital resources – systems for organising and structuring work; electronic recommendation systems; commercially available learning support materials; a broader range of websites for search
b) Visual and audio resources
c) Social resources – friends, networks, online and offline
d) Time resources

Ways of learning

a) Play – fiddling about and trial and error
b) Observing and copying high quality production
c) Producing, correcting and reproducing
d) Performing
e) Co-constructing
f) Sharing

Skills to support learning

a) Technical skills across a range of technologies and applications
b) Development of judgment
c) Networking skills
d) Collaborative skills

(Furlong and Davies, 2012: 54)

These practices are considered informal because they are under the control of the learner rather than guided by teachers or lecturers. Such informal practices might be a helpful means of designing interest-driven curricula that use pedagogies of interaction as their starting point. Pedagogies of interaction are defined here as the use of learning approaches based on social constructivism that seek to encourage learning with and through others, exploring diverse knowledges and resources formally and informally. Such pedagogies mean that students can be guided and supported in choosing and employing those strategies for learning that best support their own approach to learning. Such an approach to curriculum-making would engage but move beyond the practices of 'hanging around and geeking out' (Ito et al., 2010) and instead harness learning though customization, the exploration of diverse knowledge and resources, and learning by doing. It would also recognize super-communicators (Lenhart et al., 2008), those who communicate via multiple technologies and channels – phone calls, text messages, IMs, social network sites – and do so both more in aggregate and more frequently within each channel.

Thus, learning needs to be unbundled by acknowledging yet decentring the disciplines in a way that still enables higher education to be valued as 'higher' learning. This will mean that students choose what they want to study based solely on their interests, rather than just on what is provided for them in a degree programme. However, it would be vital to test such customized curricula to ensure this is something students want and believe they can manage, albeit with the support of tutors. It is crucial for this kind of customization to engage and enable students. One of the issues that higher education appears to have failed to address is that in distance and adult education students choose to study what interests them or what will further their careers. Students have a strongly vested interest in their learning, which is not always the case with what is put before them in higher education programmes. Many academics still believe that flexible learning has to occur within a discipline, within a university, and that it should be bounded by the quality and standards of the current systems. Bigger questions need to be asked, and bigger decisions need to be made about how (new) pedagogies of interaction can be made more widely available in schooling and higher education, what interest-driven learning might look like, and how social networking might improve and support education, especially education for the professions. It is vital to consider how digital media can be used to support, enable and reshape higher education as a space for creating interest-driven curricula, centred on pedagogies of interaction. A helpful example of this has been developed by White at the University of Oxford, based on a longitudinal study that utilizes the 'visitors and residents' concept as a framework to reassess learners' (including staff's) engagement with digital technologies.

Unbundling learning through the visitors and residents concept

In 2011 White and Le Cornu published groundbreaking research that not only unpacked and displaced the notion of digital immigrants and digital natives proposed by Prensky (2001), but provided a different model for considering how people position themselves in their use of the internet. This eloquent idea is still valuable because it is a continuum that works across the generations and not merely a binary opposition.

The argument is that people operate across an online spectrum, with the 'visitors' at one end seeing the web as a rather unruly garden shed comprising tools they use for a given task. For them, the web is functional – useful, but not something they see as an enduring component of their lives or identities. They see social networking as largely unnecessary and pointless, and hence place little value in their belonging to online spaces. At the other end of the spectrum, the 'residents' see the web as less of a tool and more of a place. For them, the distinction between online and offline is largely blurred and they have offline friends as well as a number who transcend both spaces. The web is space and place – a space to share views and a place to explore and present their identity. It is a network rather than a tool shed.

More recently, White et al. (2012) developed a detailed list of visitors' and residents' characteristics, presented in Table 5.1.

TABLE 5.1 Digital visitors and residents

Visitors	Residents
• See web as untidy garden tool shed • Defined goal or task • Select most appropriate tool for task • Need to see concrete benefit from use of a platform • Relatively anonymous • Try to avoid the creation of digital identity • Caution: identity theft, privacy • Sense that online social networking is banal and potentially a time-waster • Will use technology to maintain relationships • Web offers a set of tools to deliver or manipulate content (including conversations) • Tendency to respect (and seek out) authoritative sources • Thinking often takes place offline • Users, not members, of the web • See no value in belonging 'online'	• See web as place (park, building) where clusters of friends and colleagues meet • Live out a proportion of their life online • Distinction between online and offline increasingly blurred • Sense of belonging to a community • Have a profile in social networking platforms • Comfortable expressing their identity online • Web is a place to express opinions, to form and extend relationships, maintain and develop a digital identity • Aspect of their persona remains once logged off • See web as networks or clusters of individuals who generate content/opinion • No clear distinction between concepts of persona and content

Since the initial development of this concept, White et al. (2012) have been analysing the concept as a framework to reassess learners' (including staff's) engagement with digital technologies. Their interim findings indicate that:

1. *Students used a convenience approach to gaining information, almost always using Google as the starting point.* Thus institutions need to consider how to encourage and enable students to evaluate their sources in the context of other and more

traditional sources. Further, students need to be equipped with sound search techniques and understandings of how search engines operate. Finally, staff need to know how to equip their students with the range of critical capabilities they will need in order to evaluate information effectively to enhance their studies.

2. *Students used peers for support on assignment.* These peers were likely to be online, rather than people who were on their course or knew about the assignment. This emergency help-seeking implies that institutions need to introduce students to the notion of different understandings of knowledge and how these are established within cultures and communities. Institutions could perhaps provide more online resources in terms of expert help and lectures.

3. *Addiction and distraction.* Many students were aware of these possibilities in terms of wasting time. Discussing and sharing awareness and worries would be useful for students, as would the provision of areas within the institution that are internet and wifi free, so allowing students to choose whether to be distracted.

Whilst these are interim findings, they suggest student awareness of areas of challenge and difficulty, and highlight the gaps in the ways institutions think about student learning and knowledge management. One possibility might be to take the concept and develop it as shown in Figure 5.1 (based on White et al., 2012 and Gasser et al., 2012). The main concepts are defined as:

•   *Personal:* the way in which students use media for personal enjoyment and utilize time on their own.
•   *Academic:* the media that students use for academic study.
•   *Social:* the media students use for socializing and peer interaction.
•   *Informal:* the media places and spaces students use for informal learning and information location.

Liquid-ification and re-presentation

It is apparent that people are disrupting traditional boundaries through their use of digital media. One example of this is the merging and overlay between production and consumption – the idea that people recreate something they are already consuming, be it photographs, video or music, or all of these together. Students are making and creating opportunities and liminal arenas of which many of us are unaware. One example of this is 'vidding', whereby content is refashioned or recreated in order to present a different perspective, usually based on music videos and television programmes. The purpose of vidding is to critique, re-present and explore an aspect of the original media. For instance, anime music videos (AMVs) are usually fan made and comprise a range of clips from a variety of sources, such as films, songs and promotional trailers. These amateur videos are then posted on sites such as YouTube and AnimeMusicVideos.org. With the advent of networked media,

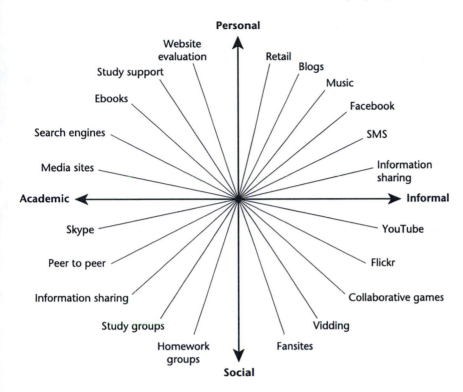

FIGURE 5.1 Rethinking learning and knowledge management

interests can be supported by platforms such as LiveJournal, Tumblr and Pinterest, and sites can be devoted to and designed for specific interest groups, such as DeviantArt, Ravelry, or fantasy sports leagues (Ito et al., 2013: 64). Yet, whilst vidding is a complex and highly skilled activity, with its sharing and learning considered important to those in the vidding community, it is not highly valued in other learning arenas.

It could be argued that traditional academic practices erode or prevent creative learning practices in young people by failing to acknowledge the playful practices involved in the use of new technologies. These playful practices are a form of liquid media – a sense of engaging with, recreating, redeveloping and re-presenting that is continually on the move. Originally, mash-ups were seen as relatively straight-forward, as something created by combining elements from two or more sources, such as music tracks. They have now become much more sophisticated with their move into films and more recently digital media. What is now occurring is a form of liquid-ification and re-presentation. Mash-ups have been discussed by Jenkins (2006) and more recently by Ito et al. (2010). We now seem to be seeing an overlap and overlay of online networks and media production tools, characterized, as boyd (2007) has argued, by persistence, searchability, replicability and engagement with invisible audiences. This is seen in the use of sharing media, creating media and publishing on social networking sites.

However, this liquid-ification brings into question issues of emotional engagement, trust and disclosure. Emotional connection has been found to be one of the strongest determinants of a user's experience, triggering unconscious responses to a system, environment or interface (Éthier et al., 2008). These feelings strongly influence our perceptions, enjoyment and pleasure, and influence how we regard our experiences at a later date; captivating a user's attention can induce a sense of immersion or presence (Robertson et al., 1997). This is a complex concept related to the physical senses and mental processes of the user, the required tasks within the environment, and the types of interaction and technology involved (Pausch et al., 1997). This engagement of the student in the learning experience is advocated to focus and improve learning (Kang et al., 2008). Emotional design at the basic level involves minimizing common emotions related to poor usability, such as boredom, frustration, annoyance, anger and confusion. Dennerlein et al. (2003) stated that during a computer task system usability may play a role in creating stressful situations that manifest themselves in various exposures to biomechanical stressors. Thus, emotional design should also focus on invoking positive emotions associated with acceptance of the system and continued usage, such as inspiration, fascination, perception of credibility, trust, satisfaction, appeal and attachment.

Technology is used to mediate a variety of sensitive actions – from online banking, to communication on social networking systems, to online counselling. Consequently, the notion of trust and the factors informing trust have received significant attention in recent years. Trust is defined here as 'an attitude of confident expectation that one's vulnerabilities will not be exploited' (Corritore et al., 2003: 740). For some, the fear and anxiety associated with making oneself vulnerable online is specifically associated with 'transactions characterized as faceless and intangible' (Beldad et al., 2010: 857). Barak and Gluck-Ofri (2007) suggest that the social environment of cyberspace is characterized by more open, straightforward and candid interpersonal communication. They found that self-disclosure in support forums was much higher than in discussion forums, in terms of both the total number and the type of disclosures. Messages in support forums were longer and included more first-voice words than those in discussion forums, and there were no gender differences linked to levels of self-disclosure.

Savin-Baden et al. (2014) used pedagogical agents to examine disclosure in educational settings. The study used responsive evaluation to explore how the use of pedagogical agents might affect students' truthfulness and disclosure by asking them to respond to a lifestyle choices survey delivered by a web-based pedagogical agent. Findings suggested that users may feel comfortable disclosing more sensitive information to pedagogical agents than to interviewers, and that emotional connection with pedagogical agents was intrinsic to the user's sense of trust and therefore likely to affect levels of truthfulness and engagement. These findings support the growing body of literature which suggests that the social environment of cyberspace is characterized by more open, straight-forward and candid interpersonal communication, and that a pedagogical agent can support this.

The disclosure of information, especially sensitive information, requires the formation of a trust relationship (Wheeless and Grotz, 1977), and Corritore et al. (2003) propose that websites can be the objects of trust. For them, the concepts of risk, vulnerability, expectation, confidence and exploitation play a key role in information disclosure in an online environment. Further, Whitty and Joinson (2009) have suggested that understandings of such social networks and veracity are central to making sense of the unique qualities of cyberspace; and studies by Yee (2006) and Bailenson et al. (2008) also indicate that issues of online and offline behaviour bear further exploration.

Augmented existence?

In the twenty-first century we lead augmented lives – lives that can be changed and enhanced through technology and surgery. Tom Caudell is seen as the person who coined the phrase 'augmented reality' while working in Boeing's Computer Services' Adaptive Neural Systems Research and Development project in Seattle. Julian Huxley linked his conceptualization of transhumanism with augmented reality and suggested that augmented reality technology would enable the human race to develop through science and technology (J. Huxley, 1927, 1957). For Aldous Huxley (A. Huxley, 1927), education was the road to emancipation, but he believed that this was blocked by unalterable bio-genetical engineering, resulting in human beings caught between different psycho-biological capabilities and the requirements of society.

To a large extent, the debates still focus on posthumanism and transhumanism. Transhumanists believe that human enhancement technologies should be widely available, that individuals should have broad discretion over which of these technologies to apply to themselves, and that parents should normally have the right to choose enhancements for their children-to-be. Posthumanism posits the idea that there are new forms of human existence which blur the boundaries between humans, nature and machines, suggesting an ideal situation in which the limitations of human biology are transcended through the use of machines. Indeed, Haraway argued that 'we are all chimeras, theorized and fabricated hybrids of machine and organism; in short, we are cyborgs. The cyborg is our ontology; it gives us our politics' (Haraway, 1985/1991: 149). However, as Herbrechter (2013: 329) argues:

> The temptation has therefore been to see posthumanism as the 'natural' successor – in analogy with the popular idea that AI, cyborgs or digital machines function as successors to the human species – to the still too humanist postmodernist/poststructuralist paradigm. Which means of course that the poststructuralist theory responsible for the birth of this posthumanism supposedly merely has a 'midwife' function and thus needs to be 'overcome'.

Whether we are cyborgs or not, our existence is augmented and our responses to 'machines' increasingly illustrate that we are prepared to trust them and reveal sensitive information to them (Savin-Baden et al., 2014). For example, in a comparison of human interviewees with virtual-world chatbots (pedagogical agents in non-learning situations), Hasler et al. (2013) found that the chatbots and the human interviewees were equally successful in collecting information about their participants' real-life backgrounds.

In the sixty-plus years since Alan Turing began work on the Turing Test (Turing 1950) to evaluate the realism of chatbots (also known as virtual assistants, pedagogical agents or HCI agents), they have become an established, although niche, educational technology. Furthermore, research into chatbot realism has suggested that anthropomorphic (human-like) chatbot appearances and voices are typically seen as desirable by the userbase (Baylor, 2011), providing the basis for most chatbot designs. Factors such as realistic eye-gaze and movement have been found to contribute significantly to the perceived quality of chatbot–user interactions (Garau et al., 2003), and might also improve student learning (Dunsworth and Atkinson, 2007). To date, research into chatbots has focused on the realism of the bots and the extent to which such realism affects user engagement. Perhaps what we are really beginning to deal with here is what Thrift (2006) has termed 'augmented existence'. This is the idea that it is not just tagging and integration that are affecting our lives but the fact that the meta-systems themselves become a new means of categorization. Yet it would seem that such augmentation is also pernicious, or at least has a pernicious side:

> The human relation to remembering is being reconfigured by the capacious, constantly updated and updatable archive that is the Internet. Every ort and fragment of digitalized life posted on a Facebook wall, on a blog, or in a tweet remain retrievable. This is an archive without an archivist, without rules of collection, and seemingly without rules of privacy. Far from encouraging purposeful self-representation or self-invention, this vast memory machine may well constrict life writing.
>
> *(Smith, 2011: 570)*

Conclusion

This chapter has explored some of the research and debates about being digitally tethered, but it is noticeable that institutions of learning still need to understand not just how, when and with whom students use technology, but also what it is that they need to enable them to work and learn effectively. Furthermore, peer-to-peer learning and collaboration are highly important, although as yet there is little research into their impact. What is also troublesome is that staff largely seem to refer to the use of social media as 'informal' learning, resulting in the segregation of (unseen) digital learning from the perceived formality of the institution. The visitors and residents concept certainly helps, as do the review and findings by Gasser et al.

(2012), considering how learning might be different, recognized differently and supported effectively. But this is just a beginning, and despite this new and innovative work, there are other issues clouding the landscape. These are discussed in Chapter 6.

6
LEARNING TOGETHER ALONE

Introduction

This chapter will examine what it means to learn in an age of digital fluency. It will explore a range of pedagogies and draw on earlier thinking in the area to examine current practices and suggest future pedagogies. Contradictions about the presence and use of social media in the classroom, in terms of when and how it is acceptable to use digital technology, will also be considered. These contradictions arise from the mixed messages circulating in the classroom, at home and in society in general about the usefulness of technology.

Collaboration and individualism

It seems that a range of new forms of learning are still relatively unrecognized or even unacceptable within formal settings, and even possibly informal ones; learning that moves beyond notions of digital literacies and digital fluency debates. For example, it is not clear how the blurred edges around particular practices – such as archiving, annotating, appropriating, mashing up, recirculating, interacting, responding, critiquing, remixing and participating across diverse social and traditional media – are managed, engineered and contended with by young people. Further, it is important to consider the potential relationships and overlap between these as thinking, acting and creating practices, and the ways in which the learning associated with developing these capabilities are valued, and by whom. For example, it is evident that many of the informal forms of digital fluency practised by teenagers are not valued or used in school; nor, in the main, are they valued by parents. Instead, creating, recreating and mashing up are predominantly viewed (at best) as teenagers messing around with technology or (at worst) as a waste of valuable studying time.

Amidst the development of these often covert capabilities and invariably highly skilled and developed ones, it is not clear how and if social norms are developed or enacted by young people or whether they have a sense of (applying) reasonable ethical norms to all these practices. For example, how do they come to know what is acceptable to adults, teachers, parents and peers (for instance, when taking photographs, placing them on Facebook and annotating them)? It appears that these practices are shifting learning structures and ethical practices in ways that are neither clearly delineated nor understood by schools and in homes, despite school guidelines and policies, and conversations with young people. There is a perception that young people sharing personal information in public places is sinister, but Ito et al. (2010: 1) argue:

> While the pace of technological change may seem dizzying, the underlying practices of sociability, learning, play, and self-expression are undergoing a slower evolution, growing out of resilient social structural conditions and cultural categories that youth inhabit in diverse ways in their everyday lives.

In 2007 Buckingham argued that there was a digital divide between in school and out of school. The situation today would seem to be different: digital tethering is now more prevalent, and more liquid than many authors imply (Thurlow, 2006, 2007; Turkle, 2011a). Further, Ellison et al. (2007) suggested that most mobile social networking practices are more concerned with thickening existing social ties than forging new ones (although it seems this is now no longer the case). Yet there would appear to be a difference in the use of digital media for learning when comparing home and school. Ito et al. (2010: 3) explain:

> We understand from this work that youth tend to be earlier adopters than adults of digital communications and authoring capabilities, and that their exposure to new media is growing in volume, complexity, and interactivity (Lenhart and Madden 2007; Lenhart et al. 2008; Roberts and Foehr 2008; Roberts, Foehr, and Rideout 2005). Research across different post-industrial contexts also suggests that these patterns are tied to broader trends in the changing structures of sociability, where we are seeing a move toward more individualized and flexible forms of engagement with media environments. Researchers have described this as a turn toward 'networked society' (Castells 1996), 'networked individualism' (Wellman and Hogan 2004), 'selective sociality' (Matsuda 2005), the 'long tail' of niche media (Anderson 2006), or a more tailored set of media choices (Livingstone 2002).

We appear to be seeing a raft of shifts in the types and formats of available media, and in the ways in which young people are adopting and adapting them for a wide range of (often unanticipated) uses.

It is clear that our society is networked, as are individuals, yet this situation seems to worry a number of researchers in the area of cognitive science. They argue that the 'always on' culture is resulting in a loss of concentration, constant shifting from one task to another and reduced performance. For example, work by cognitive scientists exploring the impact of multitasking (Rubinstein et al., 2001) indicates that it can interrupt effective concentration and learning. Glenn (2010: B6) concluded, 'self-described multitaskers performed much worse on cognitive and memory tasks that involved distraction than did people who said they preferred to focus on single tasks'. Thus, he suggested that multitaskers are not only poor performers but also unlikely to acknowledge their poor performance. Further, Ophira et al. (2009) undertook experiments that examined whether there were differences in information-processing styles between chronically heavy and light media multitaskers and found that the former performed worse on a test of task-switching ability, probably because of their inability to filter out interference from the irrelevant task set.

Studies by Mark et al. (2012) and Dabbish et al. (2011) offer a different stance on issues of multitasking and task switching in work contexts. Rather than focusing on external interruption, Dabbish et al. (2011) analysed self-interruptions, which they suggest are not well understood. Their findings indicate that self-interruption occurs more often in open offices and earlier in the day. People are more likely to interrupt themselves to return to solitary work for which they have personal responsibility. The interruptions are related to remembering something they had to do or look up. Such studies suggest that there would be value in examining young people's practices when studying and discovering if being digitally tethered enhances or distracts effective self-interruption, so that, for example, remembering they needed to look up something is facilitated by being connected to information and friends who can help.

Mark et al. (2012) suspended email for five working days for thirteen people. They concluded that although email is always perceived to speed up the pace of work, since the receiver is expected to respond quickly, without it the participants had lower stress, multitasked less and tended to focus longer on their tasks. Some participants found it more effective to read email in batches and others reported feeling relaxed without email. Consequently, the authors suggest that organizations should consider restricting, filtering or actively managing the delivery of email.

However, it is not entirely clear which multitasking activities are most disruptive or the extent to which these findings are representative of all types of learners. For example, early studies suggest that the average person concentrates on a lecture for twenty minutes (Bligh, 2000; Young et al., 2009), and it might be that short interruptions help rather than hinder learning.

Mixed messages

Despite the current culture of being always on, as mentioned in Chapter 1 schools and universities still seek to control what counts as acceptable knowledge, even though many young people can access anything they like on their phones and on computers at home, and others delight in finding ways around blocked sites at school. Crook (2012: 75) acknowledges that this perceived need to control access is

> clearly motivated by worthy ambitions to manage the personal security of students, to obstruct access to offensive material, and to sustain focus on central school tasks. However, it is not often viewed so charitably by students. Accordingly, it becomes a source of tension in this case between the felt 'Web 2.0 readiness' of students and the constraints felt necessary by schools. Such tension is reflected in a number of ways. It can sour relationships at all levels of the system – technical staff, librarians, teachers, managers and even the county education authority who were sometimes identified as the source of the imperative. Of particular concern was a species of double standard that was often perceived:

>> Yes, when teachers ask you to get like multimedia files for PowerPoints and stuff you like say to them 'I can't get them because you've blocked the sites on the Internet' so, then they say 'Oh, you can do it at home', but that's not really fair because it's the school's fault for not like, for blocking them.

Further, Ito et al. (2010: 12) argue that much of young people's learning takes place outside school, and certainly considerable amounts of school homework requires access to information and sources that are invariably blocked by school systems. There are also mixed messages about the presence and use of social media in the classroom, in terms of when and how it is acceptable to use digital technology. Sefton Green (2013a: 2) has suggested that:

> The debates about school aren't always coherent or sensible, and there are many levels to the discussion . . . I want to draw out two key propositions. The first is how we tend to conflate the idea of education and schools, and the second is how we often don't disentangle learning and formal education. Both of these kinds of lapses in thinking are part of how we might talk about young people in society at a general level: they are, however, inaccurate in ways that matter.

These contradictions arise from the mixed messages circulating in the classroom, at home and in society in general about the usefulness of technology. This is based in 'old beliefs' and a reductionist's view of technology that is not, in the main, held by young people. However, it is also noticeable that many teenagers and students choose not to use social networking sites (although the studies in this area remain somewhat sparse). Turan et al. (2013) found that the main reasons why people chose not to use social networking websites were because they were seen as a waste of time, might violate privacy or might result in addiction. The main issue seemed to be lack of trust in the use of online media: most of the students Turan et al. studied did not trust virtual friendships and did not wish to share their photographs or political views online.

Nevertheless, many teenagers *are* working at the borders – and at the spaces in between – challenging and expanding both the *intentions* of a particular piece of hardware or software and the *opportunities* offered through the media itself. These young people are making and creating opportunities and liminal arenas of which many of us are unaware. One example of this is 'vidding', whereby content is refashioned or recreated in order to present a different perspective, usually based on music videos and television programmes. This is discussed in more detail in Chapter 7.

Peer-to-peer learning

Peer-to-peer learning is generally talked about in relation to group learning in schools and universities. The focus is on sharing, supporting and guiding one another as part of a learning team. Tutor-guided learning teams are the most common form of group learning in school and universities. The tutor in this type of team sees his or her role as guiding the students through each component of the problem or challenge, and thus the students see the problem as being set within – or bounded by – a discrete subject or disciplinary area. In some situations, the tutor actually provides hints and tips on problem-solving techniques. The argument for such an approach is that students have limited skills to help them solve the problems they will encounter on their own, but the result is that students often see solutions as linked to specific curriculum content.

However, in an extensive meta-analysis that included hundreds of studies, Johnson et al. (1991) concluded that collaborative learning arrangements were superior to competitive, individualistic structures on a variety of outcomes, such as higher academic achievement, higher-level reasoning, more frequent generation of new ideas and solutions, and greater transfer of learning from one situation to another. The difference between cooperative learning and collaborative learning is that the former involves small group work to maximize student learning, which tends to maintain traditional lines of knowledge and authority. By contrast, collaborative learning is based on notions of social constructivism. As Matthews (1996: 101) puts it, collaborative learning 'is a pedagogy that has at its centre the assumption that people make meaning together and that the process enriches and enlarges them'. It is this kind of collaborative learning that is increasingly being used by young people when they create, produce and make together through social networking and practices such as vidding. Students tend to move away from formal peer-to-peer learning at school (when not required to engage in it) in order to ensure that they understand the work for themselves and gain the grades they seek. Yet often peer-to-peer learning still occurs informally through digital media.

Informal peer-to-peer learning is defined here as learning that is based on learning through interaction with peers that is not *required* by parents or a teacher, although the interaction may occur as a result of schoolwork. In this form of learning, young people support each other through informal peer support. This may occur face to face – for instance, by doing homework together on the school bus – but it is more likely to occur through informal media groups such as Facebook homework groups, sharing through Whatsapp, or texting in real time while doing homework. Most importantly, this learning is peer-led, as Ito et al. (2010: 22) explain:

> Peer-based learning relies on a context of reciprocity, in which kids feel they have a stake in self-expression as well as a stake in evaluating and giving feedback to one another. Unlike in more hierarchical and author-itative relations, both parties are constantly contributing and evaluating one another.

Our digitized, globalized society continues to offer young people a range of mixed messages, and one which remains deeply troublesome involves the relationship between individual and peer learning. In 1973 Lukes coined the term 'the ethic of individualism'. This is the notion that some students see learning within the group as an activity that is valuable only in terms of what they, as individuals, can gain from it. It is still pertinent now. The focus remains on grades of individual achievement at school and university. However, at the same time students are expected to develop an interactional stance. 'Interactional stance' captures the way in which a learner interacts with others within a learning situation. It refers to the relationships between students within groups as well as staff–student relationships at both individual and group levels. It also encompasses the way in which students interpret how they, as individuals, and others with whom they learn, construct meaning in relation to one another (Savin-Baden, 2000). Further, it may be characterized by the individual placing him/herself at the centre of the value system. Learning within the group is an activity that is valuable only in terms of personal gain for the individual.

Thus, in digital tethering, as both a practice and as a way of being, students might place high value upon collective learning experiences, but they would still be concerned about forfeiting marks by expending too much effort sharing tasks and information within the group rather than working alone. Therefore, whether in flipped classrooms or in problem-based learning, while the learning medium is team-based, the message is still individualism. This introduces questions about the purpose of peer-to-peer learning and how it can be harnessed and valued by both individuals and teams. At the same time digital tethering would seem to offer students choices about how they use information, how they share it with others (or not), the way they learn together or apart, and how they support each other in ways that current classroom practices often prevent or discourage. In many ways, informal peer-to-peer learning is the transitional link between home and school that Ito et al. (2013) argue for in their notion of connected learning, which is discussed further below.

Genres of participation

Ito et al. (2010) argue that the studies they undertook focused on cultural and social categories, rather than on variables such as age, gender and class that have been examined by other researchers. For example, they avoided categories such as technoboys and computer competent girls (Holloway and Valentine, 2003) or traditionalists and specialists (Livingstone, 2002). Instead, Ito et al. (2010) argue for genres of participation with media, which they define as a 'constellation of characteristics' that are constantly changing. The three genres are 'hanging out', 'messing around' and 'geeking out'.

Hanging out

In Ito et al.'s (2010) study, young people expressed a desire to hang around and be independent of parents, families and institutional structures. Hanging around involved fluid movement between online and offline activities, and it was noticeable that young people spent considerable time organizing and discussing the process and possibilities for hanging out as well as actually 'doing' the hanging out. They used media to facilitate hanging around through instant messaging, texting and Facebook to arrange face-to-face meetings, as well as to share their tastes, for instance in music, and post pictures on social networking sites. What is interesting about current practices is the layering that occurs: young people will hang out together in the same room but could be involved in different and possibly overlapping activities, such as playing an online game, texting others and making food. Thus, some teenagers are constantly in touch with one another online, offline *and* face to face, sharing spaces together.

Messing around

This genre was characterized by teenagers who were involved in intense exploration and engagement with new media, rather than being particularly friendship driven. It involved both 'looking around' and 'experimentation and play':

> Looking around online and fortuitous searching can be a self-directed activity that provides young people with a sense of agency, often exhibited in a discourse that they are 'self-taught' as a result of engaging in these strategies ... The autonomy to pursue topics of personal interest through random searching and messing around generally assists and encourages young people to take greater ownership of their learning processes ... As with looking around, experimentation and play are central practices for young people messing around with new media. As a genre of participation, one of the important aspects of messing around is the media awareness that comes from the information derived from searching and ... the desire and (eventually) the ability to play around with media.
>
> *(Ito et al., 2010: 57)*

What was interesting in Ito et al.'s study was that, despite the advantages enjoyed by some (such as high-speed internet connections and the latest hardware and software), the most important spaces for messing around were in either school or after-school contexts. This illustrates that a central value of informal learning is student-led exploration and the need for space and time to explore and experiment with – or alongside – others. Ito et al. (2010: 65) argue that messing around is a transitional space for geeking around:

> Although messing around can be seen as a challenge to traditional ways of finding and sharing information, solving problems, or consuming media, it also represents a highly productive space for young people in which they can begin to explore specific interests and to connect with other people outside their local friendship groups.

Geeking out

Geeking out is defined as intense engagement with technology or media exemplified through fandom or committed gaming, but not always driven by technology. The activities in this genre varied from gaming to offline activities, such as playing sports. One example of this would be a teenager spending time finding and producing information about gaming rules to share with others, so that they could all progress in an online game.

Geeking out was characterized by expertise and geek cred, and by rewriting the rules. Expertise and geek cred involved having high levels of complex knowledge in narrow domains, expertise that was recognized and often employed by others to save time and resources. Rewriting the rules transcended geeking out and messing around, as the authors of the study explained:

> there are important differences in the ways in which the rules are rewritten in each of these genres of participation. Like messing around, which involves an inchoate awareness of the need and ability to subvert social rules set by parents and institutions such as school, geeking out frequently requires young people to negotiate restrictions on access to friends, spaces, or information to achieve the frequent and intense interaction with media and technology characteristic of geeking out. Rewriting the rules in the service of geeking out, however, also involves a willingness to challenge technological restrictions – to open the black box of technology, so to speak. This practice is most often done in the service of acquiring media ... Geeking out often involves an explicit challenge to existing social and legal norms and technical restrictions. It is a subcultural identity that self-consciously plays by a different set of rules than mainstream society.
>
> *(Ito et al., 2010: 71)*

Hanging about, messing around and geeking out all require time, space and resources to experiment with autonomy in ways that are self-directed. Genres of participation

TABLE 6.1 Summary of genres of participation

Genre	Hanging out	Messing around	Geeking out
	Being independent of parents, families and institutional structures and using new media to maintain online and offline connections with friends	Intense exploration and engagement with new media, but also used to explore specific interests and to connect with other people outside their local friendship groups	Intense engagement with technology or media characterized by fandom or committed gaming but is not always driven by technology
Boundary crossing	Peer sociability ————▶	Interest-driven messing around	
		Rewriting rules ◀————————▶	
		e.g. Illegal downloading of songs to share with friends	e.g. Illegal video file sharing requiring high-level subverting of rules
		Social play ◀————	Geeky interest driven activity
Focus	Construction of spaces for offline and online friendship drives activities	Open-ended participation requiring time and resources	Highly social and engaged in terms of interest, but not expressed as being friendship driven
Type	Friendship driven	Transitional space: friendship driven and interest driven	Interest driven

are not related to types of young people, but rather to the diverse types of activities in which teenagers participate and engage: some do one; some all; some are more interest driven than others. Table 6.1 summarizes this work and suggests areas where boundary crossing is evident.

Although genres of participation are useful in offering some indication of what young people are doing in digital spaces, they offer little guidance about what this means in terms of pedagogy. The next section argues that the kind of learning that is occurring formally, informally and across the boundaries of both might be constituted as participatory pedagogies.

Participatory pedagogies

Participatory pedagogies are defined here as forms of learning and teaching that harness the use of digital media and participatory cultures and action, the details of which are provided in Table 6.2. In practice, these pedagogies are often hidden,

TABLE 6.2 Forms of participatory pedagogy

Forms of participatory pedagogy	Definition	Characteristics	Link with education theory	Key authors
New media	Media at the intersections of books, television and radio with interactive media and social networking	1. Genres of participation 2. Networked publics 3. Peer-based learning 4. New media literacy	Communities of Practice (Lave and Wenger, 1991)	Ito et al. (2013)
Produsage	Collaborative and continuous building and extending of existing content in pursuit of further improvement	1. Open participation 2. Fluid roles 3. Unfinished artefacts 4. Common property	Critical pedagogy and social action (Freire, 1972, 1974; hooks, 1994)	Bruns (2008)
Connected learning	Learning occurs across and through media and contexts by young people, often in informal and innovative ways	1. Connecting and translating between in-school and out-of-school learning 2. Learning as change in social, economic, technological and cultural context	Discovery learning (Bruner, 1991; Dewey, 1938)	Ito et al. (2010)
Mobile literacy	The ability to use social media and media for learning through the mobile web	1. Understanding information access 2. Understanding hyperconnectivity 3. Understanding the new sense of space	Transformation theory (Mezirow, 1985)	Parry (2011)
Connectivist pedagogy	Learning takes place with and through networked information and resources	1. Nurturing and maintaining connections to facilitate continual learning 2. Ability to see connections between fields, ideas and concepts is a core skill	Cooperative education (Heron, 1989, 1993; Johnson, et al., 1991, 1998)	Siemens (2008a, 2008b)

enmeshed and transcend disciplines, structures and learning boundaries. The result is that they are both difficult to locate and delineate clearly, and often informal and difficult to understand in terms of their impact on and value in education, culture and identity.

Those adopting these pedagogies recognize the popular and cultural meanings of apps, social media and tools and the ways in which young people adapt such media in both reflexive and non-reflexive ways for their own aims and purposes. They include such activities as learning through social networking, searching and retrieving information, researching information, using information, games, collaboration and shared interests. In unpacking participatory pedagogies it is important to realize that encouraging young people to become reflexive, or more reflexive, about their practices, behaviours and ethics is vital both in the development of their stance as media managers and producers and in the development of voice, agency, personalization and an ethical stance to their own practices. Participatory pedagogies comprise:

- new media;
- produsage;
- connected learning;
- mobile literacy; and
- connectivist pedagogy.

New media

This describes media at the intersections of books, television and radio with interactive media and social networking. Such media are seen as new in that they are not tied to any context, platform or situation, but are associated with culture, identity, belonging and voice. In the context of this book, they encompass informal and formal learning settings, as well as those at the interstices of both.

Produsage

Bruns (2008) argues for produsage, or the collaborative and continuous building and extending of existing content in pursuit of further improvement (Bruns, 2008; Bruns and Schmidt, 2012), characterized by:

- *Community-based activities:* produsage proceeds from the assumption that the community as a whole, if sufficiently large and varied, can contribute more than a closed team of producers, however qualified they may be.
- *Fluid roles:* produsers participate as is appropriate to their personal skills, interests, and knowledges; this changes as the produsage project proceeds.
- *Unfinished artefacts:* content artefacts in produsage projects are continually under development, and therefore always unfinished; their development follows evolutionary, iterative, palimpsestic paths.

• *Common property, individual merit:* contributors permit (non-commercial) community use, adaptation and further development of their intellectual property, and are rewarded by the status capital they gain through this process.

Connected learning

This form of learning is one in which it is recognized that learning occurs across and through media and contexts used by young people, often in informal and innovative ways. It is a means of learning, a way of delineating and analysing learning whilst experiencing changes in social, economic, technological and cultural contexts. It is also a framework for understanding learning:

> Connected learning posits that by connecting and translating between in-school and out-of-school learning, we can guide more young people to engaging, resilient, and useful learning that will help them become effective contributors and participants in adult society.
>
> *(Ito et al., 2013: 46)*

For some teachers and lecturers, there is an assumption that mechanisms and structures need to be in place to enable young people to make connections, so that they are able to translate knowledges and practices between formal and informal learning environments. Yet, for many people (of whatever age), connected learning is a central practice in their daily lives. The notion of connected learning and genres of participation is helpful but needs to be extended beyond teenagers and young people, since, as many have already noted (Crook, 2012; Merchant, 2012; Savin-Baden et al., 2010), the notion of digital natives is misplaced.

Mobile literacy

A decade ago the focus was on mobile learning, defined as learning for learners on the move (Sharples et al., 2005). Mobile literacy is based on the assumption that considerable learning takes place outside the classroom and that people create sites for learning within their surroundings. Mobile learning is a digital learning space that introduces challenges about what constitutes learning and pedagogy. It has implications for how formal schooling is carried out and how the curriculum is negotiated, and offers students opportunities to manage the relationship between formal schooling and independent, informal exploration and problem-solving. However, the terrain has shifted since 2005:

> According to the Ofcom survey, 47% of UK teenagers (12 to 15-year-olds) now own a smartphone, and this is clearly a big growth area in the mobile phone market. Furthermore, teenagers report that their use of mobiles is taking over from their use of older media. Sixty-five per cent of those with smartphones reported that they use their phone for social networking. In

addition to this, the data suggest high levels of mobile texting, music and gaming amongst teens (Ofcom, 2011). These headline statistics alone point to a rise in the availability and use of mobiles in the youth population, and certainly support claims that teenagers may be passionately engaged in mobile practices (indeed some of those surveyed describe this engagement in terms of addiction).

(Merchant, 2012: 774)

Furthermore, Katz (2006) found that students pretended to talk on the phone if walking home late at night as a signal to would-be attackers that they were in contact with someone. They would also use their phones as symbols in other social relationships: pretending to be having a mobile phone conversation to avoid talking face to face, or pretending to get a call as a way of avoiding an embarrassing social situation. Katz (2006: 11) argues that 'there is a large world of communication usage having little to do with those who are distant or virtual and everything to do with those who are collocated, socially and physically with the user'.

We now appear to be dealing with mobile literacy (as opposed to mobile learning), which Parry (2011) characterizes as:

- *Understanding information access:* using mobile devices to search for and evaluate information whilst at the same time critiquing the difference between mobile and desktop searches.
- *Understanding hyperconnectivity:* using social media to connect learners with those outside the immediate classroom context, such as using Twitter and connecting with schools in another country for language learning.
- *Understanding the new sense of space:* appreciation of how mobile devices can mediate experiences through geolocation and augmented reality apps.

Mobile literacy is also part of the new sense of connectivist pedagogy that is occurring more formally.

Connectivist pedagogy

The central premise of connectivism is that learning takes place with and through networked information and resources. This means that learning is seen not just as accessing information but also as an evaluation of the value of and relationships between different forms of knowledge. Thus, Siemens (2008a, 2008b) argues that learning takes place through the connections that students make between knowledge, opinions, resources and views accessed via search engines and online sources. Connectivist pedagogy suggests the need to ensure:

- learning and knowledge rest in diversity of opinions;
- learning is a process of connecting specialized nodes or information sources;
- learning may reside in non-human appliances;

- a capacity to know more is more critical than what is currently known;
- nurturing and maintaining connections are needed to facilitate continual learning;
- an ability to see connections between fields, ideas and concepts is a core skill;
- currency (accurate, up-to-date knowledge) is the intent of all connectivist learning activities; and
- decision-making is itself a learning process: choosing what to learn and the meaning of incoming information are seen through the lens of a shifting reality.

There would seem to be strong pedagogical links between connectivist principles (Downes, 2006; Siemens, 2008a, 2008b) and other forms of group-based peer learning in formal settings, since the approaches to learning focus on the students' ability to make connections between the forms of knowledge they encounter.

Participatory pedagogy in action: Campsmount Technology College

One weekend in December 2009 a school in Yorkshire, UK, burned down. Everything was destroyed: school records, coursework, students' contact numbers, books and computers. Nevertheless, by Monday morning, 1500 people were on the school's newly created Facebook page and the headteacher had drafted a press release and posted it on YouTube. It soon had 3000 hits. Before long, a Twitter feed and blogs had been created by staff, and the school and community were reinvented almost overnight. Documents were uploaded on to Google docs and face-to-face classes took place in vacant premises, the town hall and other local centres. The sixth form were back 'at school' within a day, with the rest following just over a week later (ap Hari, 2010). Such is the power of these media that participatory pedagogies can be mobilized in highly creative ways.

Conclusion

It seems from current research that there are shifts and changes in learning and participation, rather than a wholesale identity evolution in learners. Instead of concentrating on what young people are doing on and with the internet, perhaps the focus needs to be broadly positioned to explore the changes and structures in the way media are used to target young people, the (covert) assumptions made about their digital capabilities and the imposition of an expectation that they will have (and indeed want) transformed identities through digital media, rather than ones that are merely shifting with the times.

7

DIGITAL FLUENCY

Introduction

This chapter will present the concept of digital fluency and explore its emergence as an idea and a way of viewing current practices. It will also explore digital fluency in relation to other relatively recent concepts, such as digital literacy and electracy. The chapter also argues that a new view of digital literacy is needed – one that moves away from the idea that digital literacy comprises particular individual capabilities and instead suggests the need to embrace digital fluency. It will be suggested that digital fluency needs to incorporate a wide array of practice, such as lifewide learning, moving knowledge, disruptive media learning and vectors of transformation. The new forms of digital fluency will be defined and exemplars provided.

Literacy, fluency and electracy

The changing practices in the area of literacies seem to be perceived as eroding traditional values and ways of operating (Lea and Jones, 2011). However, it is unclear whether recent research supports this perception, or whether the concerns are more related to traditional values about how writing and literacy should be enacted. For example, Lea and Jones (2011) have argued that literacies research is interested in particular enactments of textual practice, and suggests that the new uses of literacies in relation to formulations of digital literacies seem to be dislocated from texts and focused instead on capabilities. At the same time, there have been a number of debates and arguments (such as those highlighted by Lea and Jones) about equipping young people with the necessary new media literacy skills, along with discussions about how literacies are being changed by online speech and texting.

However, work by the New Literacy Studies (NLS) movement has helped to move the focus away from what occurs in the minds of individuals and towards the importance of understanding literacy in the context of interaction and social practice. As Gee (n.d.) points out, some of the theories that have informed this movement to date have omitted 'the person as agent, who utters (writes) the words with (conscious and unconscious) personal, social, cultural and political goals and purposes'. Wood et al. (2011a, 2011b) suggest that texting enhances rather than disrupts the learning of spelling and grammar, while students with dyslexia prefer to use the small screens of mobile phones rather than large-screen computers.

Thus, many of the debates seem to centre on what are the acceptable and less acceptable ways of communicating in terms of grammar and spelling, as well as in terms of etiquette and how social media spaces should be used. However, whether they are writing texts for formal assignments or participating in student forums, there remain challenges about communication, representation and digital fluency. Students in new learning spaces, such as university, do not necessarily know how to represent and locate themselves textually, because their past school texts were often required to be authoritarian. Yet, in personal media spaces such as Facebook and Tumblr, texts are informal, mistakes are disregarded and ease of communication is central.

Miller and Bartlett (2012) reflect that a number of frameworks have been proposed in the ongoing effort to define what information literacy is and thus what it means to be 'literate'. Whilst many of these share overlapping attributes and emphases, they often disagree, too. Shifts in the use of social media sites, and online media use in general, have prompted a redefining of literacy in a bid to capture these changes, yet the debates about what constitutes digital literacy remain troublesome, especially given that some digital literacy frameworks, such as that delineated by Gurak (2001), are just transpositions of existing frameworks into digital contexts, so that the literacies are focused on locating, organizing, understanding and evaluating information using digital technology.

Ulmer (2003) suggests that merely transferring and transforming literacy on to the internet in the form of ready-made papers placed on websites is not enough. Instead, he argues that it is vital to create pedagogies that will enable the integration of internet practices with literate skills in new and innovative ways. Thus, he has developed the concept of 'electracy':

> What literacy is to the analytical mind, electracy is to the affective body: a prosthesis that enhances and augments a network of organic human potential ... If literacy focused on universally valid methodologies of knowledge (sciences), electracy focuses on the individual state of mind within which knowing takes place (arts).
>
> *(Ulmer, 2003)*

The notion of electracy as prosthesis fits with digital tethering, in that many people see their devices as attachments and fashion statements, and being tethered as a component or extension of their identity. Hobbs (2008) defined four approaches to new literacies: media literacy, information literacy, critical literacy and media management. More recently, she has suggested that students who are digitally literate can access, analyse, create, reflect and take action (Hobbs, 2011). Whilst helpful on one level, surely we would expect most students to be able to achieve all of these anyway, both in school and at university.

I would suggest that digital fluency is a concept that should be used instead of both digital literacy and electracy, as we are now seeing diverse forms of digital fluency. Digital literacy is the ability to assemble knowledge, evaluate information, search and navigate, as well as locate, organize, understand and evaluate information using digital technology. By contrast, digital fluency is the ability to use digital media, of whatever sort, to manage knowledge and learning across diverse offline and online spaces. It includes the ability to understand complex issues such as how identity can be established and faked, to evaluate the trustworthiness and accuracy of information, and to understand the subtext of digital media and information, and then place it within a wider context. Thus, digital capabilities comprise the range of skills and understandings needed to operate digital media and collaborate and share with others, as well as being digitally literate and fluent.

Digital fluency

There have been many definitions of digital fluency, and these often overlap and indeed collide with definitions and arguments about digital literacy and even multimodality. Yet, I feel that digital fluency is different from the definitions of digital literacy proposed by Lea and Jones (2011) and the arguments for multimodality proposed by Kress (2003).

The post-war generation tended to be seen by media producers as individual, passive consumers, whereas in the 2000s digital media became increasingly participatory, as Karaganis argued in 2008:

> Although it is tempting to see technological change as an independent driver of this process, there is powerful reciprocity at work: New technologies take hold only in the context of accompanying cultural innovation as their latent possibilities are explored. This interdependence means that technologies are not merely received but, through processes of adoption, socially defined and, eventually, socially embedded in new collective and institutional practices.
>
> *(Karaganis, 2008: 6)*

In 2015 social networking, whether messaging and sharing on Facebook or vidding, is embedded within and across many cultures worldwide. The result is that the distinctions (if any) between production, sharing, distribution, consumption and re-sharing are blurred, which in turn has created new forms of digital culture and diverse forms of participation.

Miller and Bartlett (2012) argue that a completely new mixture of competencies is required for living and working in the online world. They have termed these competencies digital fluency (rather than digital literacy), and group them into three components:

- *Net savviness:* a practical understanding of the way the internet works, such as the basics of how search engines generate results, and how identity can be established and faked.
- *Critical evaluative techniques:* the knowledge and use of basic checks, techniques and principles that can be applied to assess the trustworthiness and accuracy of information.
- *Diversity:* the extent to which users' online consumption is broad, varied and diverse, such as whether they realize the subtextual ideological basis of a site, comment or opinion piece, and place it within a wider context.

(Paraphrased from Miller and Bartlett, 2012: 39)

Miller and Bartlett (2012) argue that it is vital to place digital fluency at the heart of learning, but suggest that young people are not digitally fluent. For instance, particular internet practices make it difficult to tell the difference between truth claims. Some examples they present include:

- *pseudo-sites and propaganda:* sites that are not what they seem and yet are designed to appear trustworthy;
- *skittering:* the practice of merely scanning pages and spending little more than five minutes reading an article; and
- *bouncing:* visiting only one to three pages of the thousands available.

Further, they note:

> 44 per cent of 12–15 year olds who use search engines make some type of critical judgment about search engine results, thinking that some of the sites returned will be truthful while others may not be (Ofcom 2011, p.47). However, 31 per cent believe that if a search engine lists information then it must be truthful and 15 per cent don't consider the veracity of results but just visit the sites 'they like the look of'. These proportions have not changed since 2009, suggesting that nearly half of 12–15 year olds who use search engine websites are not critically aware of the provenance of their content (Ofcom 2011, p.47).

(Miller and Bartlett, 2012: 40)

However, this notion of digital fluency does not address issues of online representation, presentation and performance, nor those of changing identities (possibly in pernicious ways) that can or should introduce questions about the ways in which honesty, safety and ethics are lived out in such mutable spaces.

Whilst the notion of digital fluency tends largely to be centred on people and their capabilities, at the same time there has been an increasing fluidity in the realms of technology. The emergence of social network sites in the early 2000s promoted a high degree of interest and interaction but the sites in the main remained separate. Now, in 2015, sites are more rhizomatic, so users share their profiles across sites as well as collating their data from apps there, whether it be sports information or diet trackers.

This brings with it challenges about data sharing. For example, people's contacts become available across a wide range of sites and in 2007 the 'social' graph began to be recognized as a key marketing tool. The social graph is defined as the links between people in a system (Fitzpatrick and Recordon, 2007) and is now seen as highly valuable for advertising, since third-party developers can build software on top of the social graph, so connecting people to advertising and other sites via their Facebook Friends lists.

Digital fluency has therefore been aided by changes in technology, making it easier to communicate and share information with others. At the same time, engagement with social networking sites has become more media-centric than in former years. Today, activities, photographs and achievements, rather than profiles, are shared. Such interaction with technologies in these ways introduces questions about the power relationship between the users and the corporate producers. Digital fluency today brings with it the challenge of commodification of participation (Burwell, 2010), exemplified by the appropriation of social networking sites by media corporations. It also introduces questions about the extent to which users have agency; whether they are under surveillance; whether they have truly independent choice or are steered by the extent to which the affordances of social networking sites result in communicative capitalism (Dean, 2005: 51). Digital fluency at one level is now no longer about mere net savviness, but rather can be seen as a deeply contested marketing tool, in terms of the ways in which organizations configure their technology for their users. This raises questions about the relative benefits for those technology users. However, realizing the diverse pedagogical opportunities that digital fluency and digital participation can offer should enable institutions to shift away from technological determinism and recognize the benefits of new and valuable learning gateways.

New digital fluencies

Digital fluency is a concept which captures the sense of there needing to be a balance between and across spaces in higher education, so that account is taken of knowledge, content, conceptions and acquisition, as well as of ontology, values and beliefs, uncertainty and complexity. Such a stance recognizes that learners and teachers are not apolitical, acultural or disembodied beings. They are often disturbed and uncomfortable, and need to have a sense of how their presuppositions impact on and interact with those of others in different digital spaces.

Although some of this is occurring in/on the social networking sites, a number of different and overlapping digital fluencies still need to be recognized. These digital fluencies reach beyond current definitions and are presented below.

Lifewide learning

Barnett (2011) suggests that lifewide learning is characterized by learning in different spaces simultaneously and across the learner's lifeworld. Further, he argues:

> This concept – of lifewide learning – poses in turn profound questions as to the learning responsibilities of universities: do they not have *some* responsibility towards the *totality* of the students' learning experiences? Does not the idea of lifewide *education* open here, as a transformative concept for higher education? In sum, the idea of lifewide education promises – or threatens – to amount to a revolution in the way in which the relationship between universities, learners and learning is conceived.
>
> *(Barnett, 2011: 22; original emphasis)*

What is important about his idea of lifewide education is that learning is not only seen to be happening in many spaces, but within and across simultaneous spaces which are often competing for the learner's attention. This conception of learning is useful because of the two distinctions that Barnett makes: namely, that learning should connect with the learner's wider life and lifewide learning should include informal and experiential learning. In many ways this can be linked to the idea of unbundling learning (as mentioned in Chapter 6). However, what needs to be incorporated into Barnett's concept is the digital, so that what we have is *digital lifewide learning*, as presented in Table 7.1 on page 97.

This kind of digital lifewide learning meets many of the eight classifications of learning spaces that Barnett suggests the university might use to value this kind of learning:

a) *Authorship:* What degree of ownership does the learner have in the activity in question? To what degree can the learner author her own activities? Where does the power lie in the framing of a learning space?

b) *Accountability:* To whom is the learner accountable? What form does that accountability take?

c) *Responsibility:* For what range of activities is the learner responsible? Is the learner responsible for other people?

d) *Framing:* How bounded are the activities of the learning space? To what degree are they regulated by formal and tacit rules and conventions?

e) *Sociability:* To what degree is the activity of the learning space personal and to what degree is it a matter of interaction and even possibly collaboration?

f) *Visibility:* How public is the activity?

g) *Complexity:* What is the level of the intellectual demand? How complex is the activity?

h) *Money:* How is the activity financed? What are its costs? Is there an income stream attached? Is the learner responsible for managing the income?

(Barnett, 2011: 33)

In the context of digital fluency these capabilities as yet remain largely unrecognized, and probably undervalued in many (often traditional) university programmes; but these are the kinds of capabilities that enable many students to progress through their courses.

Moving knowledge

It is noticeable that there has been considerable discussion about knowledge construction and reconstruction in relation to social media use and sharing across the internet. Yet at the same time there is also a new language of performance: performing knowledge. This perhaps reflects the need to rethink (again) what counts as knowledge as well as the way it is used – and indeed performed. The idea of Mode 1 and Mode 2 knowledge would now seem to be redundant. Gibbons et al. (1994) argued for Mode 1 and Mode 2 knowledge. The former is propositional knowledge that is produced within academia, separate from its use; the academy is considered the traditional environment for the generation of Mode 1 knowledge. Mode 2 knowledge transcends disciplines and is produced in, and validated through, the world of work. Knowing in this mode demands the integration of skills and abilities in order to act in a particular context. Barnett's (2004) Mode 3 knowledge is where one recognizes that knowing is the position of realizing and producing epistemological gaps. Such knowing produces uncertainty because, 'No matter how creative and imaginative our knowledge designs it always eludes our epistemological attempts to capture it' (Barnett, 2004: 252).

The merging of knowledges across social and academic lives is prompting many of us to rethink what might be meant by knowledge these days. Patently, social media focuses on the social even though it might be used in academia for other purposes. Yet, because it is social, and designed for that very intention, the knowledge used within social networking focuses on the performative: the way knowledge is shared, identity performed, the means by which views are presented or hidden. Knowledge is no longer the stuff of solid textbooks; instead, we have types, levels and formulations of knowledge.

Admittedly, to some extent, this has always been the case when we consider the ways in which knowledge has been passed down and shared across generations. Dawn (2010) argues that a great deal of Western culture is built on stories or ideas that come from the Bible and the diverse narrative styles that appear in it. She shows how these stories have become enmeshed in Western culture, using examples such as the tales of Adam and Eve, the ten plagues of Egypt and the prodigal son, and

TABLE 7.1 Lifewide learning and digital lifewide learning

Activity	Type	Space	External value	Form of learning	Value to students
Essay writing	Formal, within a course	On campus	Credited	Formal	Low
Fieldwork	Formal, within a course	Off campus	Credited	Formal and experiential	Medium
Running sports club	Voluntary	On campus	Linked to course but unaccredited	Informal and experiential	High
Critiquing essays for friends	Voluntary	On campus	Unaccredited	Informal	Medium
Holiday language learning	Voluntary	On campus	Unaccredited	Informal and experiential	High
Digital lifewide learning					
Vidding	Voluntary	Digital space	Unaccredited	Informal and experiential	High
Blogging	Voluntary	Digital space	Unaccredited	Informal and experiential	High
Peer-to-peer support	Voluntary	Digital space	Linked to course but unaccredited	Informal	High
Team project using Whatsapp	Voluntary	Digital space	Linked to course but unaccredited	Informal	High
Facebooking	Voluntary	Digital space	Unaccredited	Informal	High

explains how such narratives have influenced everyone from Shakespeare to Monty Python. However, as Hides (2005: 327) argues:

> The Internet's de-centred structure and purported promiscuity with respect to content are taken as axiomatic expressions of the postmodern, post-ideological, pragmatic landscape. Through its displacement of traditional authority structures and processes, e-learning is claimed to enable alienated students to participate, and to allow all students to learn more effectively, with less difficulty and more enjoyment. Nonetheless, the proliferation of e-learning re-inscribes the questions of the status of knowledge and its relation to power within these new techno-cultural forms.

In many spaces e-learning continues to reinforce the borderlands of knowledge, leaving students stranded between the desire to explore and experiment and the requirements to cover content. More than ten years later, teaching in higher education is no longer about broadcasting knowledge, but about enabling students to become synthesizers and critics of multiple knowledges and knowledge sources.

Some years ago, Perkins (1999: 8–10) suggested the categories of knowledge as being ritual, inert, conceptually difficult and foreign:

- Ritual knowledge, 'a routine and rather meaningless character'. It feels, he argues, 'like part of a social or an individual ritual: how we answer when asked such-and-such, the routine that we execute to get a particular result'. Names and dates are often little more than ritual knowledge.
- Inert knowledge, suggests Perkins, 'sits in the mind's attic, unpacked only when specifically called for by a quiz or a direct prompt but otherwise gathering dust'.
- Conceptually difficult knowledge is encountered as troublesome in all curricula but perhaps particularly in mathematics and science. A mix of misimpressions from everyday experience (objects slow down automatically), reasonable but mistaken expectations (heavier objects fall faster), and the strangeness and complexity of scientists' views of the matter.
- 'Foreign' or 'alien' knowledge is that which 'comes from a perspective that conflicts with our own. Sometimes the learner does not even recognize the knowledge as foreign.'

Students need to be able to transcend all of these during the processes of knowledge creation, knowledge consumption and knowledge performance. In managing these knowledges students will develop a digital fluency that is transformative personally and pedagogically.

Yet, however knowledge is viewed, one of the central challenges for teachers is in deciding what knowledge is used and how it is presented, or even performed, to students. Another challenge for staff is how to enable students to critique that knowledge on offer, that knowledge placed before them, and the way that it is performed to them. Perhaps we need to embrace disruptive media for learning and rethink what liquid learning might be, not as just theoretical ideals but as practical means of enabling and facilitating new forms of learning and teaching through disruptive media.

Vectors, trajectories and rhizomes of transformation

Today we are dealing with new epistemologies of educational performance and rampant presentations of knowledge. Many academics too rarely get beyond the first page of a Google search. What we seem to forget is that amidst the debates about technology and pedagogy and the need for 'new skills', many students (and indeed staff) already have these capabilities but become overwhelmed by the choice and range of information available to them. The role of the educator would now seem to be to steer students through these lurid lures of knowledge performances, to help them to stay critical and focused, and to harness the capabilities that they have already developed in school and college. For many students, these capabilities have already enabled them to achieve university entrance and success in other areas of their lives, as well as to take a stance towards knowledge. Yet, for other students, it is not always clear what learning matters and what does not. There have been, for some years, suggestions of 'unlearning' (Hedberg, 1981): the idea that obsolete knowledge is deleted while new knowledge is created. However, such a stance appears misplaced since it is impossible to clear what we have already learned; instead, we need to reflect on the learning and change and adapt. We might improve or become more reflexive, but it seems unlikely that we unlearn.

Studies such as those reviewed by Gasser et al. (2012), offer interesting perspectives on learning, evaluation and the developing skills and capabilities of young people. In one example, they explain that:

> In the formal education context, skill is defined according to adult normative and prescriptive ideas about what youth ought to know how to do. In the informal context, skill is often transferred through peer learning, such as the techne-mentor and -mentee relationship.
>
> *(Gasser et al., 2012: 29)*

Such skill and mentorship are evident in the invention that for many students and young people is the central plank of being tethered and being fluent with digital media. Nevertheless, notions of invention vary from complex examples of vidding to innovative but more straightforward options. One example of the latter is Scratch, a programming environment developed at MIT. The software means that creating stories and simulations is relatively straightforward through the linking of digital Lego-type blocks. Scratch was launched in 2007 to enable people to learn computing and mathematical concepts. Resnick (2012) explained that it was designed to be:

- *More tinkerable*. To create programs in Scratch, you snap together graphical blocks into stacks, just like LEGO bricks, without any of the obscure syntax (square brackets, semi-colons, etc.) of traditional programming languages. Thus, it is easier to 'tinker' with Scratch – quickly trying out new ideas, then continually modifying and refining.
- *More meaningful*. Scratch supports many different types of projects (games, stories, animations) and many different types of media (graphics, photos, sounds, music), so it can engage people with a wide diversity of interests, even people who had never imagined themselves as programmers.
- *More social*. The Scratch website hosts a vibrant online community with more than 1 million registered members. You can share and get feedback on your own projects, remix other people's projects, or join a 'collab' to create collaborative projects.

Resnick argues that young people learn to become creative thinkers who explore new ideas and new directions, develop systematic reasoning and learn to collaborate in diverse ways by using Scratch.

More recently, Minecraft has become even more popular. Although at first glance it appears to be merely a block-y kind of video game, its non-linear gameplay is very appealing, as is the sharing of ideas, strategies and solutions that occur offline (in the playground). There is a high level of fandom and the best Minecraft players demonstrate their creations to others through Twitch.tv, which streams live games for audiences to watch.

Disruptive media learning?

The term 'disruptive media learning' was adapted from a business model in which disruptive technology helps to create new and different markets and value networks, which then disrupt existing markets. The term 'disruptive technologies' was coined by Bower and Christensen (1995). These were aimed at high-level executives who made the future funding and purchasing decisions in companies. They argued that leading-edge companies invariably lost their competitive edge because they believed that recognizing and following customer demand were central to continued growth and success. Bower and Christensen (1995: 53) suggest that disruptive innovations need to be made, independent from the mother company, so that its executives and directors have the opportunity to realize the potential of the innovation 'at arm's length'. The argument is: 'if the corporation doesn't kill them off itself, competitors will'.

In terms of higher education, disruptive media learning is based on the premise that innovative experimentation needs to occur and be supported by and within the organization, whilst not affecting the overall learning and teaching of the university. Thus, disruptive media learning examines, experiments, develops and researches the impact of such technologies on learning, the learners and the institution. In practice, it is invariably set aside from the organization, and staff are seconded to disruptive media labs to undertake experiments which may or may not be successful, with the successful ones then implemented more broadly at a later stage, across the institution. The hope is that by disrupting and displacing existing notions of learning and knowledge creation, new models will emerge.

The ideas behind such disruption are not new: they can be traced back to the work of Schumpeter (1934). In the 1980s, the use of problem-based learning was seen as a form of learning that could interrupt and disable the organizational culture as well as be disrupted by it (Savin-Baden, 2000). For example, problem-based learning can prompt 'creative destruction' (Schumpeter, 1934) in an organization, whereby the innovation challenges and destroys established practice. New innovations are intended to displace old innovations. This, in turn, is expected to create a pattern whereby new solutions are generated through the solving (or managing) of problems. This may be the case in many organizations, but difficulties arise when innovations such as problem-based learning or new forms of disruptive learning media are merely bolted on to existing courses, leading staff to believe that they are new innovations. Today, in many universities, the nearest anyone seems to get to being disruptive is to introduce an interactive mode of learning into a traditional programme, such as problem-based learning, activity-led learning or action learning sets.

New and emerging technologies tend to interrupt hierarchical learning trajectories, resulting in opportunities for liquid learning and rhizomatic research. Yet it seems we have few maps to navigate this landscape, and little idea how to deal with these vectors of transformation. Consequently, our students travel in multiple directions and collect multiple knowledge sources, yet then mostly fail to understand how best to manage the knowledges they have acquired or how to critique them effectively. Turkle (2005: 14) has argued:

> The dramatic changes in computer education over the past decades leave us with serious questions about how we can teach our children to interrogate simulations in much the same spirit. The specific questions may be different, but the intent needs to be the same: to develop habits of readership appropriate to a culture of simulation.

Her argument in 2011 remains similar (Turkle, 2011a). Nevertheless, it is unclear whether this argument is valid, whether indeed it is a problem, or whether it is just a different form of interrogation: they *choose* which games to play; they decide if the media (and which apps) are any good. Perhaps we are dealing with different ways/ forms of 'reading' and 'interrogating' that we have not yet come to understand. Perhaps what is really needed is to locate and understand learning differently: not merely as something that occurs across a space–time continuum but rather as a vector. Seeing the direction of travel as a vector, a line of fixed length and direction without a fixed position, would mean learning spaces and digital fluency cease to have a sense of fixed linearity and position. It could be suggested that there is little difference between a vector and a trajectory, although in fact the divergence is one of power. Such liquid spaces and spaces of digital fluency transcend the existing structures of higher education and become catalysts to shift beyond linear learning journeys. Such a perspective might also be seen as a sense of living with the oblique, the idea that spaces should be the fusion of movement and dwelling (Virilio, 1997), so that the space is essentially ludic (i.e. playful). Learning, play, fluency and liquidity need to be coupled so that students develop the ability to work and learn with a sense of boundary pushing and pedagogic interruption.

Conclusion

Participatory culture, characterized by the use of Facebook and YouTube, prompts or encourages the democratization of media production, bringing with it the suggestion that young people are both central to the digital age and key players in its formulation and (re)creation. There are also a number of debates about how, when and by whom different media genres – such as vidding, machinima and sequential art – should be used (and in what context) as new modes of presentation, re-presentation and representation. However, what is central to all these debates is the concept of value and identities: who values what and why and in what context? What results in something being given more or less value, and why are some media more effective in tethering to identities than others? Much of this remains unclear, but tethered identities are explored further in Chapter 8.

8
TETHERED IDENTITIES?

Introduction

As change occurs across the globe, it is suggested here that identities are not only increasingly multiple but also that they are tethered in diverse ways. In the past identity and self were seen as static entities. It is now recognized that this was misplaced and that context is important in understanding identity in higher education. In the 1970s and 1980s learning context was recognized as being important in supporting students in developing their ability to learn effectively. The work of Bernstein was influential in arguing for the importance of pedagogic identities and the ways in which they are influenced within the academy. Haraway and Hayles have been at the forefront of discussions about identity in digital spaces, and Ito et al. have been influential by examining how youth culture and identity might be understood. Thus, along with the raft of sociologists who have examined identity, there is a broad literature on this subject, but relatively little that has analysed tethered identities and what this might mean for learning in higher education.

This chapter examines the notion of tethered identities from a number of angles, beginning with a short overview of earlier perceptions of identities and then analysing the notion of friendship identities. It then explores the impact of context collapse on identities and suggests that this has resulted in many of us becoming what Lammes terms 'cartographers on tour'. The second part of the chapter examines some of the darker concerns relating to identity, such as security, secrets and suspicion. The final section suggests that our tethered identities are related to Plato's metaxis and the notion of in-between-ness.

Shifting identities?

Bernstein (1992) argued that, through their experiences as students, individuals within higher education are in the process of identity formation. He suggested that this process may be seen as a student constructing a pedagogic identity that will change according to the different relationships that occur between society, higher education and knowledge. Pedagogic identities are defined as those that 'arise out of contemporary culture and technological change that emerge from dislocations, moral, cultural, economic and are perceived as the means of regulating and effecting change' (Bernstein, 1992: 3). Thus, pedagogic identities are characterized by the emphases of the time. For example, in the traditional disciplines of the 1960s, students were inducted into the particular pedagogical customs of those disciplines, whereas students' pedagogic identities of the 1990s were characterized by a common set of market-related, transferable skills.

Authors such as Buber (1964) seem to have a perception of selfhood that is static; there remain questions to be answered about the extent to which identity shifts, as well as role shifts, are more likely to occur in some environments than others. Hall (1996: 3–4) has argued:

> identity does *not* signal that stable core of the self, unfolding from beginning to end through all the vicissitudes of history without change ... Nor – if we translate this essentialising conception to the stage of cultural identity – is it that collective or true self hiding inside the many other, more superficial or artificially imposed 'selves' ... identities are never unified, and in late modern times, increasingly fragmented; never singular, but multiply constructed across different ... discourses, practices and positions.

Thus, it is argued here that what is needed instead is not a static view of self but a liquid view, a sense of multiple identities that shift and change with time.

Turkle (2005) suggests that computers are not merely objects that make our lives more efficient but subjects that are intimately and ultimately linked to our social and emotional lives. The result then is that computers change not only what we do but how we think about the world and ourselves. Such suggestions would seem to be exemplified in perspectives on and studies into virtual reality and immersion (for example Žižek 2005; Hayles 1999), as well as in studies about identity positions in virtual worlds. However, Clark (2003: 174) has argued:

> Human–machine symbiosis, I believe, is simply what comes naturally. It lies on a direct continuum with clothes, cooking ('external, artificial digestion'), bricklaying, and writing. The capacity to creatively distribute labor across biology and the designed environment is the very signature of our species, and it implies no real loss of control on our part. For who we are is in large part a function of the webs of surrounding structure in which the conscious mind exercises at best a kind of gentle indirect control.

Meanwhile, the growth of the games culture has prompted much discussion about the impact of games on identity and the ways in which they not only position players but send strong messages about race, power and class (e.g. Nakamura, 2010), and the creation of spatial stories.

Lammes reviewed real-time strategy games in which players explore and master environments through digital mapping. The player becomes an imaginary cartographer while creating a spatial story around himself/herself:

> According to de Certeau these two conceptions of spatiality [maps and tours] are both incongruous dimensions of contemporary culture: we are confronted with a static representation of the world we live in, while at the same time sensing our space in a dynamic and more personal way. As place and space, maps and tours necessitate one another and come into being through two-way movement. Even more, a map always presupposes a tour, since one first needs to go somewhere to give an objective spatial account of it (de Certeau 1984: 117–121).
>
> *(Lammes, 2008: 87–88)*

Lammes suggests that these games help to improve spatial awareness and draws on the work of Fuller and Jenkins (1995), who suggest that digital games and new media should be seen as spatial stories, since players construct a narrative by travelling through space. Thus, space and tours are seen as a more spatial experience that is both known and changeable, whereas places and maps are seen as stable and timeless. Whilst this is a useful distinction between space and place, and there is still a sense that place is seen as a more stable identity than space, the polarity is perhaps less stark in 2015, when location finders, GPS systems and digital maps on mobile devices result in collisions of space and place.

Perhaps more of an issue here is identity tourism, a metaphor developed by Nakamura (2000) to portray identity appropriation in cyberspace. Such appropriation makes it possible to play with different identities without encountering the risk associated with racial differences in real life. However,

> One of the dangers of identity tourism is that it takes this restriction across the axes of race/class in the 'real world' to an even more subtle and complex degree by reducing non white identity positions to part of a costume or masquerade to be used by curious vacationers in cyberspace.
>
> *(Nakamura, 2000)*

We travel through cyberspace, putting on and taking off identities as we cross fluctuating boundaries and bounce between our virtual and real-life worlds; and identity tourism offers opportunities to 'play away' from other identities. Yet staff have certainly questioned the extent to which in-world identities have spilled over into work or home identities and impacted on or prompted reformulations of other identities in other worlds. This is illustrated in Table 8.1.

Sinclair refers to this sense of having a left-behind identity in relation to her disquiet about the relationship between her real-life and Second Life identities

TABLE 8.1 Identities in flux

	Characteristics	Purpose or function	Relationship with other 'identities'	Example
Identity tourism	Wholehearted appropriation of another identity	Playing away from other, more responsible, identities	Different and invariably subversive, often pernicious	Changing racial or sexual identity for deceitful purposes
Identity expansion	Several, but often the same voices in a wide range of spaces, a kind of expanded voice	To increase profile and voice across digital spaces	Similar, copied and stretched	The use of multiple blogs and websites
Identity multiplication	Different identities in diverse spaces	Identity exploration in different spaces and contexts	Different from one another but with a sense of coherence relating to real-life identities	Creating avatars in different virtual worlds and games
Changelings	Residual identity which has a sense of being a left-behind identity	A denial of current other identities or a mirroring of real-life identities due to ambivalence about them	Either dislocated from other identities or strongly copied	Avatars that are used transgressively or are used as copies of other stronger identities
Shapeshifters	A transformation into a different form and persona	Unclear, but usually a choice related to solving a difficulty of some kind	Usually the same, it is the form that is usually different	Shift to another form such as animagi in Harry Potter, or characters in the X Men films

Source: Savin-Baden, 2010: 75.

(Savin-Baden and Sinclair, 2010). However, some scholars suggest that it is important to have a clear conceptual understanding of who we are in cyberspace, since without it we risk being confused (e.g. Floridi, 2011). Those who argue for such a stance seem to be suggesting that separating and being honest about identities brings with it some kind of honesty or morality, yet this seems to be misplaced. Similarly, Kimmons and Veletsianos (2014: 8) argue that the ability to undertake identity explorations relies on the

> user's ability to separate the legion of one's virtual, exploratory selves from the real life or traditionally viewed unitary self. In the Web 2.0 world, however, one's ability to do this diminishes as anonymity declines, real life connections are replicated in the virtual medium, web resources are used for surveillance, and sites like Facebook and LinkedIn seek to present 'authentic', unitary selves that are similar to the selves expressed in real life.

This stance seems to be similarly misplaced, since identity exploration does not require a clear separation of identities, but a recognition that identities are not just multiple and fluid but overlap and shift according to context. Although later in their article Kimmons and Veletsianos do acknowledge that context has some relevance, they still hold on to the notion of some kind of unitary self. For example, they argue that Facebook is built on the premise that people have authentic identities and that those identities are expressed online. Yet work by Madge et al. (2009) suggests that while the use of Facebook can support student engagement and integration at university, students still largely use it as a social tool. These authors suggest students adopt a wide variety of 'different place-based and online-networks to develop and sustain their settling-in process and maintain and develop social networks' (Madge et al., 2009: 152).

Further, Kimmons and Veletsianos also argue that online identities are mere fragments of themselves and that people tend neither to play a part nor act out identities. Yet this sense of just using what they term 'acceptable identity fragments' would seem to suggest that people merely use online splinters of themselves rather than making specific decisions and choices about what is revealed, acted, dramatized and performed. Attrill and Jalil (2011) argue that issues of identity and disclosure are strongly connected online and this is borne out by the studies into disclosure to pedagogical agents mentioned in Chapter 6. However, research indicates that self-disclosure, in some instances, is different from face to face, indicating that intimate disclosure tends to occur faster online. For example, Leung (2002) found that using instant messaging increased the level of disclosure when compared with offline communication. Attrill and Jalil (2011) found that this was the case, too, although to some degree those people who were more favourably disposed towards forming online relationships were more likely to report it and disclose more. Yet they also found that this disclosure was quite superficial, in that people tended to disclose only interests and personal views; and although there might be more online exchanges than face to face ones at the same stage of a relationship, the former were no more in depth than the latter. Thus, as discussed in detail in Chapter 9, honesty, disclosure and revelation remain complex issues to manage in a networked society, and the amount of truthful information divulged tends to be proportionate to people's perception of privacy and risk.

Identity form-ations?

Opportunities to explore separate identities in distinct spaces are occurring, so it is important to recognize these and locate and study the ways in which they are played, and how they affect learning. Identities will be played out differently according to the diverse online groups with which it is possible to engage; we are all enactors of our own spatial stories and practices and we have different values and spatial limits. Identities then might be delineated as multiple, multifaceted, but perhaps shaped as follows:

- *Spatial identities:* the many mobile and polyvalent identities that are played in diverse media spaces, whether Twitter, Facebook, blogs or email. Largely there will be some degree of crossover between them, and some kind of stability, even though we might choose to represent ourselves differently on Facebook than we do in a work email conversation. These identities are enacted through digital media and each enactment tends to prompt a different kind of performance, invariably guided by the norms, cultures and affordances of both the software and the users of these spaces.
- *Networked identities:* in 2008 Ryberg and Larsen suggested that networked identities represented the idea that identities were constructed in multidimensional and complex ways across overlapping online and offline networks across school, work and spare time and that individual identities exist and become real through such networks. Since then, further research has supported their theory, but also indicates the emergence of visibility and status hierarchies with such networks. For example, Kozinets (2010: 24) suggested this was less about status per se and more about 'visibility and identity expressions'. Networked identities differ from spatial identities as the former are specifically located in, and in relation to, given networks, rather than in the broader spatial zones of the latter, although of course there is overlap between the two. Literature on networked identities has grown, although there are still questions about the production of networked reputations, credibility and status. For academics, it is interesting to consider whether and how much Twitter and other social media can bring high status and identity recognition without the need for academic publications and large-scale grant funding.
- *Place-based identities:* these identities are strongly located in relation to the places we inhabit, and tend to be relatively stable and ordered. Place-based identities, then, often relate to roles and positions such as home and work, but are also located in communities where people feel a sense of belonging.

- *Mapped identities:* these identities tend to be imposed identities. For example, they might be provided by school reports, external data, job profiles or human resources records. They are seen as static and objective, although in many ways they are not; they are in fact identities mapped on to us by others.
- *Identities on tour:* there is often a sense of play with these identities. They are not static, and do not have anything sinister about them (unlike identity tourism). Instead, they are dynamic, and the purpose and point of view of the traveller are central. Thus, when working in areas such as mixed and augmented reality, people might create legitimate space and places for identity exploration and (re)formation.
- *Frontier identities:* these identities tend to overlap with and overlay on to other spaces, and also tend to be twilight identities, in the sense that identities sit beside one another and come to the fore when one is required over another. Yet there are other frontiers which might be said to have a mediating quality, because they can be both the point of contact and the point of collision between two areas. For example, increasingly complex and sophisticated software means that we can be tagged in real life, within and across cyberspace – and such tagged identities may or may not cross over one another.
- *Interstitial identities:* metaxis (or metaxy) is a word used by Plato to describe the condition of 'in-between-ness' that is one of the characteristics of being human. Plato applied it to spirituality, describing its location as being between the human and the divine. Whelan (2008) expands the notion of metaxis for the modern age, claiming that 'we humans are suspended on a web of polarities – the one and the many, eternity and time, freedom and fate, instinct and intellect, risk and safety, love and hate, to name but a few'. Metaxis has also been defined as the state of belonging completely and simultaneously to two different autonomous worlds (Linds, 2006). The idea of metaxis reflects the state of being of many people who are digitally tethered: they live, work and perform in and across in-between spaces simultaneously.
- *Bridged identities:* these are identities created to link with other exterior worlds, such as virtual worlds, discussion forums and gaming worlds. Such identities might be located through the creation of avatars or by using avatars for identity play (playing with avatar identity in ways that are seen as fun and sometimes trite (Savin-Baden, 2010)). Thus, bridged identities are linked to other (alien) identities, such as other territories and no-man's land. For example, the bodily markers that are used to present ourselves in life, clothes, ethnicity, gender and speech may be re-presented (differently) in virtual worlds but they also indicate choices about how we wish to be seen or the ways in which we might like to feel differently. However, as Nakamura (2010: 430) suggests, we might be aware that these kinds of media (games and virtual embodiment) create social factions of race and gender, while accurate images of gender and cultural realties might be rare.
- *Left-behind identities:* Žižek (1999), in his deconstruction of *The Matrix*, suggests that the deletion of our digital identities could turn us into 'non-persons', but

it might be more accurate to say that we could become changelings, or have left-behind identities. Thus, as we shift and move identities across online contexts, rather than deleting those that become superfluous, we tend to leave them behind. Such identities then become part of the junk spaces of the internet – left behind and forgotten avatars, discarded blogs or Facebook profiles, along with those that remain when someone dies, which may evoke memories, sadness or sinister thoughts for some.

Playing at the borders of identity seems to be an attempt to disrupt the mind/body polarity by focusing on a resituated and often repositioned body. However, it is not entirely clear whether young people realize or question the extent to which online identities spill over into work or home identities and have impacted on or prompted reformulations of other identities in other worlds. These could be seen as spatial identities on tour. Perhaps it is more complex and we need to have a new set of space/place identities that reflect squashed polarities, chaotic overlaps and new configurations of space and place. For example, in areas such as trust and cyber-influence, past assumptions have centred on external threats that are place-based and can be mapped, but in the twenty-first century these are no longer valid.

Thus, it would seem that digital tethering is transforming identities and territories across personal zones, work geographies and interactive spaces. Such transformations are affecting our identities and sense of space and place, so there is a sense of being disparate as well as holding homogenized identities. For example, the ways we perform on Twitter may or may not reflect real-life identities or the identities we have adopted in MySpace or in work-related discussion forums. It could be – and increasingly is – argued that cyberspace has resulted in a sense of multiple identities and disembodiment, or even different forms of embodiment. Further, the *sense* of anonymity, and the assumption that this was what was understood through one's words rather than one's bodily presence, is becoming increasingly unmasked in cyberspace. For example, Steils (2013: 242–250) developed a typology of learner identity in virtual worlds by showing how students seek to manage their identities through their avatars. This typology portrays learner identity across five dimensions that are summarized below.

Dimension one: dislocated avatars

The first dimension concerns the utilization of default avatars. In this dimension the avatar was positioned as merely functional. No emotional attachment to the avatar was indicated, and participants basically ignored the appearance of the avatar.

Dimension two: representative avatars

The second dimension considers an understanding of the avatar as a representation of oneself in functional terms. Although the avatar's appearance seemed closely connected to (or was at least an approximation of) the physical world appearance of the user, students described the relationship to the avatar in terms of functional representation and rendered the avatar as an object or tool.

Dimension three: avatars as toys and tools

The third dimension portrays an understanding of the avatar as a tool and object for playful engagement, as well as a status object. The avatar was here positioned as an object that could be customized and played with to take on various appearances.

Dimension four: avatars as extensions of self

The fourth dimension relates to students who declared their respective avatars as extensions of themselves, both visually and emotionally. The avatars were described as closely related to the users in corporeal appearance and possibly by name, and students were emotionally and psychologically attached to them.

Dimension five: avatars as identity extensions

In this dimension, students engaged with their avatars and the virtual world in terms of 'laboratories for the construction of identities' (Turkle 1996: 184; 1999). Thus, the avatar ventured into dimensions of exploring notions of potential, new or alternative identities for the user in the context of the virtual world by using this as a testing ground for the physical world and also explored possibilities beyond its boundaries.

Context collapse

Not having opportunities to explore identities and operate differently in different spaces, as Floridi (2011) suggests, or operating only with identity components, as suggested by Kimmons and Veletsianos (2014), rather seems to lock down the freedoms inherent in living online. Authors such as Seymour (2001) have suggested that although the physical body is invisible, meanings, mannerisms, behaviours and unstated assumptions are clearly visible in online communication. Further, studies suggest that users of immersive virtual worlds may adjust their identities to match those of their avatars.

Yet, amidst all these shifting identities, it would seem that issues of context are no longer as useful as they once were in helping to locate and position identities. boyd coined the phrase 'context collapse' and has argued:

> The underlying architecture of the digital environment does not provide the forms of feedback and context to which people have become accustomed. The lack of embodiment makes it difficult to present oneself and to perceive

the presentation of others. As people operate through digital agents, they are forced to articulate their performance in new ways. Additionally, the contextual information that they draw from does not have the same implications online. Situational context can be collapsed with ease, thereby exposing an individual in an out-of-context manner.

(boyd, 2002: 12)

Whilst contexts may have collapsed, as boyd suggests, it is evident that those using social networking sites do have a sense of their (imagined) audience. Yet the varied, mainstream and often linked (Facebook and Twitter) sites could be said to be resulting in multiple context collapse. Thus, articulating performance in new ways can be seen as a means of enacting different forms and types of status online. The result is that context collapse has affected the ways in which identity status is played out and the new ways in which status is developed and valued.

Identity status

Identity status is defined here as the way in which people enact and develop their status (largely consciously) online. In the main, this usually relates to the way in which a person chooses to portray their identity in terms of their professional life, but it can also refer to the position they adopt in social groups, such as sports groups on Facebook or playing out friendship identities on MySpace in youth cultures. The developing of status can occur through having multiple followers, multiple Twitter and Facebook accounts, often posting across as many sites as possible, and the tweeting and retweeting of one's own work. It can also occur through the creation of drama and gossip on social media sites. Three types of identity status are evident: professional status, friendship status and participatory pioneering.

Professional status

The use of social media for self-promotion in academia has grown considerably in the last five years. Many academics – and many more journalists, use social networking for self-promotion. Breaking news, sharing ideas and creating informal networks are positive and useful uses of media such as Twitter. Despite this, such sites of self-promotion are either not valued or under-valued by the more traditional members of the academy. Those who do use social media well have seen their work very quickly being referenced across the globe. Some researchers have been able to promote their important empirical findings to a much wider audience, while for others academic fame has been achieved based on relatively little research! However, sharing early research findings can mean people easily become susceptible to public scrutiny in ways that they had not anticipated. The result is that whilst reputations can be enhanced, they can also be harmed, as representations are or can be reframed by others, making personal and social interactions more visible and volatile.

Friendship status

Friendship-driven teen practices indicate that identity status and teen cultures are being developed through digital tethering. Yet, at the same time, teenagers are creating new norms and practices – such as how to deal with drama and conflicts in digital social spaces. boyd (2010) suggests that social media are used not only to maintain and sustain friendships but to create drama and generate attention – often to allay fears about unpopularity. Acts of drama on social media tend to be continuations of face-to-face drama, thus spaces such as Facebook provide platforms for dramas to be (re)created, played out and often extended. However, although social networking sites can be used to spread rumours and gossip through news feeds, most of this tends to spread through instant messaging and text messaging:

> The public, persistent, searchable, and spreadable nature of mediated information affects the way rumors flow and how dramas play out. The explicitness surrounding the display of relationships and online communication can heighten the social stakes and intensity of status negotiation.
>
> *(boyd, 2010: 112)*

It is important to note that work by Larsen and Ryberg (2011) suggests that youth experience and sensibility, on the one hand, and the media's portrayal of youth uses of social media, on the other, are markedly different. The public discourses emphasize risk, predators and bullying, whereas young people themselves argue that they simply report such dangers, and they overwhelmingly see social networking spaces as sites of friendship and affirmation.

Friendship hierarchies are developed through social networking sites such as Facebook and MySpace, where people are encouraged to indicate who their top friends are. This is controversial, because teenagers tend not to rank their friends hierarchically and they have different friends in different contexts – friends from the bus, friends from class, friends from clubs. Although boyd (2010) suggested that deleting a friend on Facebook is seen as unacceptable, in 2015 the culture and practice of doing just that are now less clear: attitudes may vary across cultures or it may be more acceptable in 2015 than it was in 2012. boyd (2010) examined the intersection of social media with making friends, performing friendships, articulating friendship hierarchies and navigating status, attention and drama. Surveys have and still do indicate that most teens use social media to socialize with people they already know or with whom they are already loosely connected (Ito et al., 2010). Within these friendship groups, issues of status occur both offline and online.

Participatory pioneering

This is the process by which people learn and teach each other collaboratively through digital media to invent, create and remix in ways that are both pioneering and disruptive in their use of media. Vidding is one example of this. Others are: Mixlr, which enables users to host a radio show or produce a podcast using high-quality audio that can be shared or exported to Dropbox or Soundcloud; Vine, for (very) short video sharing; and the hugely popular Instagram, where users take pictures and videos, apply digital filters to them and share them on a variety of social networking sites. Common to all of these is that engagement in them is shared, and support is provided for improving and developing media by peers, both offline and online.

Other forms of media that also involve sharing and discussing what has been created by others are not essentially participatory pioneering. These include apps such as Snapchat, which offers fifteen-second photo and video sharing, and WeChat, which provides multimedia communication and contact information, and seems to be overtaking Facebook in terms of its popularity among young people.

Despite youth interest and creativity in using digital media, critics still focus on the impact of media on people rather than on what they do with it. These increasingly interactive and participatory cultures have a range of benefits, including: 'opportunities for peer-to-peer learning, a changed attitude toward intellectual property, the diversification of cultural expression, the development of skills valued in the modern workplace, and a more empowered conception of citizenship' (Jenkins, 2009: xii). The teaching, sharing and collaboration that are central to participatory pioneering result in increased identity status for those creating and teaching others, so that fandom is created around a particular person or group.

Conclusion

Social media offer opportunities for people to interact and change media landscapes, and thus they become explorers and tourists who work out their identities as they travel. Phones, fashion and hanging out with the cool and the popular are all key markers of social identity and status. Yet, at the same time, norms about what is acceptable change with technology, and in many cases both adults and teens are still working out how, when and with whom to articulate identities in social media spaces. Despite many people being comfortable and at ease with these technologies, there remains much concern about security, secrecy and the extent to which there is more or less danger than we are being led to believe. This is explored in Chapter 9.

9

DIGITAL SURVEILLANCE AND TETHERED INTEGRITY

Introduction

This chapter examines the way in which surveillance and privacy are affected in online spaces and analyses the research findings to date. It suggests that the concepts and practices associated with privacy have become increasingly complex, and that this remains an area that many users of social networking sites still find troublesome. Furthermore, it introduces some questions about what types of ethics need to be considered in relation to being digitally tethered.

The chapter argues that rather than focusing just on surveillance, privacy and disclosure as issues, it is perhaps more helpful to engage with the possibilities for creating and sustaining some forms of tethered integrity in order to cope with the shifts and changes that are occurring continually across cyberspace. The final section of the chapter offers practical suggestions for managing privacy and surveillance.

Privacies?

Despite numerous media scare stories, many students do in fact care about and wish to protect their personal information in cyberspace. However, it is unclear whether they are aware of the extent to which their personal information is stored and tracked. For instance, Facebook expects its users to provide their real identities, and all of their information can be manipulated and classified through the company's huge database. Most students still, it seems, have open profiles and share email addresses and even phone numbers. Yet there are extensive debates relating to internet privacy, and authors such as Floridi (2011) argue that people need to have a clear conceptual understanding of who they are in cyberspace, since without this there is a risk of confusion and impasse (although it is not clear who will be confused).

Privacy, per se, is not straightforward. There are a number of ways in which it can be delineated, and it is useful to consider each of these in relation to digital tethering:

- Expressive privacy is the desire to protect oneself from peer pressure or ridicule in order to express one's own identity (DeCew, 1997).
- Informational privacy is the protection of information relating to finances, personal information and lifestyle (DeCew, 1997).
- Institutional privacy is the protection of personal information and monitoring by organizations such as governments and banks through CCTV, genetic screening and credit cards.
- Social privacy is discussed by Raynes-Goldie (2010), who found that the young people in her study were particularly concerned about access to their personal information, as opposed to institutional privacy. In the study she found that users attempted to ensure their social privacy by using pseudonyms, setting up false accounts, regularly deleting wall posts and photographs, and untagging themselves from other people's posts.

It is increasingly evident that many people who use social networking sites choose to be what Westin et al. (1991) termed 'privacy pragmatists', in that they are prepared to share information for personal gain, for instance on Facebook, to maintain networks with friends and family. Based on their survey data, Westin et al. argued that people could be grouped into one of three categories:

- *The privacy fundamentalists:* largely distrustful of organizations that ask for personal information and concerned about the safety and accuracy of computerized information. They are in favour of laws and regulatory actions and will generally choose privacy over consumer-service benefits.
- *The privacy pragmatics:* weigh up the benefits of various consumer opportunities against the intrusiveness of providing personal information and increasing government power, but want to retain the ability to opt out of even non-evaluative uses of their personal information, such as in compilations of mailing lists.
- *The unconcerned:* generally trustful of organizations that collect their personal information, comfortable with existing organizational procedures, ready to forgo privacy claims to secure consumer-service benefits, and against the enactment of new privacy laws or regulations.

Brandtzaeg et al. (2010) compared the experiences and usage patterns of younger and older Facebook users. They found that all age groups had diverse friends and acquaintances, but younger users were more skilled in their Facebook usage, and the various groups' open public profiles were different. A table from this study vividly reflects age-related differences in usage, preferences and concerns about privacy (Table 9.1).

TABLE 9.1 General comparison of the younger adult sample and the older adult sample in regard to social practices and privacy

	Younger People (Sample 1)	*Older People (Sample 2)*
Sociability		
Usage	Use it less, but check their accounts multiple times a day for a few minutes at a time and as a substitute for instant messaging, SMS and email.	Use FB for fewer but longer sessions, replace to some extent SMS and telephone calls. Use it more often than before.
Family	Report somewhat frequent contact with cousins and relatives because of FB, little contact with their parents.	Report contact with extended family and follow their children's use. Those with children older than twenty have quite frequent contact with them.
Friends	Mainly contact existing friends whom they see in their everyday lives.	Mainly contact existing friends whom they see in their everyday lives.
Purpose	Microcoordination, purposeful use, flirting, photo sharing, general contact with friends for private reasons.	A kind of a nostalgic communication and curiosity, and less purposeful use, keep in touch with family, and keep up to date with old friends, photo sharing.
Content sharing		
Photo and video	Often post large numbers of photos from parties and social events. Some also post their own videos.	Post some family and holiday photos, but seldom. Do not upload videos.
Status update and wall posts	Seldom use status updates; girls use wall posts more than boys.	Use status updates and wall posts more often than the younger sample.
Privacy		
Sharing control	Confident in their FB usage and more knowledgeable about content-sharing practices.	Less confident in their FB usage, some report accidents related to sharing and asking for help from their children on how to use FB.
Third-person effect	Likely to see that other people have more risk to privacy.	Perceive the risk to the privacy of others as greater than to their own privacy. Think that younger people are more transparent and exposed to a greater risk of having their privacy violated compared to themselves.
Social surveillance	Think they have too many friends, and clean up photos and wall posts. Some find having adult family members as FB friends to be problematic.	Some complain about too many friends, but not as much as the younger ones. Those with younger children report surveillance and parental control as their motivation for using FB.

(continued)

TABLE 9.1   *(continued)*

	Younger People (Sample 1)	*Older People (Sample 2)*
Self-presentation	Looking good, positive and authentic. Untagging bad or unpleasant photos. A concern is that friends in the network also create and define the user's self-presentation.	Looking good, positive and sporty. Often brag about holidays and travelling.
Pictures without consent	Report a number of cases in which others upload photos of them without their consent. Also comment on pictures.	Report a number of cases in which others upload photos of them without their consent, but not as common in this age group.
Privacy concern	Quite high awareness. Think of FB presence in terms of future job prospects. Find it less likely that FB itself will use their pictures and information.	They are concerned, but not as aware of the usage and protection strategies as the younger ones. Some are afraid that burglars will use FB as a tool to determine whether they are home.

Source: Brandtzaeg et al., 2010: 1018–1019.

As a result of their findings, Brandtzaeg et al. (2010: 1025) suggest that certain privacy design principles should be adopted. These are summarized below:

- *Design for privacy salience:* to ensure the core features of the privacy settings are clear and visible to all users.
- *Design with a focus on privacy purpose:* so that users understand the purpose of the privacy settings.
- *Design for restrictions on friends:* for example, no friend suggestions, since having too many friends can result in privacy problems.
- *Design for multiple social circles and forms of social capital:* provide users with simple tools, so that they can create different relationships and levels of confidentiality.
- *Design for control over content sharing:* provide tools to ensure that users can see how the content will be visible and accessible.
- *Make restrictive default settings:* for children and older adults.

These design principles are valuable and bring to the fore some of the dilemmas that are currently experienced in relation to online privacy.

Privacy dilemmas

Despite many clear and useful definitions, there is an increasing view that privacy is an embedded cultural and social practice which encompasses issues such as risk, trust, morality, danger and identity (Dourish and Anderson, 2006). Thus, in this model, privacy necessarily becomes a series of trade-offs in terms of what is shared and what is withheld. Some years ago, there was much discussion of the 'privacy paradox', an idea proposed by Barnes (2006). This suggested that, whilst adults are concerned about invasions of privacy, teens freely give up their personal information because they are unaware of the public nature of the internet. Although some authors still hold to this idea, Tufekci (2008) showed that the privacy paradox is not a paradox at all, and many others have suggested it is more of a dilemma than a paradox. For example, Utz and Krämer (2009) suggest that more people are changing their default privacy settings and their concern about privacy is influenced by the social practices of others' norms. In particular, they note that choosing privacy settings is a dynamic process which indicates that users are indeed concerned with the privacy question. Meanwhile, Brandtzaeg et al. (2010) have suggested that social network users experience a dilemma between their desire for privacy and their desire to share and be sociable. They argue that the more people believe that their privacy is protected, the more they feel able to share.

Glass bedrooms

Pearson (2009) argued that the metaphor of a glass bedroom was being adopted by users of social networking sites, who saw them as not entirely private but not fully public; rather a bridge with its own semiotics. The idea is that private exchanges take place whilst users are inside the glass bedroom, with varying degrees of friends and strangers passing by. In terms of privacy and surveillance, this metaphor is useful because of the private/public nature of social networking sites. For example, in MySpace and Facebook, exchanges are generally undertaken with an awareness of others beyond the glass. Yet, at the same time, people may use jokes, slogans and codes in public spaces or create smaller private groups, thereby creating an outside and an inside. This means that whilst surveillance is often still perceived as being institutional (as discussed below), the glass bedroom indicates that this is not the case. As users exchange information, the process of tagging and sharing makes information increasingly public. Consequently, material that may originally have been intended only for close friends is shared by others, thereby disrupting the boundaries of public and private spaces.

Privacy and insider attacks

In recent years, real-time location sharing has become widely adopted. Conventional (offline) privacy attacks are undertaken by persistently targeting someone's whereabouts and habits in order to build up a profile of them and their behaviour. Online privacy attacks tend to employ similar tracking practices. Whilst, as discussed above, there are privacy dilemmas and research suggests that people's attitudes to privacy differ from their actual practices, there do seem to be some interesting online and offline differences. For example, online privacy attacks tend to occur in spaces such as immersive worlds and banking websites, whereas location sharing attacks (stalking, burglary) occur offline as result of location sharing apps that provide information about physical position, such as a person being away on holiday. A study by Kostakos et al. (2011) found that users who are both central to their local and global social networks and possess many friends are more likely to share locations readily and are therefore most likely to be at risk.

Our open, accessible, online society has resulted in a level of tracking that many of us would rather not contemplate. By default, our mobile phones are set to track us, often without our knowledge, so that our Twitter feeds can be analysed and visualized, our movements and shopping habits followed, and indeed most of our activities discovered by someone else with relative ease. To some extent, this has resulted in an overarching lack of trust, because essentially we are all insiders now; and whilst some people are only mildly suspicious of this, others are much more so. In day-to-day life, in the main, this open but hidden knowledge is already accepted and ignored, but being insiders means that security, privacy and trust boundaries have been breached, and it is difficult to decide how security might be maintained in a post-security world.

Chivers et al. (2013) suggest that insider attacks tend to occur through misuse of authority, electronic assaults and violations of security, and they define insiders as those who work within a defined boundary and have privileges or trust within that boundary. A boundary may encircle a place of work, an organization or a nation, and such a boundary is considered to be the first line of defence for most countries and organizations. The expectation is that people will work within boundaries and conform to both organizational policies and the correct modes of operating within physical and electronic systems. Chivers et al. (2013: 18) argue that:

> Examples of security violations by insiders include 'home grown' terrorism, espionage, theft of industrial secrets, sabotage, and employee fraud. We also include in our definition of insider a person or element of a system that has been subverted to act for an external attacker, because the detection problem is the same: the system cannot be protected at the perimeter, and the attacker has acquired some degree of internal authority. Examples of such attacks include the coercion or social engineering of employees, including using such techniques to subvert employees' electronic equipment. Attacks may involve a single major incident, such as terrorist attack, sabotage, or theft, or may take place over a long period.

Insider attacks are interesting because most companies and institutions fail to recognize that they are a possibility, or at least assume that any attack is much more likely to come from outside. Certainly, most ministries of defence around the world traditionally assumed that the employees within their walls are 'patriotic and therefore safe', apart from the expected handful of double agents. However, this is no longer the case. Enforcing security now carries a huge financial cost and therefore the protection of some areas is prioritized over that of others. Of course, this raises the questions: what should be left unsecure and what might the consequences be? Furthermore, it is important to consider whether there is now any real possibility of true privacy or secure identities. It seems that our identities can be stolen, borrowed, and even used against us, perhaps not imminently but certainly in the future.

However, although privacy is a complex concern and surveillance is big business, Palen and Dourish (2003: 131) have noted that disclosure can be used to limit, rather than increase, accessibility; thus, academics tend to upload their articles to decrease requests for them. Further, as Tufekci (2008: 34) remarks, 'making it clear that you are in a relationship or that you are politically conservative or that religion is very important to you or that you cannot stand (or you live for) hip hop ... can be considered fair warning to people who may not be compatible with you'. Although considerable research has explored privacy, relatively little has examined using disclosure in this way to limit accessibility or the extent to which taking a clear stand on beliefs, hobbies and political views may provide some degree of protection from unwanted interest. Nevertheless, privacy seems to be one component of the increasingly complex landscape of digital surveillance.

Digital surveillance

Surveillance is defined here as the monitoring of activities and behaviour in order to influence, manipulate and manage people's lives. In the context of digital tethering, such monitoring occurs in online spaces, and it is often viewed as more sinister and secretive than other kinds of surveillance. In 2008 Zimmer coined the term 'Search 2.0' to describe the loss of privacy which occurs through the aggregation of users' online activities. In practice, Search 2.0 enables companies to track and aggregate data in ways that were previously impossible, since in the past people's data were scattered across diverse sites. Now, as a result of social networking sites, personal data can be mined and cross-referenced, sold and reused, so people are now being classified by others because they have chosen to share their own data. Zimmer (2008) suggested that there should be better formal regulation and changes in the way social media are designed, but this has not yet occurred and there is no sign of it happening in the future. Instead, we live in a world of liquid, participatory and lateral surveillance.

The term 'liquid surveillance' was developed by Lyon (2010), building on the work of Bauman. As mentioned in Chapter 2, Bauman (2000) argued that we have moved into 'liquid modernity', an era of constant change, ambivalence and uncertainty. Liquid modernity is thus a chaotic continuation of modernity, yet until the rise of social networking the solidity of technology initially seemed to overlay this notion of liquidity. Now, though, Lyon argues that everyone can be targeted and sorted through data flows and regimes of in/visibility. He also suggests that surveillance is a central theme in Bauman's depiction of modernity. What is particularly useful in the context of an analysis of social networking sites is the way in which Bauman (1987: 168) sees consumer seduction as a substitute for repression:

'conduct is made manageable, predictable and hence non-threatening, by a multiplication of needs rather than by a tightening of norms'.

Social networking sites seem to be somewhat panoptical, and although, as Foucault noted, Bentham's (1787/1995) original perspective was of a closed space and the watched were unaware of the watcher, the openness and who is watching whom can be troublesome:

> the major effect of the Panopticon: to induce in the inmate a state of conscious and permanent visibility that assures the automatic functioning of power ... Bentham laid down the principle that power should be visible and unverifiable. Visible: the inmate will constantly have before his eyes the tall outline of the central tower from which he is spied upon. Unverifiable: the inmate must never know whether he is being looked at at any one moment; but he must be sure that he may always be so. In order to make the presence or absence of the inspector unverifiable, so that the prisoners, in their cells, cannot even see a shadow.
>
> *(Foucault, 1975/1977: 201)*

Yet it seems that there is a shift away from the idea of the panopticon through self-surveillance. Surveillance is liquid, Lyon (2010: 332) argues, because it no longer keeps its shape but rather flows and is mobile:

> In a convenient confluence with liquid fear, liquid surveillance joins forces with everything from emergency preparedness drills to neighbourhood watches. In this way it also helps to beget its alter egos. If everyone is responsible for surveillance duty, everyone is also responsible for seeing to it that they are not surveilled against their will. Evading surveillance is in this view a problem of individual biography, not of institutional responsibility.

There also appears to be an interesting parallel between open social networking sites and the (relatively) closed institutional sites. For example, the way in which technology is employed in many universities is resulting in an institutional panopticon, where visibility and calculability are still in many instances not seen as problematic. There is a sense, too, that closed virtual learning environments are the ultimate twenty-first-century panopticon, where everything is visible, and for students or staff not to be seen in these spaces is a punishable offence.

Poster (1990) coined the term 'participatory surveillance' when arguing that current communication systems and databases constitute a super-panopticon. Here, individuals are not just disciplined but actively participate in their own surveillance by contributing information. Subsequently, Albrechtslund (2008) suggested that the term 'participatory surveillance' should be adopted more positively to describe the playful and social aspects of surveillance. Yet the term 'surveillance' itself is still so associated with watching and control that it is imbued with too much textual negativity for this to occur. Perhaps we are all just players and watchers now.

Or perhaps Koskela's (2004) argument for the term 'empowering exhibitionism' is more useful, as it describes the practice of revealing your (very) personal life, so that in the process of exhibiting it you can claim 'copyright' over it. More recently, Albrechtslund and Lauritsen (2013) have argued for a stronger conceptualization of participatory surveillance, suggesting that surveillance is strongly affected by how participation is negotiated and the ways in which actions and intentions in relation to surveillance are translated.

Surveillance, then, is affected by context, permissions, participation and levels of honesty. Yet, at the same time, we also seem to be engaged with what could be termed participatory exhibitionism, as we all share our own – and other people's – films and photos on Facebook. Perhaps it would be more accurate to say that we are dealing with Andrejevic's lateral surveillance:

> Lateral surveillance, or peer-to-peer monitoring, understood as the use of surveillance tools by individuals, rather than by agents of institutions public or private, to keep track of one another, covers (but is not limited to) three main categories: romantic interests, family, and friends or acquaintances.
>
> *(Andrejevic, 2005: 488)*

Lateral surveillance – whereby a person might track their children's communications, monitor their lover's phone calls or use a webcam to spy on their neighbours – can appear more sinister than extensive government tracking, perhaps because many of us believe that the latter form of top-down surveillance has always existed. Nevertheless, it has become a type of informal law enforcement and micro-inquiry into other people's lives. Thus, we market-research, verify and run checks on friends and colleagues, so that 'In an era in which everyone is to be considered potentially suspect, we are invited to become spies – for our own good' (Andrejevic, 2005: 494).

The ethics of being digitally tethered

Ethics have become an increasingly difficult topic in recent years. In general, the term is used to refer to the principles of rights and moral conduct, but ethics are becoming ever more complex, both because of the transfer of material across cyberspace and because notions of rights and truths have changed. For example, a number of scandals – including those relating to the 'tearoom trade' (Humphreys, 1970), Thalidomide (Knightley et al., 1979) and Alder Hey Hospital (*Royal Liverpool Children's Inquiry Report* (*The Redfern Report*), 2001) – have resulted in public outrage about the way in which people were treated during research studies. Humphreys (1970) conducted an ethnographic study into anonymous homosexual encounters in public restrooms/lavatories (known as 'tea-rooming' in the US and 'cottaging' in the UK). He recorded participants' vehicle licence plate numbers and later interviewed them in their homes under false pretences, at which time he confirmed that over 50 per cent of the men were outwardly heterosexual. In the Thalidomide scandal, a drug developed in Germany for use as a sedative was prescribed to pregnant mothers as a treatment for morning sickness. It was administered with insufficient testing and its use led to significant birth defects among thousands of infants worldwide. Finally, in the 1990s it was discovered that several UK hospitals, including Alder Hey Children's Hospital, Liverpool, were keeping children's organs, often hearts, without authorization.

In academia, such scandals have resulted in a shift towards highly procedural mechanisms in research practice. While following these closely affords some protection, there is now a widespread feeling that all angles must be covered, in some cases with little regard for people with cultural differences or those whose notion of consent differs from traditional Western views. Thus, keeping data confidential and gaining (written) informed consent can become merely performative compliance with the requirements of ethics committees and review boards. In terms of digital media, authors such as Pavlik (2012) suggest that there are two major issues: errors of commission and errors of omission. The former include practices such as using anonymous sources, phone hacking and making up sources, whereas the latter include not asking tough questions of politicians and failing to exclude unnecessary violence from films and news clips.

This appears to offer a straightforward distinction, but in fact digital ethics are more complex than this. Thus, several questions (following Pavlik, 2012) need to be considered in relation to digital tethering:

1.   What counts as digital manipulation? Pavlik suggests:

> In general, the types of digital media manipulations possible include: 1) the addition or subtraction of content; 2) composite imagery or constructed images, where multiple video or still images or their audio equivalents are merged into one seamless image; 3) synthetic images, video or audio, where completely real-looking scenes are created artificially depicting events that might have taken place or that might take place in the future; and 4) animations.

2.   Should we expect privacy from cameras orbiting the earth, which can offer a public service of views of the polar icecap in summer, yet can also show the impact of natural disasters on communities and personal lives?
3.   What counts as privacy? Is it acceptable to use a webcam to spy on the person who is baby-sitting your child or to film your university roommate as a joke?

Being digitally tethered, and practices associated with digital tethering, introduce questions and confusions about what counts as ethics, responsibility and judgement, and about who decides where the boundaries of these might fall.

Turing tests and WikiLeaks

As mentioned in Chapter 5, chatbots have become an established educational technology. Morrissey and Kirakowski (2013) identified seven themes that influence users' perceptions of realistic chatbot–user interactions. These were:

- maintenance of themed discussions;
- responding to specific questions;
- responding to social cues;
- using appropriate linguistic register;
- greetings and personality;
- giving conversational cues; and
- inappropriate utterances and damage control.

The notion of trustworthiness has been identified as particularly important in sensitive situations, and essential in the formation of an emotional connection between a user and a chatbot (Savin-Baden et al., 2013). Furthermore, Corritore et al. (2003: 70) have suggested that websites can be objects of trust, in which trust is defined as 'an attitude of confident expectation that one's vulnerabilities will not be exploited'.

What is the relationship between civil behaviour, free speech and transparency, as in the examples provided below by Pavlik (2012)?

> UCLA student Alexandra Wallace used her mobile phone to create a video and posted it to YouTube in March 2011 and it quickly went viral. The problem was her video was a rant against Asians and their alleged misuse of cell phones in the library and beyond. In response to her video posting, Wallace received death threats and she removed the video and apologized.
>
> In 2010 Julian Assange's WikiLeaks digitally published hundreds of thousands of classified government and military documents. Was this transparency a good thing? Was it a crime? Was it ethical for media organizations to publish stories based on the information contained in the massive WikiLeaks digital data-trove? Bill Keller, former *New York Times* executive editor, argued the First Amendment should protect WikiLeaks, and the media should come to its defence.

As Pavlik (2012) asks, how many of us would 'be proud to have our digital media actions, or inactions, reported, emulated, distributed on Facebook, Twitter or via our hometown, national or global media for family or friends to read, watch or listen to on the evening news or digital display?'

Honesty and veracity

The nature of honesty is defined by people and contexts, and whilst posting messages can be viewed as one's own business at one level, at another it can be offensive, cause offence and result in employers taking action if what is posted is deemed to be unethical. It is important when we are adopting particular identities on social networking sites that we ensure that we position ourselves in a way that helps us to avoid the prejudice *for* similarity and *against* difference. Central to honesty is the idea of veracity – the idea that there is a sense of responsibility built into what is represented, portrayed and displayed, without deliberately overstating what has occurred, or exaggerating how an audience 'witnesses' what is presented.

Criticality, reflexivity and integrity

The word 'critical' derives from a set of Greek words including *krisis* (a turning-point), *kritikos* (a judge or decision-maker) and *krinein* (to discriminate). Criticality requires that when searching for information, posting on sites or texting, it is important to strive for critical awareness and a reflexive stance. Willig (2001) identifies two types of reflexivity – personal and epistemological – and whilst these are discussed in relation to research they are useful in terms of operating ethically when digitally tethered.

Personal reflexivity is an examination of the way our experiences affect the choices we make and epistemological reflexivity involves analysing and exploring how our belief systems shape our choices and decisions. Maintaining integrity is also a complex activity, partly because our perspectives change and move over the course of life, as do those of our friends, contacts and work colleagues. Integrity relates very much to the way we situate ourselves, respond to others, as well as the extent to which we lurk, flame or ignore people with whom we are tethered.

Tethered integrity

'Tethered integrity' captures the idea that many of those who are always on, those who are digitally tethered, do in fact have a degree of integrity about their use of social networking sites. Whilst some studies indicate that youth have more integrity in this area than adults (Brandtzaeg et al., 2010), there is also an increased recognition of the power of such sites to manipulate what is shared, what is bought and the ways in which people behave. However, there are also other questions to be asked about the extent to which it is ethical always to be 'on message', whatever the situation; whether people are in interpersonal situations, interviews, meal meetings, concerts or lectures. Should people always be digitally engaged? How ethical is it to be digitally engaged constantly? Such concerns remain unresolved and relate very much to personal, family and work practices and values. Thus, perhaps tethered integrity should include the following judgements:

- Informed choice about which social networking sites are used and which are not, as well how they are used and the privacy that is not only espoused but implemented.
- Recognition and realistic control over the personal information that is shared, in ways that illustrate an appreciation of the personal benefit gained over the privacy lost.
- Understanding the cost of surveillance and making informed choices about what that means in practice and whether it can be managed realistically.

- Being aware of phone tracking and tracking through apps such as Twitter, and making decisions about how this might be managed (or not).
- Being aware of data mining programs such as:
  - PRISM which is a clandestine mass electronic surveillance data mining program, launched in 2007. This program collects stored internet communications based on demands made to internet companies such as Google.
  - XKeyscore. This is a system used by the United States National Security Agency for searching and analysing the internet data it collects worldwide every day. It was revealed in July 2013 in Australia.
  - Tempora, a clandestine security electronic surveillance program established in 2011 and operated by the British Government Communications Headquarters (GCHQ). Tempora uses fibre-optic cables to gain access to large amounts of internet users' personal data.
- Whether to use a site such as Prism Break (http://prism-break.org/en/), which offers useful alternatives and guidance, as well as clarifying issues such as the fact that Microsoft Windows is affected by PRISM and so is highly likely to compromise privacy.

Levels of digital integrity

This section suggests ways in which it is possible to increase, although not ensure, personal security. Although some people are more concerned than others, just being aware of what is available is important, even if it is not adopted.

High

This level is one on which people may choose to use their own server, block all surveillance traffic and use encryption wherever possible. Some examples of the software to enable this are described below, based on guidance from Estep (2013).

- Using Tor, a free software package that prevents anyone from learning location and browsing habits. This is an effective tool against network surveillance and traffic analysis.
- Encrypting files and email using software such as Pretty Good Privacy Essentially. This uses key cryptography, so that messages can be decrypted only though a personal key file and the sender's public key. You can even encrypt files so that only a specific person can open them. This is probably rather complicated for most people, but it is useful for the more technically savvy who want to communicate securely.
- Employing StartPage.com rather than Google for searching. It advertises itself as 'the world's most private search engine' and allows anonymous searching via Google. It is one of the few search engines that do not collect or share any personal information. Another example is DuckDuckgo.

- Using Pidder, rather than Facebook, as this is a private social network that uses encrypted communication and offers the option of anonymity.
- Taking the battery out of your phone. Whilst this might seem excessive, the only way to disable a phone's tracking/recording capacity is to remove the battery. Note that many of the most recent smartphones have been fitted with non-removable batteries.

Medium

Medium levels are for those who use social networking sites but accept that in doing so they are subject to inevitable surveillance and location tracking. The suggestions here are therefore largely based on ensuring personal physical safety at home and work, and protection from virus attack.

- Using a secure wireless connection, so that other users can neither use it nor introduce unwanted and possibly dangerous traffic via it.
- Employing an effective firewall and keeping it turned on, as well as using anti-spam and anti-spyware. It is important to know which services and sites are trying to send and receive data over your connection.
- Deleting cookies regularly. Cookies are invariably used to track and collect data about you and the sites you visit. A useful plug-in to deal with this is DoNotTrackMe.
- Disconnecting your webcam as this can be activated secretly (without the indicator light being turned on), so you won't even know that you are being watched or recorded.

Low or no integrity

Despite much warning about these dangers, many people leave both location tracking and wireless connection on permanently, and do not log out of internet sites. Whilst most of them will not come to any immediate harm, data will be collected on them, their behaviour will be tracked and their personal safety and privacy could be at risk. And they are at even more risk of identity theft. For example, Zeus is a Trojan horse used for malicious and criminal tasks, such as stealing banking and credit card information. Further, as Giles (2010) explained: 'The key to successful malware lies in tricking users into unwittingly installing it. And now even dilettante hackers can spread their malware by paying more technically adept criminals to do it for them.'

Government surveillance and the monitoring of our shopping habits have both occurred for many years, but they are now much more sophisticated. Yet, amidst all of this, people do still have a choice about what they engage with. By employing high digital integrity and moving platforms and social networking sites, privacy – of a sort – can still be maintained to some degree. The question is the extent to which people are really concerned.

Conclusions

A considerable body of research indicates that young people and students are aware of privacy issues and surveillance, and some go to considerable lengths to ensure that they make wise choices about their privacy. Yet sophisticated government surveillance software and easy-to-use malware mean that privacy and safety have become both complex and difficult to manage. Some people might argue that paranoia is the best option, but it would seem that many of us, and young people in particular, are beginning to develop various forms of digital wizardry in order to manage these difficulties. Perhaps we are facing brinkmanship rather than experiencing digital wizardry, as is explored in the final chapter.

10
WIZARDS AND BRINKMANSHIP

Introduction

The final chapter of this book examines issues connected to the digital condition of higher education and examines some of the ideas, suggestions and agendas that are being promoted. It suggests that play, performance and improvisation have rather been lost and need to be regained, whilst also proposing that the idea of a university has been mislaid. In the context of such losses and the marketization of learning, it is argued that, perhaps contrastingly, students have *not* lost their way. They have become capable users of digital technologies who are able to engage with the wider debates about power and politics. Nevertheless, students who are digitally fluent and digitally tethered are still challenged by the shifts and flows of the digital world, which continues to create spaces of change and interruption, and by issues of privacy and trust, which are not only continually contested but constantly on the move.

Brinkmanship?

Higher education seems to be in rather a troubled and troubling space. There is a loss of creativity and improvisation, along with a tendency towards repletion and boundary management. As the digital world runs away with itself and us, many people (administrators) want to lock things down and ensure that quality is neither compromised nor improvised. Yet our world has changed in ways that have resulted in both losses and gains. It seems that brinkmanship, the idea of pursuing a dangerous policy to the limits of safety before stopping, is occurring at both institutional and personal levels, resulting in a somewhat chaotic series of digital spaces. The increasing accountability of academia to government agendas, the subjugation of education to market forces and increased 'cultural suspicion'

(O'Neill, 2002) have resulted in not only inconsistency but confusion of role and purpose:

> *In theory* the new culture of accountability and audit makes professionals and institutions more accountable *to the public*. This is supposedly done by publishing targets and levels of attainment in league tables, and by establishing complaint procedures by which members of the public can seek redress for any professional or institutional failures. But underlying this ostensible aim of accountability *to the public* the real requirements are for accountability *to regulators, to departments of government, to funders, to legal standards*. The new forms of accountability impose forms of central control – quite often indeed a *range of different and mutually inconsistent* forms of central control.
>
> *(O'Neill, 2002: 52–53; emphasis added)*

The targets and attainments demanded in 2002 continue apace worldwide. The increasingly striated and stratified school and university sector is trying to rebuild itself amidst the surrounding forces of marketization, pernicious ideologies and digital surveillance that threaten its very being and purpose.

Despite the changes that have occurred since the advent of Web 2.0, there seems to be a tendency to delineate people in relation to attributes and capabilities, rather than recognize the importance of learner identity and diversity. It is vital to examine what people are doing with technologies, how they are creating them and learning through them, and to ask questions about the relative values of forms of digital fluency that are about skill sets rather than fluency per se. For example, notions such as 'the internet of things', which was originally about supplying everything with unique identifiers but is now more often used to refer to connectivity and ubiquitous computing, continue to introduce questions about the impact of tagging on security as well as moral decision-making, agency and personal privacy.

Despite this shift away from unique identifiers, there are also plenty of studies relating to technology and personal engagement with digital media that give cause for concern:

> It has been estimated that 20% to 29% of teenagers and young adults feel addicted to cell phone usage (Jancin, 2011; Konijn et al., 2008). In a large study of teenagers, 'hypertexters' were found to have a number of social, adjustment, and psychological issues. A 'hypertexter' was defined as a student who self-reported an average of 120 texts or more times, per day, on school days. They comprised 20% of the sample. Even when controlled for age, gender, race, parental education, and household structure, 'hypertexters' were more depressed, twice as likely to have tried alcohol, more likely to be binge drinkers, and were one third more likely to be current users of marijuana. They were more likely to have skipped classes and got lower grades than other students (Jancin, 2011).
>
> *(Clayson and Haley, 2012: 27)*

Turkle (2011:29b) also believes that there are some worrying behaviours, suggesting that technology has become akin to a phantom limb – but presumably without the phantom pain. She also argues that technology offers the 'illusion of companionship without the demands of friendship'.

Yet it is not merely being tethered that is troublesome. The challenges are also to do with a technology versus intimacy debate, and are more related to underlying assumptions about how technology is mediated, and how media and networks can be used for learning purposes. One such example concerns the subtext, ideas and practices that are implicit in the idea of technology-enhanced learning (TEL). For a number of researchers, TEL is seen as a series of practices sweeping across higher education with relatively little critique, along with other terms such as 'engagement', 'quality' and 'harnessing'. Bayne (2014), for example, has argued that TEL is more about technology than learning. Certainly, the number of projects funded by the European Union over the last ten years would seem to support this view:

> 'TEL', far from being an unexceptionable and neutral term simply in need of clearer definition, is in fact a deeply conservative discourse which reduces our capacity to be critical about digital education, and fails to do justice equally to the disruptive, disturbing and generative dimensions of the academy's enmeshment with (digital) technology.
>
> *(Bayne, 2014: 348)*

Bayne argues that TEL is really about neither enhancement nor learning, since it focuses merely on the instrumental, drawing on Biesta's (2006) rather misplaced critique of the 'learnification' of education. Many academics wholeheartedly support this 'learnification', since the shift from teaching to learning has focused more on learning context, learner identity and the recognition that many learners understand better than the teachers who are teaching them how they learn. Biesta argues that a focus on learning 'makes it far more difficult, if not impossible, to ask the crucial educational questions about content, purpose and relationships' (Biesta, 2012: 36), but does not really explain why this might be the case.

I suggest that Biesta's ideals do not fit much with the digital age; rather, they are suggestive of teachers who feel the need to teach students something and to manage the content that they think needs to be taught. The university of the Middle Ages called itself the *studium*, since the term *universitas* generally meant community or corporation; thus, in the context of the *studium*, *universitas* referred to the student body. Towards the end of the medieval period, however, these distinctions were lost and the term *universitas* was adopted for both.

The function of the university both then and now is the pursuit of learning. Many of the difficulties that remain today in higher education are caused by the focus on disciplinarity and content coverage; instead, the focus should be on seeing students as producers and creators of knowledges and media who operate in and through widespread networks and are active rather than passive recipients of diverse digital knowledges. Much of the technology that is being used in learning environments has not been designed in the first place for that purpose, and nor do many academics see the technology as useful for learning per se. It seems that learning *about* learning technology and using diverse digital media are seen as just another burden. For example, Hil's (2012) text *Whackademia* drew on interview data from university staff who argued that their institutions were corporate and bureaucratized and that virtual learning environments and emails were seen merely as mechanisms that supported formulaic forms of pedagogy. Yet, although these views are widespread across academia, they also seem to point to an erosion of the academic voice in the current system. It appears that academics no longer recognize that they have a stance, a position, a voice (call it what you will) that can, and should, challenge an overly systemized and bureaucratized organization. Critiquing, questioning and, where necessary, disrupting and subverting should be seen as central planks of academia. To lose these abilities is to lose our position. What is needed is a change in perspective:

> [W]e may ... begin to ask: what are the varieties and complexities in juvenile media culture? Moreover ... we may begin to change the perspective of the panics by respecting children's own perceptions and asking for their evaluations of their media cultures. Asking such questions and respecting children's answers does not necessarily imply a populist embrace of everything they say and the media they favour. But it does open a space of dialogue between adult and juvenile judgments, tastes and pleasures – a space that adults may learn as much from as children.
>
> *(Drotner, 1999: 619)*

Staff and students in higher education need to embrace spaces of dialogue, and respect and understand what learning and teaching mean to one another. This is because we are now redefining our notions of learning – as both about learning with others and with other things – in ways we have not done previously. For some, such a stance undermines learning as a focal point of education, yet there needs to be clarity about whether these other concepts that are being peddled as pedagogies are really undermining what higher education is and is for, and what learning means.

If we decentre the human (as Edwards (2014) suggests) then people just become resources. Instead, we need to see the university, and indeed learning, not just as a space to be filled with content, but as a space for the harnessing of technology and useful systems for pedagogic ends, not the other way around. We need to examine the digital flow in people's lives and how they reshape 'things'. There is also a need to abandon efforts to codify people's lives by using signs, signposts and maps, because in higher education this is creating a position of brinkmanship, whereby assumptions are being made that it is possible to teach digital fluency while expecting students to leave their social media at the door of the lecture hall. Instead, we should do what Fuller (2010) suggests and ensure that higher education is a place of creativity, filled with moments of experimentation.

Living moments of experimentation

Play and performance seem to have been misplaced in the lexicon of higher education. Instead there is too much repetition and reuse of materials; we should be deeply worried about the very idea of 'reusable learning objects', never mind help to construct them. Lectures and even lecturers are captured and replayed so we are just knowledge reproducers, instead of being living moments of experimentation, and creators and improvisers of new knowledges.

Fuller (2010) asks: what difference does university make if everything produces knowledge or is in the business of knowledge production? His stance is Humboldtian. He argues for the importance of the lecture and suggests that many academics today do not really understand its premise or the important synergy between research and teaching. The university is not just about passing on knowledge. It is about the exploration of wisdom and knowledge: *sapere aude* – 'dare to be wise' or 'dare to know' – was originally used by Horace, but it is more often cited in relation to Kant's seminal essay, *What is Enlightenment?* Fuller asks: how do you prepare a generation to dare to know, to think for themselves? For Fuller, hiring lecturers to give lectures where what they speak about is reducible to PowerPoint presentations means it isn't/shouldn't be worth hiring/ hearing; nor, I suggest, is it likely to reflect an increasingly needed Humboldtian research–teaching nexus. Freedom, for Fuller, is not innate; it is learned, and therefore one needs to discover what one needs to know to be free. Lectures should raise problems and questions for students, not just pass on knowledge. Being free involves discrimination and making judgements. There is a need for staff to have the capacity to improvise, enquire and take intellectual risks. If we are able to record things or deliver the same lecture accurately in the same way time and again, we will be replaced. The 'value added' of the university for Fuller is the exposition of people's writing through the lecture; a lecturer is the exemplification of someone who thinks for himself/herself. Further, Fuller (2010: 2) argues:

> Historically speaking, a specific institution has best promoted a form of intellectual freedom that has managed to serve as a vehicle for the progressive transformation of society. That institution is the university, especially in its nineteenth-century reincarnation as the seat of 'academic freedom', as theorized by 'philosophy', understood as both the foundation and the ultimate unifier of all specialized forms of knowledge. This idea was largely the invention of Wilhelm von Humboldt, who saw himself as applying the lessons of Immanuel Kant's critical philosophy, which formalized many aspects of the previous century's Enlightenment movement. Humboldt envisaged that as increasing numbers of people received a university educa- tion, they would become intellectually empowered, so as to take decisions of public import for themselves in democratic forums.

Pedagogy and play remain rarely linked, except in spaces such as virtual worlds and serious games, yet in our digitally tethered world these are the kinds of spaces which can be intellectually empowering. It is this creativity and improvisation, this exploration of liminal spaces and the sense of the in-between, which offer students new learning spaces that transcend what they learn in social spaces and academic spaces, spaces that are perhaps digital intervals.

Digital intervals?

Digital media help us to stand inside and outside our worlds at the same time. News feeds invade lecture theatres; students check our references and ideas as we speak. There was an idea that the university offered 'the gift of the interval', the central idea of which was that it was possible to become critical of oneself and the world only by being outside it. Yet, in many ways, digital media also offer intervals; perhaps digital intervals are now central (or they should be) to our performance. In Elizabethan playhouses performances were lit by candles, which led to the introduction of 'intervals', when burned-down candles were replaced. Perhaps perpetual tethering will result in spent academics and burned-out students. It might be that those who are digitally tethered are ahead of the game – forerunners of new interconnections between learning and research. Perhaps, though, students are mere dupes of cognitive capitalism, since global corporate interests in learning tend to prompt, encourage and further particular behaviours, and encourage students to think of themselves as customers rather than undergraduates. Are they really global citizens who are deeply and diversely connected? Are they just connected to their own self-interested, self-serving networks. It could also be argued that those who are digitally tethered will simply aid the drift away from a higher education concerned with critical thinking and critical reason, as many authors have suggested. However, I suggest that students and young people are often more critical than we acknowledge. Ito et al. (2013: 47) have argued:

> Our hypothesis is that in order to develop these cross-cutting repertoires of practice, young people need concrete and sustained social networks, relationships, institutional linkages, shared activities and communication infrastructures that connect their social, academic, and interest-driven learning. It is not enough for young people to have knowledge 'in their head' and expect that they can apply it appropriately and effectively in varied settings on their own. They need caring adults, supportive peers, shared cultural references, and authentic ways of contributing to shared practices in order to mobilize their skills and knowledge. In contrast to the voluminous literature and research on cognitive and individual models of transfer, there has been very little work that looks more ecologically at the relational, infrastructural, and institutional settings that undergird effective translation and transfer between formal instruction and varied practices. The connected learning approach is an effort to propose a proactive research and design agenda that addresses this gap.

Connected learning, then, does appear to offer one way forward. Nevertheless, some of the questions that still bear exploration are whether new learning spaces are being created through social media and what students are learning, where they are learning, and who they are learning it from. The adapting and adopting of different media by students and young people do seem to be accelerating the creation of new spaces and landscapes of learning. For them, knowledges and media are both universally accessible and globally located, which for university staff means that students (rather than the staff themselves) are digital and intellectual risk-takers. Students can be seen as both risk takers and at risk, since it would be easy to confuse activities such as blogging and exchanging easy opinions with intellectual criticality, and we need to be wary of this, as Benhabib argued in an interview:

> It's certainly the case that the blogosphere and listservs create a kind of conversation. They are quick; they move in real time and they permit the back and forth of exchange. But democracy and democratic decision making is not just about an exchange of opinions and views, it is also about deliberating about how to live together over a period of time ... So it is important not to confuse democracy with the unfettered exchange of opinion alone ... [T]hese new [technological] developments are certainly helpful in terms of challenging the monopoly of existing powerful media, but they are not enough to organize people as citizens.
>
> (Wahl-Jorgensen, 2008: 966)

Perhaps what we are seeing is hypersociality overtaking criticality in higher education. Ito (2007) suggested that hypersociality occurs through the interaction of childhood, commodity capitalism and communication technologies. It is typified by students and young people being highly engaged in mass media in ways that are active, interactive and peer-based, where stories and ideas are shared and there is a sense of digital flow.

Digital flow?

Digital flow is defined here as the ways in which people move almost seamlessly across diverse media, taking their information and identities with them. Thus, people are able to manage their position within the reservoir of media possibilities, and are participants rather than just passive consumers in the digital cultures they create. The flows between media occur across the permeable boundaries of creation, distribution, sharing and consumption. Search engines may organize our experiences. Wikipedia disembeds our knowledge and we are tagged and surveyed more than we will ever appreciate, although of course at the same time many of us realize this and flow between sites and media, invariably with a sense of agency and a clarity of choice that those who watch us choose not to believe or guess at. Nevertheless, privacy remains in a state of flux: not only can privacy no longer be assumed, but we are on the verge of not really understanding what counts as privacy and what does not. It seems that it is managed by social norms, yet these too are on the move.

At one end of the spectrum, commentators such as Selwyn (2012) suggest that we are still in an 'EdTech bubble'. Meanwhile, at the other end, the likes of Turkle (2010, 2011b) blame digital tethering practices (children competing with texting for parents' attention) for many of society's ills. Yet it seems a leap to blame technology for major societal shifts. Turkle (2010) has suggested that people's desire to engage with robots has a sense of the uncanny. This is because, for some, engaging with robotics offers people opportunities to connect with something emotionally and feel supported, even loved, without the need to reciprocate.

Whilst Turkle finds this unsettling in terms of what is 'real' and what is simulated, what is perhaps more poignant is what appears to be a kind of pernicious selfishness. Preferring a robot over a parent because the robot is perceived to understand, care or listen more, not only seems misplaced but shows a prodigious naivety about the human condition. Tethering to phones and computers presents interesting challenges, yet marrying robots and substituting them for loved ones seems a step too far. People fatigue is worrying especially since research indicates that the disclosure of information, especially sensitive information, requires the formation of a trust relationship. For example, Corritore et al. (2003) suggest that the concepts of risk, vulnerability, expectation, confidence and exploitation play key roles in information disclosure in an online environment. Emotional connection has been found to be one of the strongest determinants of a user's experience, triggering unconscious responses to a system, environment or interface. However, Culley and Madhavan (2013: 578) have cautioned that 'as the agent becomes increasingly morphologically similar to a human, it is also likely that operators will engage in correspondence bias more frequently by ascribing human motivations, reasoning abilities and capabilities to this non-human system'. Student willingness to disclose sensitive information to chatbots has been attributed partially to those chatbots being *almost* like a person (Savin-Baden et al., 2013).

There are questions to be considered, such as whether we really do have relationship fatigue and prefer robots. I suspect not. Yet there is little doubt that most people are digitally tethered, at least to some degree. For young people, there is an increasing engagement with participatory politics – peer-based acts through which young people seek to influence political and public issues (Cohen and Kahne, 2012). Many students and young people also centre their lives on networked publics – spaces that are created, structured and restructured around networked technologies. 'A public' is seen as a highly accessible space where diverse audiences gather to share what Livingstone (2005: 9) calls 'a common understanding of the world, a shared identity, a claim to inclusiveness, a consensus regarding the collective interest'. Yet government agendas still focus on forms of digital governance and there is a certain perniciousness to current practices, as Williamson (2014: 548) explains:

> the policy network is deploying these database pedagogies [Williamson is referring here to networked social media, new learning analytics and adaptive

software applications] as part of its approach to creating a new 'governable space' in education, a space in which governing is increasingly to be done by collecting and compiling individual learner data in order to calculate and predict their future needs and to generate prescriptions for future pedagogy. This is governing being done not through intervening in the national space of the education system but by resculpting and re-educating the mind and body of the learner for a pedagogized future − a shift in the space of governance and its governing practices from the state to the individual subject, facilitated by sophisticated software products.

There needs to be a shift away from digital governance and a creation of new learning flows, along with a recognition that students will bring all their different kinds of learning capabilities to the classroom. They should not be required to leave behind the sophisticated abilities that they have developed through networked publics, contained in some kind of hidden mediascape.

Tethered liquidity

The question that still remains unanswered is the extent to which it really matters just how tethered we are. The ways in which we operate in/on the internet do seem largely to mirror current society, but things are just shared (faster) on a bigger and wider stage than they used to be. Learning is also on the move; lives are liquid. For adults, digital tethering may mean engagement with networked publics and participatory politics, although more often it is about keeping in touch with friends and family and relying on a mobile phone.

Implicit in all this tethering is that its impact on learning in higher education remains under-researched. The views of teachers and students about the value of digital technology still differ markedly in many schools and universities. What learning means appears to be more contested than ever, yet social media and networks should be offering us some purchase on the ways in which students consider and enact learning. We need to create learning spaces that allow for tethered liquidity − the sense that students are tethered to their technology whilst also on the move. Such spaces should enable students and young people to study across social space, times and cultural communities. Learning needs to be seen as embedded across geographies as well as physical and virtual realms, so that home/school/work/leisure/play become spaces for learnings, criticalities and creativities to develop, with reflection, re-enactment and repetition as central components. Learning a module of some subject is no longer enough. What matters is shaping learning so that it enables students to engage in participatory politics and networked publics, undertake problem management and become digital citizens, whose brinkmanship is based on a desire to mess around in order to understand and transform their learning lives in liquid ways, so that learning leaks across the various boundaries of their worlds.

Conclusion

But what of wizardry? It is surely just the ability to transform things in clever ways – without, one hopes, them getting entirely out of hand. Many people are pinning their hopes on the digital creations of the future, but there is no wizardry here. There is no Narnia where we are transported through the wardrobe (and into virtual realities), where time moves at a different pace; nor, unlike Harry Potter, can we apparate and use a time turner to transport ourselves and manage our lives differently. What we *are* dealing with is the need to gain some old ground and not be satisfied with

> the baseless fabric of this vision,
> The cloud-capped towers, the gorgeous palaces,
> The solemn temples, the great globe itself –
> Yea, all which it inherit – shall dissolve,
> And like this insubstantial pageant faded,
> Leave not a rack behind.
> > (Shakespeare, 1610–1611/2004:
> > *The Tempest*, Act IV, Scene 1)

There is little question that we are experiencing technology learning lag in higher education worldwide, but perhaps we need to be tethered not only to technology but to the idea of a university, as Oakeshott (1989: 30) suggested:

> A university will have ceased to exist when its learning has degenerated into what is now called research, when its teaching has become mere instruction and occupies the whole of an undergraduate's time, and when those who came to be taught come, not in search of their intellectual fortune with a vitality as unroused or so exhausted that they wish only to be provided with a serviceable moral and intellectual outfit.

If a university education centres on the pursuit of learning, then we need to recognize that being digitally tethered is not an unfettered compression of time and space. Although our students and their liquid learning lives are located and positioned, to a large extent, by market forces, government agendas and relational challenges, they will still question and oppose us and the systems we inhabit. They will not be bounded nor stay still. This is our challenge.

GLOSSARY

Alt-avatar – the creation of an alternative avatar to the one used on a more everyday basis. Often used by staff for social purposes, or to remain unnoticed by students if they are in-world and wish to be anonymous.

Augmented reality – the live view of a physical world environment whose elements are merged with computer imagery, thus it places emphasis on the physical, so that information from virtual space is accessed from within physical space. An example would be the projection of immersive virtual worlds into a physical space such as a real-life conference.

Augmented virtuality – where the virtual space is augmented with aspects from physical space, so there is a sense of overlay between the two spaces.

Avatar – the bodily manifestation of oneself in the context of a three-dimensional virtual world.

Blogs (weblogs) – personal websites consisting of regularly updated entries displayed in reverse chronological order.

Chatbots – characters not controlled by a user within a virtual world or website. Chatbots are also known as 'non-player characters (NPCs)' or pedagogical agents that can be commanded to do certain actions by the facilitator, such as moving around.

Conditions of flexibility – the fifteen issues Barnett (2014) believes will promote flexible provision in higher education.

Digital capabilities – the range of skills and understandings needed to operate digital media, collaborate and share with others and be digitally literate and fluent.

Digital connectivity – the opportunity to be always connected to the internet and to people in some way through digital media.

Digital fluency – the ability to use digital media, of whatever sort, to manage knowledge and learning across diverse offline and online spaces. It includes the ability to understand complex issues, such as how identity can be established and faked, the ability to evaluate the trustworthiness and accuracy of information, and the ability to understand the subtext of digital media and information and place it within a wider context.

Digital knowledge – an informed understanding of the power and impact of digital media in terms of the way it can be used and harnessed in particular settings for particular purposes.

Digital learning – learning that takes place specifically through digital media such as virtual worlds, blogs, Tumblr, kik and YouTube, searching, but in a cohesive way. Digital learning is not merely about acquiring chunks of information from spaces such as Wikipedia; it is learning that is organized and choate.

Digital literacy – the ability to assemble knowledge and to evaluate, search for and navigate through information in the digital world, as well as to locate, organize, understand and evaluate information using digital technology.

Digital media – text, audio, video and graphics that are electronically transmitted over the internet or computer networks.

Digital spaces – those spaces in which communication and interaction are assisted, created or enhanced by digital media.

Digital tethering – constant interaction and engagement with digital technology, the sense of being 'always on', 'always engaged', characterized by wearing a mobile device, texting at dinner, or driving (illegally) while 'Facebooking'.

Disciplinarity – all that is seen as central to a given discipline: its pedagogy, values, beliefs, rhetorics and expected norms that are embodied by the academics who guard it.

Disjunction – a sense of fragmentation of part – or all – of the self, characterized by frustration and confusion, and a loss of sense of self, which often results in anger and the need for right answers.

Embodiment – the interaction of the body, material places and social spaces towards the development of meaning.

Flaming – posting or sending offensive messages over the internet, often on online discussion forums.

Friendship–driven genres of participation – participation online that emerges from (largely) age-related friendship groups, so that the media practice within this category emerges from local face-to-face friendships (Ito et al., 2010).

Group scribbles – software that allows students and staff to 'write' on sheets similar to Post-It notes, and manage the movement of these electronic notes jointly within and between public and private spaces.

Haptics – the use of technology that creates a sense of touch, such as vibration or movement, in order to enhance visual engagement in immersive virtual worlds.

Identities:

- **Bridged identities** – identities created to link with other exterior worlds. Such identities might be located through the creation of avatars or by using avatars in identity play (playing with avatar identity in ways that are seen as fun and sometimes trite) (Savin–Baden, 2010).

- **Frontier identities** – identities that tend to overlap and overlay on to other spaces but also tend to be twilight identities in the sense that identities sit beside one another and come to the fore when one is required over another.
- **Identities on tour** – dynamic identities: the purpose and point of view of the traveller are central.
- **Identity tourism** – a metaphor developed by Nakamura (2000) to portray identity appropriation in cyberspace. Such appropriation makes it possible to play with different identities without encountering the risk associated with racial difference in real life.
- **Interstitial identities** – metaxis (or metaxy) was used by Plato to describe the condition of 'in-between-ness' that is one of the characteristics of being human.
- **Left–behind identities** – the idea that, as we shift and move identities across online contexts, rather than deleting them, we tend to leave them behind.
- **Mapped identities** – usually imposed identities, provided by, for example, school reports, external data, job profiles and human resources records. Thus, these identities are seen as static and objective, even though in many ways they are not; they are in fact identities that others map on to us.
- **Networked identities** – the idea that identities are constructed in multidimensional and complex ways across overlapping online and offline networks in school, work and spare time and that individual identities exist and become real through such networks (Ryberg and Larsen, 2008).
- **Place-based identities** – identities that our strongly located in relation to the places we inhabit and tend to be relatively stable and ordered.
- **Spatial identities** – identities enacted through digital media. Each enactment tends to prompt a different kind of performance, invariably guided by the norms, cultures and affordances of both the software and the users of those spaces.

Interest-driven genres of participation – participation that has developed from specific activities, so the interest is more important than the friendship.

Lateral surveillance – the use of surveillance tools by individuals (rather than by agents of institutions, public or private), to keep track of one another.

Learner identity – an identity formulated through the interaction of learner and learning. The notion of learner identity moves beyond, but encapsulates, the notion of learning style, and encompasses positions that students take up in learning situations, whether consciously or unconsciously.

Learning context – the interplay of all the values, beliefs, relationships, frameworks and external structures that operate within a given learning environment.

Learning nexus – the connection made between different types of learning, whether face to face, learning though digital media, or lectures and group work.

Limen/liminal – threshold, often referred to as a betwixt-and-between state.

Liminality – characterized by a stripping away of old identities and an oscillation between states, it is a betwixt-and-between state and there is a sense of being in a period of transition, often on the way to a new or different space.

Liquid learning – characterized by emancipation, reflexivity and flexibility, so that knowledge and knowledge boundaries are contestable and always on the move.

Liquid learning spaces – open, flexible and contested, spaces in which both learning and learners are always on the move so that curricula are delineated with and through the staff and students, they are defined by the creators of the space(s).

Liquid surveillance – the idea that through data flows and regimes of (in)visibility everyone is being targeted and sorted (Lyon, 2010).

Lurking – the action of reading chatroom discussions, group or message-board postings, but not contributing.

Machinima – a word developed by combining 'machine' and 'cinema' to describe the process of creating films in immersive virtual worlds so that computer-generated imagery (CGI) is rendered using real-time, interactive, three-dimensional engines instead of professional three-dimensional animation software.

Mixed reality – a method for integrating virtual and physical spaces much more closely so that physical and digital objects coexist and interact in real time.

MMORG – massively multiplayer online role-playing game. The focus in these games is on role-play as opposed to MUVEs. The games tend to have some form of progression, social interaction within the game and an in–game culture.

Moodle – a free software e-learning platform designed to help educators create online courses. Its open-source licence and modular design allow for global development.

MUVE – multi-user virtual environment. Whereas MMORGs are games-related, MUVEs are environments such as immersive virtual worlds that are not usually seen as games. Thus, MUVE is a more general reference to a virtual world.

Net generation – the generation that has barely known a world without computers, the World Wide Web, highly interactive video games and mobile phones. For many of this generation, instant messaging, rather than the telephone or email, is the primary form of communication.

Non-player characters (NPCs) – characters not controlled by a user within Second Life. Also known as chatbots, NPCs can be commanded to perform certain actions by the facilitator, such as move around.

Online tone – hearing what is being 'said' in an online context, particularly in discussion forums, and being able to locate anger, distress and pleasure without the use of emoticons. The ability to 'read' voices is something that needs to be developed by facilitators.

Pedagogies of interaction – the use of learning approaches based on social constructivism that seek to encourage learning with and through others, exploring diverse knowledges and resources formally and informally.

Photorealism – originally the genre of painting based on photography, but now also used in immersive virtual worlds to describe the highly realistic reproduction of objects and buildings from real life.

Pirate code – a code of conduct used for governing pirates. Each pirate crew tended to have its own code for discipline and the division of stolen goods.

Privacy:

- **Expressive privacy** – the desire to protect oneself from peer pressure or ridicule in order to express one's own identity (DeCew, 1997).
- **Informational privacy** – the protection of personal information relating to finances, lifestyle, etc. (DeCew, 1997).
- **Institutional privacy** – the protection of personal information and monitoring by organizations such as governments and banks through CCTV, genetic screening and credit cards.
- **Social privacy** – ensuring privacy on social media sites by using pseudonyms and false accounts and by regularly deleting wall posts and photographs and untagging oneself from other people's posts.

Podcast – a digital media file, or a series of such files, that is distributed over the internet.

Posting – (verb) publishing a message on an online forum or discussion group; (noun) a message published on an online forum or discussion group.

Problem-based learning – an approach to learning where the focus is on problematic situations, rather than content. Students work in small teams and are facilitated by a tutor.

Problem-solving learning – teaching where the focus is on students solving a given problem by acquiring the answers expected by the lecturer, answers that are rooted in the information supplied to the students in some way. The solutions are bounded by the content and students are expected to explore little extra material other than that with which they have been provided in order to discover the solutions.

Problem-based learning online – a generic term which captures that vast variety of ways in which problem-based learning is being used synchronously and asynchronously, on campus, or at a distance. It represents the idea that students learn through web-based materials, including text, simulations, videos and demonstrations, and resources such as chatrooms, message boards and environments that have been purpose-built for problem-based learning.

Proxemics – the study of spatial distances between individuals in different cultures and situations.

Qualia – a term used in philosophy to describe the subjective quality of conscious experience. In virtual worlds it tends to be used to refer to the illusion and extent of being present in an environment.

Scaffolding – concept based on Vygotsky's (1978) zone of proximal development. Individualized support designed to facilitate a student's ability to build on prior knowledge and to generate and internalize new knowledge is provided by the tutor or other students. The support is pitched just beyond the current level of the student.

Search 2.0 – the loss of privacy which occurs through the aggregation of users' online activities (Zimmer, 2008).

Second Life – a three-dimensional virtual world created by Linden Lab and set in an internet-based world. Residents (in the form of self-designed avatars) in this world interact with each other and can learn, socialize, participate in activities, as well as buy items from and sell items to one another.

SLOODLE (simulation-linked object-oriented dynamic learning environment) – this brings together Second Life and the virtual learning environment Moodle. It comprises the product itself, SLOODLE software; the SLOODLE community, a group of users and developers; and the research studies relating to SLOODLE for academic and product development.

Spatial interaction – model developed by Benford and colleagues (Benford and Fahlén, 1993; Benford et al., 1994) that provides flexible support for managing conversations between groups and can also be used to control interactions among other kinds of objects.

Technological determinism – a strong determinist stance that has been promoted and popularized by Prensky (2001) and affirmed further by Tapscott (2008), whereby it is argued that those who have grown up in a digital age are necessarily different and that 'connectivity' is damaging to students.

Teleport – transferring from one location to another in an immersive virtual world almost instantaneously, this can occur by being offered a teleport by another avatar or choosing to teleport yourself to a new location.

Tethered integrity – the idea that many of those who are 'always on', who are digitally tethered, have a degree of integrity about their use of social networking sites.

Text chat – the means of communicating in immersive virtual worlds by typing a response to another avatar in-world.

Threshold concept – the idea of a portal that opens up a way of thinking that was previously inaccessible. The result is a transformed understanding, or interpreting, or viewing something without which the learner cannot progress. 'Such a transformed view or landscape may represent how people "think" in a particular discipline, or how they perceive, apprehend, or experience particular phenomena within that discipline (or more generally)' (Meyer and Land, 2003: 1).

Transition – shifts in learner experience caused by challenges to a person's life-world. Transitions occur in particular areas of students' lives, at different times and in distinct ways. The notion of transitions carries with it the idea of movement from one place to another and the necessity of taking up a new position in a different place.

Transitional learning – learning that occurs as a result of critical reflection upon shifts (transitions) that have taken place for the students personally (including viscerally), pedagogically and/or interactionally.

Troublesome knowledge – Perkins (1999) described conceptually difficult knowledge as 'troublesome knowledge'. This is knowledge that seems to be, for example, counter-intuitive, alien (emanating from another culture or discourse) or incoherent (discrete aspects are unproblematic but there is no organizing principle).

Troublesome spaces – places where 'stuckness' or 'disjunction' occurs.

Vidding – where content is refashioned or recreated in order to present a different perspective, usually based on music videos and television programmes in order to critique, re-present and explore an aspect of the original media.

Viral methodologies – instead of research methodologies being specifically 'located' in areas such as post-structuralism and constructivism, the underlying theories are seen as mutable and liquid.

Virtual ethnography – methodology that seeks to understand, from a sociological perspective, what people 'do' on the internet (Hine, 2000).

Virtual learning environment (VLE) – a set of learning and teaching tools involving online technology designed to enhance students' learning experience: for example, Blackboard, WebCT, Moodle.

Virtual patients – simulations or representations of individuals that are designed by facilitators as a means of creating a character in a healthcare setting.

Virtual reality – a simulated computer environment in either a real or an imaginary world. Most virtual reality emphasizes immersion, so that the user suspends disbelief and accepts it as a real environment and uses head-mounted displays to enhance this.

Web 2.0 technologies – now a somewhat dated term, but refers to the development of social software such as a wiki or blogs, which have become user-driven and facilitate information sharing and social networking.

Webinars – conducting live meetings, seminars or presentations via the internet.

Weblip – an instant messaging system that aims to connect users to other Weblip users currently viewing the same website. Rather than using a chat window, it uses an overlaying animated avatar that stands at the bottom of the browser's window.

Wikis – server software that allows multiple users to contribute to, and edit, web page content.

World of Warcraft – a highly popular massively multiplayer online role-playing game (MMORPG) developed by Blizzard Entertainment. Players control an avatar to explore locations, defeat creatures and complete quests. The game is set in the world of Azeroth.

REFERENCES

Albrechtslund, A. (2008) Online social networking as participatory surveillance, *First Monday*, 13 (3). Online. Available http://firstmonday.org/article/view/2142/1949 (accessed 12 June 2014).

Albrechtslund, A. and Lauritsen, P. (2013) Spaces of everyday surveillance: Unfolding an analytical concept of participation, *Geoforum*, 49: 310–316.

Anderson, C. (2006) *The Long Tail: Why the Future of Business is Selling Less of More*, New York: Hyperion.

Andrejevic, M. (2005) The work of watching one another: Lateral surveillance, risk, and governance, *Surveillance and Society*, 2 (4): 479–497.

ap Hari, G. (2010) The school they couldn't kill. Online. Available www.agent4change.net/events/bett-2010/534-the-school-they-couldnt-kill-we-are-campsmount.html (accessed 12 November 2013).

Arnab, S., Lim, T., Carvalho, M.B., Bellotti, F., de Freitas, S., Louchart, S., Suttie, N., Berta, R. and De Gloria, A. (2014) Mapping learning and game mechanics for serious games analysis, *British Journal of Educational Technology*, 46 (2). Online. Available http://dx.doi.org/10.1111/bjet.12113 (accessed 2 November 2014).

Aristotle (1995) *Poetics*, edited and translated by St. Halliwell, Cambridge, MA: Harvard University Press.

Attrill, A. and Jalil, R. (2011) Revealing only the superficial me: Exploring categorical self-disclosure online, *Computers in Human Behavior*, 27 (5): 1634–1642.

Ausubel, D.P., Novak, J.S. and Hanesian, H. (1978) *Educational Psychology: A Cognitive View*, New York: Holt, Rinehart & Winston.

Baeten, M., Kyndt, E., Struyven, K. and Dochy, F. (2010) Using student-centred learning environments to stimulate deep approaches to learning: Factors encouraging or discouraging their effectiveness, *Educational Research Review*, 5: 243–260.

Bailenson, J.N., Yee, N., Blascovich, J. and Guadagno, R.E. (2008) Transformed social interaction in mediated interpersonal communication, in E. Konjin, M. Tanis, S. Utz and A. Linden (eds), *Mediated Interpersonal Communication* (77–99), Mahwah, NJ: Lawrence Erlbaum Associates.

Barak, A. and Gluck-Ofri, O. (2007) Degree and reciprocity of self-disclosure in online forums, *CyberPsychology and Behavior*, 10 (3): 407–417.

Barnes, S.B. (2006) A privacy paradox: Social networking in the United States, *First Monday*, 11 (9). Online. Available http://firstmonday.org/htbin/cgiwrap/bin/ojs/index.php/fm/article/view/1394/1312 (accessed 6 June 2014).

Barnett, R. (1994) *The Limits of Competence*, Buckingham: Open University Press/SRHE.

Barnett, R. (2003) *Beyond All Reason: Living with Ideology in the University*, Buckingham: Open University Press/SRHE.

Barnett, R. (2004) Learning for an unknown future, *Higher Education Research and Development*, 23 (3): 247–260.

Barnett, R. (2007) *A Will to Learn*, Maidenhead: McGraw Hill.

Barnett, R. (2011) Lifewide education: A new and transformative concept for higher education, in N. Jackson (ed.), *Learning for a Complex World: A Lifewide Concept of Learning, Education and Personal Development* (22–38), Bloomington, IN: Author-House.

Barnett, R. (2014) *Conditions of Flexibility*, York: Higher Education Academy.

Barron, B. (2004) Learning ecologies for technological fluency: Gender and experience differences, *Journal of Educational Computing Research*, 3 (1): 1–36.

Barron, B. (2006) Interest and self-sustained learning as catalysts of development: A learning ecologies perspective, *Human Development*, 49: 193–224.

Bauman, Z. (1987) *Legislators and Interpreters*, Cambridge: Polity Press.

Bauman, Z. (2000) *Liquid Modernity*, Cambridge: Polity Press.

Baylor, A.L. (2011) The design of motivational agents and avatars, *Educational Technology Research and Development*, 59 (2): 291–300.

Bayne, S. (2014) What's wrong with 'technology enhanced learning?, in S. Bayne, C. Jones, M. de Laat, T. Ryberg and C. Sinclair (eds), *Proceedings of the 9th International Conference on Networked Learning*: 347–350.

Bazalgette, C. and Buckingham, D. (2013) Literacy, media and multimodality: A critical response, *Literacy*, 47 (2): 95–102.

Beetham, H. and Sharpe, R. (eds) (2013) *Rethinking Pedagogy for a Digital Age: Designing and Delivering E-Learning*, London: RoutledgeFalmer.

Beldad, A., de Jong, M. and Steehouder, M. (2010) How shall I trust the faceless and the intangible? A literature review on the antecedents of online trust, *Computers in Human Behavior*, 26 (5): 857–869.

Belenky, M.F., Clinchy, B.M., Goldberger, N.R. and Tarule, J.M. (1986) *Women's Ways of Knowing*, New York: Basic Books.

Benford, S., Bowers, J., Fahlén, L.E. and Greenhalgh, C. (1994) Managing mutual awareness in collaborative virtual environments, in *Proceedings of the Conference on Virtual Reality Software and Technology*, Singapore: 223–236.

Benford, S.D. and Fahlén, L.E. (1993) A spatial model of interaction in virtual environments, in G. De Michelis, C. Simone and K. Schmidt (eds), *Proceedings of the 1993 European Conference on Computer Supported Cooperative Work, ECSCW '93, Milano*: 109–124.

Bennett, S., Maton, K. and Kervin, L. (2008) The 'digital natives' debate: A critical review of the evidence, *British Journal of Educational Technology*, 39 (5): 775–786.

Bentham, J. (1787/1995) *The Panopticon Writings*, edited by M. Bozovic, London: Verso (accessed at: http://cartome.org/panopticon2.htm, 8 May 2014).

Bergmann, J. and Sams, A. (2012) *Flip Your Classroom: Reach Every Student in Every Class Every Day*, New York: International Society for Technology in Education.

Bernstein, B. (1971) *Class, Codes and Control: Theoretical Studies towards a Sociology of Language*, London: Routledge & Kegan Paul.

Bernstein, B. (1992) Pedagogic identities and educational reform. Mimeo. Paper presented at the Santiago Conference, Chile, April.

Bernstein, B. (1996) *Pedagogy: Symbolic Control and Identity*, London: Taylor & Francis.

Bernstein, B. (2001) From pedagogies to knowledges, in A. Morais, I. Neves, B. Davies and H. Daniels (eds), *Towards a Sociology of Pedagogy: The Contribution of Basil Bernstein to Research* (363–368), New York: Peter Lang.

Biesta, G. (2006) *Beyond Learning: Democratic Education for a Human Future*, Boulder, CO: Paradigm.

Biesta, G. (2012) Giving teaching back to education: Responding to the disappearance of the teacher, *Phenomenology and Practice*, 6 (2): 35–49.

Bligh, D.A. (2000) *What's the Use of Lectures?*, San Francisco, CA: Jossey-Bass.

Blikstein, P. (2013) Digital fabrication and 'making' in education: The democratization of invention, in J. Walter-Herrmann and C. Büching (eds), *FabLabs: Of Machines, Makers and Inventors* (203–222), Bielefeld: Transcript.

Bloom, B. (1956) *Taxonomy of Educational Objectives*, 2 vols, New York: Longmans Green.

Boughey, C. (2006) Texts, practices and students learning: A view from the South. Keynote speech Higher Education CloseUp3, University of Lancaster, 24–26 July.

Bower, J.L. and Christensen, C.M. (1995) Disruptive technologies: Catching the wave, *Harvard Business Review*, 73 (1): 43–53.

boyd, d. (2002) FACETED ID/ENTITY: Managing representation in a digital world, Master of Science in Media Arts and Sciences, Massachusetts Institute of Technology, September 2002. Online. Available www.danah.org/papers/Thesis.FacetedIdentity.pdf (accessed 12 June 2014).

boyd, d. (2007) Why youth (heart) social network sites: The role of networked publics in teenage social life, in David Buckingham (ed.), *MacArthur Foundation Series on Digital Learning – Youth, Identity, and Digital Media Volume* (119–142), Cambridge, MA: MIT Press.

boyd, d. (2010) Friendship, in M. Ito et al., *Hanging out, Messing around, and Geeking out* (79–116), Cambridge, MA: MIT Press.

Brandtzaeg, P.B., Lüders, M. and Skjetne, J.H. (2010) Too many Facebook 'friends'? Content sharing and sociability versus the need for privacy in social network sites, *Journal of Human–Computer Interaction*, 26 (11–12): 1006–1030.

Bruer, J.T. (1993) *Schools for Thought: A Science of Learning in the Classroom*, Cambridge, MA: MIT Press.

Bruner, J. (1991) *Acts of Meaning*, Cambridge, MA: Harvard University Press.

Bruns, A. (2008) *Blogs, Wikipedia, Second Life, and Beyond: From Production to Produsage*, New York: Peter Lang.

Bruns, A. and Schmidt, J.-H. (2012) Produsage: A closer look at continuing developments, *New Review of Hypermedia and Multimedia*, 17 (1): 3–8. Online. Available http://eprints.qut.edu.au/48818/1/Produsage_Editorial.pdf (accessed 9 June 2014).

Buber, M. (1964) *Daniel: Dialogues on Realization*, New York: Holt, Rinehart, & Winston.

Buckingham, D. (2007) *Beyond Technology: Children's Learning in the Age of Digital Culture*, Malden, MA: Polity.

Buckingham, D., Burn, A., Parry, B. and Powell, M. (2014) *Developing Media Literacy: Culture, Creativity and Critique*, Abingdon: Routledge.

Burwell, C. (2010) Rewriting the script: Toward a politics of young people's digital media participation, *Review of Education, Pedagogy, and Cultural Studies*, 32 (4–5): 382–402.

Callaghan, M.J., McShane, N. and Gómez Eguíluz, A. (2014) Using game analytics to measure student engagement/retention for engineering education, *Proceedings of 11th International Conference on Remote Engineering and Virtual Instrumentation (REV)*: 297–302.

Callon, M. (1986) Some elements of a sociology of translation: Domestication of the scallops and the fishermen of St Brieuc Bay, in J. Law (ed.), *Power, Action and Belief: A New Sociology of Knowledge* (196–223), London: Routledge & Kegan Paul.

Calvani, A., Cartelli, A., Fini, A. and Ranieri, M. (2008) Models and instruments for assessing digital competence at school, *Journal of e-Learning and Knowledge Society*, 4 (3): 183–193.

Calvino, I. (1995) *Six Memos for the Next Millennium*, Toronto: Vintage Canada.

Carvalho, L. and Goodyear, P. (eds) (2014) *The Architecture of Productive Learning Networks*, New York: Routledge.

Castells, M. (1996) *The Rise of the Network Society*, Vol. 1: *The Information Age: Economy, Society and Culture*, Cambridge, MA, and Oxford: Blackwell.

Chivers, H., Philip, P., Shaikh, A.M., Clark, J. and Chen, H. (2013) Knowing who to watch: Identifying attackers whose actions are hidden within false alarms and background noise, *Information Systems Frontiers*, 15 (1): 17–34.

Clark, A. (2003) *Natural-Born Cyborgs: Minds, Technologies, and the Future of Human Intelligence*, Oxford: Oxford University Press.

Clark, L.S. and Alters, D. (2004) Developing a theory of media, home, and family, in S.H. Hoover, L.S. Clark, D. Alters, J. Champ and L. Hood, *Media, Home, and Family* (35–50), New York: Routledge.

Clayson, D.E and Haley, D.A. (2012) An introduction to multitasking and texting: Prevalence and impact on grades and GPA in marketing classes, *Journal of Marketing Education*, 35 (1): 26–40.

Cockburn, C. (1998) *The Space between Us: Negotiating Gender and National Identities in Conflict*, London: Zed Books.

Cohen, C. and Kahne, J. (2012) *Participatory Politics: New Media and Youth Political Action*, Oakland, CA: Youth and Participatory Politics Research Network. Online. Available http://ypp.dmlcentral.net/sites/all/files/publications/YPP_Survey_Report_FULL.pdf (accessed 21 May 2014).

Collins, A. and Ferguson, W. (1993) Epistemic forms and epistemic games: Structures and strategies to guide inquiry, *Educational Psychologist*, 28 (1): 25–42.

Collins, A. and Halverson, R. (2009) *Rethinking Education in the Age of Technology: The Digital Revolution and Schooling in America*, New York: Teachers College Press.

Conradi, E., Kavia, S., Burden, D., Rice, D., Woodham, L., Beaumont, C., Savin-Baden, M. and Poulton, T. (2009) Virtual patients in Virtual World: Training paramedic students, *Medical Teacher*, 31 (8): 713–720.

Corritore, C.L., Kracher, B. and Wiedenbeck, S. (2003) On-line trust: Concepts, evolving themes, a model, *International Journal of Human–Computer Studies*, 58(6): 737–758.

Cover, R. (2006) Audience interactive: Interactive media, narrative control and reconceiving audience history, *New Media and Society*, 8 (1): 139–158.

Cox, R., Kontianen, S., Rea, N. and Robinson, S. (1981) *Learning and Teaching: An Evaluation of a Course for Teachers in General Practice*, London: University Teaching Methods Unit, Institute of Education.

Crook, C.K. (2008) *Web 2.0 Technologies for Learning: The Current Landscape – Opportunities, Challenges and Tensions*, London: BECTA.

Crook, C.K. (2012) The 'digital native' in context: Tensions associated with importing Web 2.0 practices into the school setting, *Oxford Review of Education*, 38 (1): 63–80.

Crystal, D. (2008) 2b or not 2b?, *Guardian*, 5 July.

Culley, K.E. and Madhavan, P. (2013) A note of caution regarding anthropomorphism in HCI agents, *Computers in Human Behavior*, 29 (3): 577–579.

Dabbish, L., Mark, G. and González, V.M. (2011) Why do I keep interrupting myself? Environment, habit and self-interruption, in *Proceedings of the International Conference on Human Factors in Computing Systems, CHI 2011, Vancouver, BC, Canada, May 7–12, 2011*: 3127–3130.

Davies, P. (2006) Threshold concepts: How can we recognise them?, in J.H.F. Meyer and R. Land (eds), *Overcoming Barriers to Student Understanding: Threshold Concepts and Troublesome Knowledge* (70–84), London: Routledge.

Dawn, M. (2010) *The Writing on the Wall: High Art, Popular Culture and the Bible*, London: Hodder & Stoughton.

Dean, J. (2005) Communicative capitalism: Circulation and the foreclosure of politics, *Cultural Politics*, 1 (1): 51–74.

de Certeau, M. (1984) *The Practice of Everyday Life*, translated by Steven Rendall, Berkeley: University of California Press.

DeCew. J.W. (1997) *In Pursuit of Privacy: Law, Ethics, and the Rise of Technology*, Ithaca, NY: Cornell University Press.

Dede, C. (1995) The evolution of constructivist learning environments: Immersion in distributed, virtual worlds, *Educational Technology*, 35 (5): 46–52.

Deleuze, G. and Guatarri, F. (1988) *On the Line*, translated by John Johnston, New York: Semiotexte.

Dennerlein, J., Becker, T., Johnson, P., Reynolds, C. and Picard, R.W. (2003) Frustrating computers users increases exposure to physical factors, in *Proceedings of the International Ergonomics Association, Seoul, Korea*. Online. Available http://affect.media.mit.edu/pdfs/03.dennerlein-etal.pdf. (accessed 19 April 2013).

Dewey, J. (1938) *Experience and Education*, New York: Collier and Kappa Delta, Pi.

Drotner, K. (1999) Dangerous media? Panic discourses and dilemmas of modernity, *Paedagogica Historica*, 35 (3): 593–619.

Dourish, P. and Anderson, K. (2006) Collective information practice: Exploring privacy and security as social and cultural phenomena, *Human–Computer Interaction*, 21 (3): 319–342.

Downes, S. (2006) Learning networks and connective knowledge. Instructional Technology Forum Paper 92. Online. Available http://it.coe.uga.edu/itforum/paper92/paper92.html (accessed 28 November 2010).

Downes, S. (2012) Connectivism and connective knowledge essays on meaning and learning networks. Online. Available www.downes.ca/me/mybooks.htm (accessed 18 November 2013)

Dunsworth, Q. and Atkinson, R.K. (2007) Fostering multimedia learning of science: Exploring the role of an animated agent's image, *Computers and Education*, 49: 677–690.

Economist, The (2013) The attack of the MOOCs, 20 July. Available www.economist.com/news/business/21582001-army-new-online-courses-scaring-wits-out-traditional-universities-can-they (accessed 6 June 2014).

Edwards, R. (2014) Spatial theory in networked learning, in S. Bayne, C. Jones, M. de Laat, T. Ryberg and C. Sinclair (eds), *Proceedings of the 9th International Conference on Networked Learning*: 526–532.

Ellison, N.B. and boyd, d. (2013) Sociality through social network sites, in W.H. Dutton (ed.), *The Oxford Handbook of Internet Studies* (151–172), Oxford: Oxford University Press.

Ellison, N., Steinfield, C. and Lampe, C. (2007) The benefits of Facebook 'friends': Social capital and college students' use of online social network sites, *Journal of Computer-Mediated Communication*, 12: 1143–1168.

Engeström, Y. (1987) *Learning by Expanding: An Activity-Theoretical Approach to Developmental Research*, Helsinki: Orienta-Konsultit.

Entwistle, N.J. (1981) *Styles of Learning and Teaching*, New York: John Wiley & Sons.

Entwistle, N. (2008) Threshold concepts and transformative ways of thinking in research into higher education, in R. Land, J.H.F. Meyer and J. Smith (eds), *Threshold Concepts within the Disciplines* (21–35), Rotterdam: Sense Publishers.

Entwistle, N.J. and Ramsden, P. (1983) *Understanding Student Learning*, London: Croom Helm.

Eriksen, T.H. (2001) *Tyranny of the Moment: Fast and Slow Time in the Information Age*, London: Pluto Press.

Estep, E. (2013) 7 powerful ways to maintain your privacy and integrity. Online. Available www.collective-evolution.com/2013/06/13/7-powerful-ways-to-maintain-your-privacy-and-integrity-online/ (accessed 12 May 2014).

Éthier, J., Hadaya, P., Talbot, J. and Cadieux, J. (2008) Interface design and emotions experienced on B2C web sites: Empirical testing of a research model, *Computers in Human Behavior*, 24 (6): 2771–2791.

Eva, K.W., Neville, A.J. and Norman, G.R. (1998) Exploring the etiology and content specificity: Factors influencing analogic transfer and problem solving, *Academic Medicine*, 73 (10): S1–S5.

Eynon, R. (2009) Mapping the digital divide in Britain: Implications for learning and education, *Learning, Media and Technology*, 34 (4): 277–290.

Ferguson, R.F. (2006) Racial and ethnic disparities in home intellectual lifestyles, in *Getting it Done: Raising Achievement and Closing Gaps in Whole School Systems: Recent Advances in Research and Practice*, conference report, Cambridge, MA: Harvard University. Online. Available www.agi.harvard.edu/events/2008Conference/GETTING_IT_DONE_02_24_09.pdf (accessed 2 November 2014).

Fisher, M. (2010) The co-production of social contagion: A comparative analysis of two social networking sites. Online. Available http://digitalcase.case.edu:9000/fedora/get/ksl:fiscop00/fiscop00.pdf (accessed 14 February 2014).

Fitzpatrick, B. and Recordon, D. (2007) Thoughts on the social graph. Online. Available http://bradfitz.com/social-graph-problem/ (accessed 14 February 2014).

Floridi, L. (2011) The construction of personal identities online, *Minds and Machines*, 21: 477–479.

Freire, P. (1972) *Pedagogy of the Oppressed*, London: Penguin Books.

Freire, P. (1974) *Education: The Practice of Freedom*, London: Writers and Readers Co-operative.

Freire, P. (1997) *Pedagogy of the Heart*, New York: Continuum.

Foucault, M. (1975/1977) *Discipline and Punish: The Birth of the Prison*, translated by A. Sheridan, London: Penguin Books.

Fuller, M. and Jenkins, H. (1995) Nintendo and new world travel writing: A dialogue, in S. Jones (ed.), *Cybersociety: Computer-Mediated Communication and Community* (57–72), Thousand Oaks, CA: Sage.

Fuller, S. (2010) *The Sociology of Intellectual Life: The Career of the Mind in and around the Academy*, London: Sage.

Furlong, J. and Davies, C. (2012) Young people, new technologies and learning at home: Taking context seriously, in special issue of *Oxford Review of Education: The Educational and Social Impact of New Technologies on Young People in Britain*, 38 (1): 45–62.

Garau, M., Slater, M., Vinayagamoorthy, V., Brogni, A., Steed, A. and Sasse, M.A. (2003) The impact of avatar realism and eye gaze control on perceived quality of communication in a shared immersive virtual environment, in *Proceedings of the SIGCHI Conference on Human Factors in Computing Systems*: 529–536.

Gasser, U., Cortesi, S., Malik, M. and Lee, A. (2012) Youth and digital media: From credibility to information quality. Berkman Center for Internet and Society. Online. Available http://ssrn.com/abstract=2005272 (accessed 13 February 2014).

Gee, J.P. (2004) *What Video Games Have to Teach Us about Learning and Literacy*, Basingstoke: Palgrave Macmillan.

Gee, J.P. (n.d) The new literacy studies and the 'social turn'. Online. Available www.schools.ash.org.au/litweb/page300.html (accessed 6 December 2006).

Gibbons, M., Limoges, C., Nowotny, H., Schwarzman, S., Scott, P. and Trow, M. (1994) *The New Production of Knowledge: The Dynamics of Science and Research in Contemporary Societies*, London: Sage.

Gibbs, G. and Simpson, C. (2005) Conditions under which assessment supports learning, *Learning and Teaching in HE*, 1: 3–31.

Giles, J. (2010) Cyber crime made easy, *New Scientist*, 205 (2752): 20–21.

Gilster, P. (1997) *Digital Literacy*, New York: Wiley.

Giroux, H.A and Giroux, S. (2004) *Take Back Higher Education*, London: Palgrave.

Glenn, D. (2010) Divided attention, *Chronicle of Higher Education*, 56 (21): B6–B8.

Goodyear, P. and Carvalho, L (2014) Design for networked learning: Framing retains between participants' activities and the physical setting, in S. Bayne, C. Jones, M. de Laat, T. Ryberg and C. Sinclair (eds), *Proceeding of 9th International Conference on Networked Learning*: 137–144.

Goodyear, P. and Dimitriadis, Y. (2013) *In medias res*: Reframing design for learning, *Research in Learning Technology*, 21 (S1): 1–13.

Greenhow, C. and Robelia, B. (2009) Old communication, new literacies: Social network sites as social learning resources, *Journal of Computer-Mediated Communication*, 14 (4): 1130–1161.

Gustavsson, I., Alves, G., Costa, R., Nilsson, K., Zackrisson, J., Hernandez-Jayo, U. and Garcia-Zubia, J. (2011) The VISIR Open Lab Platform 5.0 – an architecture for a federation of remote laboratories, in *Proceedings of REV 2011, Brasov* [CD].

Gurak, L. (2001) *Cyberliteracy*, New Haven, CT: Yale University Press.

Haggis, T. (2004) Meaning, identity and 'motivation': Expanding what matters in understanding learning in higher education?, *Studies in Higher Education*, 29 (3): 335–352.

Hahn, T.N. (2003) *Joyfully Together: The Art of Building a Harmonious Community*, Berkeley, CA: Parallax Press.

Hall, G. (2009) Fluid notes on liquid books, in T.W. Luke and J.W. Hunsinger (eds), *Putting Knowledge to Work and Letting Information Play: The Center for Digital Discourse and Culture* (33–53), Blacksburg VA: Center for Digital Discourse and Culture. Available www.cddc.vt.edu/10th-book/ (accessed 3 November 2014).

Hall, S. (1996) Introduction: Who needs 'identity'?, in S. Hall and P. du Gay (eds), *Questions of Cultural Identity* (1–17), London: Sage.

Hämäläinen, R., Manninen, T., Järvelä, S. and Päivi Häkkinen, P. (2006) Learning to collaborate: Designing collaboration in a 3-D game environment, *Internet and Higher Education*, 9 (1): 47–61.

Hamdan, N., McKnight, P., McKnight, K. and Arfstrom, K. (2013) A review of flipped learning. Flipped Learning Network. Online. Available www.flippedlearning.org/cms/lib07/VA01923112/Centricity/Domain/41/LitReview_FlippedLearning.pdf (accessed 6 June 2014).

Hanh, T.N. (2003) *Joyfully Together: The Art of Building a Harmonious Community*, Berkeley, CA: Parallax Press.

Haraway, D. (1985/1991) A cyborg manifesto: Science, technology, and socialist-feminism in the late twentieth century, in D. Haraway, *Simians, Cyborgs and Women: The Reinvention of Nature* (149–181), New York: Routledge.

Hasler, B.S., Tuchman, P. and Friedman, D. (2013) Virtual research assistants: Replacing human interviewers by automated avatars in virtual worlds, *Computers in Human Behavior*, 29: 1608–1616.

Haug, K.H. (2006) Students' development of assessment criteria and enhancement of learning potential. Paper presented at the European Conference on Educational Research, University of Geneva, 13–15 September.

Hayles, K. (1999) *How We Became Posthuman: Virtual Bodies in Cybernetics, Literature and Informatics*, Chicago, IL: University of Chicago Press.

Hedberg, B. (1981) How organizations learn and unlearn, in P. Nystrom and W.H. Starbuck (eds), *Handbook of Organizational Design*, Vol. 1, London: Cambridge University Press.

Heidig, S. and Clarebout, G. (2011) Do pedagogical agents make a difference to student motivation and learning?, *Educational Research Review*, 6 (1): 27–54.

Herbrechter, S. (2013) Posthumanism, subjectivity, autobiography, *Subjectivity*, 5: 327–347.

Heron, J. (1989) *The Facilitator's Handbook*, London: Kogan Page.

Heron, J. (1993) *Group Facilitation*, London: Kogan Page.

Hides, S. (2005) The ideology of performative pedagogies: A cultural symptomology, *E-Learning*, 2 (4): 227–240.

Hil, R. (2012) *Whackademia: An Insider's Account of the Troubled University*, Sydney: University of New South Wales Press.

Hine, C. (2000) *Virtual Ethnography*, London: Sage.

Hobbs, R. (2008) Debates and challenges facing new literacies in the 21st century, in S. Livingstone and K. Drotner (eds), *International Handbook of Children, Media and Culture* (431–447), London: Sage.

Hobbs, R. (2011) Digital and media literacy: tapping into popular culture, *NASSP Principal Leadership*, 12 (1). Online. Available www.nassp.org/tabid/3788/default.aspx?topic=Digital_and_Media_Literacy (accessed 7 November 2014).

Hockings, C., Cooke, S., Yamashita, H., McGinty, S. and Bowl, M. (2008) Switched off? A study on disengagement among computing students at two universities, *Research Papers in Education*, 23 (2): 191–201.

Holloway, S.L. and Valentine, G. (2003) *Cyberkids: Children in the Information Age*, London: RoutledgeFalmer.

Holyoak, K.J. (1991) Problem solving, in D.N. Osherson and E.E. Smith (eds), *Thinking: An Invitation to Cognitive Science* (117–146), Cambridge, MA: MIT Press.

hooks, b. (1994) *Teaching to Transgress*, London: Routledge.

Hounsell, D. (2003) Student feedback, learning and development, in M. Slowey and D. Watson (eds), *Higher Education and the Lifecourse* (67–78), Milton Keynes: SRHE and Open University Press.

Hounsell, D. (2007) Towards more sustainable feedback to students, in D. Boud and N. Falchikov (eds), *Rethinking Assessment in Higher Education* (101–113), London: Routledge.

Hull, C.L. (1935) The conflicting psychologies of learning: A way out, *Psychological Review*, 42: 491–516.

Humphreys, L. (1970) *Tearoom Trade: A Study of Homosexual Encounters in Public Places*, London: Duckworth.

Huxley, J. (1927) *Religion without Revelation*, London: E. Benn.

Huxley, J. (1957) *Transhumanism*, London: Chatto & Windus.

Huxley, A. (1927) *Proper Studies*, London: Chatto & Windus.

Ingold, T. (2012) Towards an ecology of materials, *Annual Review of Anthropology*, 41: 427–442.

Ito, M. (2007) Technologies of the childhood imagination: Yu-Gi-Oh!, media mixes, and everyday cultural production, in J. Karangis (ed.), *Structures of Participation in Digital Culture* (88–111), New York: Social Science Research Council.

Ito, M., Baumer, S., Bittanti, M., boyd, d., Cody, R., Herr-Stephenson, B. et al. (2010) *Hanging out, Messing around, and Geeking out*, Cambridge, MA: MIT Press.

Ito, M., Gutiérrez, K., Livingstone, S., Penuel, B., Rhodes, J., Salen, K., Schor, J., Sefton-Green, J. and Watkins, S.C. (2013) *Connected Learning: An Agenda for Research and Design*, Irvine, CA: Digital Media and Learning Research Hub.

Jancin, B. (2011) Hypertexting by teens linked to increased health risks, *Clinical Psychiatry News*, 14 February. Online. Available www.clinicalpsychiatrynews.com/specialty-focus/childadolescent-psychiatry/single-article-page/hypertexting-by-teens-linked-to-increased-health-risks/e0ceb4aade.html (accessed 29 October 2014).

Jenkins, H. (2006) *Convergence Culture: Where Old and New Media Collide*, New York: New York University Press.

Jenkins, H. (2009) *Confronting the Challenges of Participatory Culture: Media Education for the 21st Century*, Cambridge, MA: MIT Press.

Jewitt, C. (2008) Challenge outline: New literacies, new democracies. Online. Available www.beyondcurrenthorizons.org.uk/wp-content/uploads/bch_challenge_paper democracies_carey_jewitt.pdf (accessed 2 May 2014).

Jewitt, C. and Kress, G. (2010) Multimodality, literacy and school English, in D. Wyse, R. Andrews and J. Hoffman (eds), *The Routledge International Encyclopaedia of English, Language and Literacy Teaching* (342–353), London: Routledge.

Johnson, D.W., Johnson, R.T. and Smith, K.A. (1991) *Cooperative Learning: Increasing College Faculty Instructional Productivity*, ASHE–ERIC Higher Education Report 4, Washington, DC: George Washington University, School of Education and Social Development.

Johnson, D.W., Johnson, R.T. and Smith, K.A. (1998) *Active Learning: Cooperation in the College Collaborative Learning Classroom*, Edina, MN: Interaction Book Company.

Johnson, L. and Renner, J. (2012) Effect of the flipped classroom model on secondary computer applications course: Student and teacher perceptions, questions and student achievement, doctoral dissertation, University of Louisville.

Johnson, L., Adams, S. and Cummins, M. (2012) *2012 Horizon Report*, Austin, TX: The New Media Consortium. Online. Available http://net.educause.edu/ir/library/pdf/HR2012.pdf (accessed 2 May 2014).

Juul, J. (2013) *The Art of Failure: An Essay on the Pain of Playing Video Games*, Cambridge, MA: MIT Press.

Kandiko, C.B. and Mawer, M. (2013) *Student Expectations and Perceptions of Higher Education*, London: King's Learning Institute.

Kang, M., Kim, J. and Park, M. (2008) Investigating presence as a predictor of learning outcomes in e-learning environment, in J. Luca and E. Weippl (eds), *Proceedings of World Conference on Educational Multimedia, Hypermedia and Telecommunications*: 4175–4180.

Karaganis, J. (ed.) (2008) *Structures of Participation in Digital Culture*, New York: Social Science Research Council.

Katz, J.E. (2006) *Magic in the Air: Mobile Communication and the Transformation of Social Life*, New Brunswick, NJ: Transaction.

Kelly, K. (2006) Scan this book!, *New York Times*, 14 May. Online. Available www.nytimes.com/2006/05/14/magazine/14publishing.html?ex=1305259200en=c07443d368771bb8ei=5090&_r=1& (accessed 12 June 2014).

Kerly, A., Hall, P. and Bull, S. (2007) Bringing chatbots into education: Towards natural language negotiation of open learner models, *Knowledge-Based Systems*, 20: 177–185.

Kiili, K. (2005) Digital game-based learning: Towards an experiential gaming model, *Internet and Higher Education*, 8: 13–24.

Kiley, M. and Wisker, G. (2009) Threshold concepts in research education and evidence of threshold crossing, *Higher Education Research and Development*, 28 (4): 431–441.

Kimmons, R. and Veletsianos, G. (2014) The fragmented educator 2.0: Social networking sites, acceptable identity fragments, and the identity constellation, *Computers and Education*, 72: 292–301.

Kinchin, I., Cabot, L.B. and Hay, D.B. (2010) Visualising expertise: Revealing the nature of a threshold concept in the development of an authentic pedagogy for clinical education, in J.H.F. Meyer., R. Land and C. Baillie (eds), *Threshold Concepts and Transformational Learning* (81–95), Rotterdam: Sense Publishers.

Knightley, P., Potter, E. and Wallace, M. (1979) *Suffer the Children: The Story of Thalidomide*, New York: Viking Press.

Konijn, E.A., Utz, S., Tanis, M. and Barnes, S.B. (2008) *Mediated Interpersonal Communications*, New York: Routledge.

Koskela, H. (2004) Webcams, TV shows and mobile phones: Empowering exhibitionism, *Surveillance and Society*, 2 (2/3): 199–215. Online. Available www.surveillance-and-society.org/articles2(2)/webcams.pdf (accessed 28 February 2014).

Kostakos, V., Venkatanathan, J., Reynolds, B., Sadeh, N., Toch, E., Shaikh, S.A. and Jones, S. (2011) Who's your best friend? Targeted privacy attacks in location-sharing social networks, in *UbiComp '11 – Proceedings of the 2011 ACM Conference on Ubiquitous Computing*: 177–186. Online. Available http://opus.bath.ac.uk/27149/ (accessed 17 May 2014).

Kozinets, R.V. (2010) *Netnography: Doing Ethnographic Research Online*, London: Sage.

Krause, K. and Coates, H. (2008) Students' engagement in first-year university, *Assessment and Evaluation in Higher Education*, 33 (2): 277–304.

Kress, G. (2003) *Literacy in the New Media Age*, Abingdon: Routledge.

Kress, G. and van Leeuwen, T. (2001) *Multimodal Discourse: The Modes and Media of Contemporary Communication*, London: Hodder Arnold.

Kress, G., Jewitt, C., Jones, K., Bourne, J., Franks, A. and Hardcastle, J. (2005) *English in Urban Classrooms*, London: Routledge.

Kuh, G.D., Kinzie, J., Buckley, J.A., Bridges, B.K. and Hayek, J.C. (2007) *Piecing Together the Student Success Puzzle: Research, Propositions and Recommendations*, ASHE Higher Education Report 32, no. 5, San Francisco, CA: Jossey-Bass.

Lameras, P., Savin-Baden, M., Petridis, P., Dunwell, I. and Liarokapis, F. (2014) Fostering science teachers design for inquiry-based learning by using a serious game. Paper presented at the 14th IEEE International Conference on Advanced Learning Technologies – ICALT2014 Advanced Technologies for Supporting Open Access to Formal and Informal Learning, Athens, 7–10 July.

Lammes, S. (2008) Spatial regimes of the digital playground: Cultural functions of spatial practices in computer games, *Space and Culture*, 11: 260–272.

Land, R. (2006) Paradigms lost: Academic practice and exteriorising technologies, *E-Learning*, 3 (1): 100–110.

Land, R. and Bayne, S. (2006) Issues in cyberspace education, in M. Savin-Baden and K. Wilkie (eds), *Problem-based Learning Online*, Maidenhead: McGraw-Hill.

Lankshear, C. and Knobel, M. (2003) *New Literacies: Changing Knowledge and Classroom Learning*, Buckingham: Open University Press.

Larsen, M.C. and Ryberg, T. (2011) Youth and online social networking: From local experience to public discourses, in E. Dunkels, G.M. Frånberg and C. Hällgren (eds), *Youth Culture and Net Culture: Online Social Practices* (17–40), New York: IGI global.

Lave, J. and Wenger, E. (1991) *Situated Learning: Legitimate Peripheral Participation*, Cambridge: Cambridge University Press.

Latour, B. (1987) *Science in Action: How to Follow Scientists and Engineers through Society*, Milton Keynes: Open University Press.

Lea, M.R. and Jones, S. (2011) Digital literacies in higher education: Exploring textual and technological practice, *Studies in Higher Education*, 36 (4): 377–393.

Leander, K.M. and McKim, K.K (2003) Tracing the everyday 'sitings' of adolescents on the internet: A strategic adaptation of ethnography across online and offline spaces, *Education, Communication and Information*, 3 (2): 211–240.

Leander, K., Phillips, N. and Taylor, K.H. (2010) The changing social spaces of learning: Mapping new mobilities, *Review of Research in Education*, 34: 329–394.

Leeson, P.T. (2009) The invisible hook: The law and the economics of pirate tolerance, *New York University, Journal of Law and Liberty*, 4 (2): 139–171.

Leggo, C. (2011) A heartful pedagogy of care: A grandfather's perambulations, in J.A. Kentel (ed.), *Educating the Young: The Ethics of Care* (61–83), New York: Peter Lang.

Lenhart, A., Arafeh, S., Smith, A. and Rankin Macgill, A. (2008) *Writing, Technology and Teens*, Pew Internet and American Life Project, Washington, DC: Pew/Internet. Online. Available www.pewinternet.org/pdfs/PIP_Writing_Report_FINAL3.pdf) (accessed 6 June 2012).

Lenhart A. and Madden, M. (2007) *Teens, Privacy & Online Social Networks*, Pew Internet and American Life Project. Online. Available www.pewinternet.org/2007/04/18/teens-privacy-and-online-social-networks/ (accessed 2 November 2014).

Leontiev, A. (1981) *Problems of the Development of Mind*, Moscow: Progress Press.

Leppänen, S., Pitkänen-Huhta, A., Piirainen-Marsh, A., Nikula, T. and Peuronen, S. (2009) Young people's translocal new media uses: A multiperspective analysis of language choice and heteroglossia, *Journal of Computer-Mediated Communication*, 14: 1080–1107.

Leung, L. (2002) Loneliness, self-disclosure and ICQ ('I Seek You') use, *CyberPsychology and Behavior*, 5: 241–251.

Linds, W. (2006) Metaxis: Dancing in the in-between, in J. Cohen-Cruz and M. Shutzman (eds), *A Boal Companion: Dialogues on Theatre and Cultural Politics* (114–124), New York: Routledge.

Ling, R. and Pederson, P. (2005) The socio-linguistic of SMS: An analysis of SMS use by a random sample of Norwegians, in R. Ling and P. Pedersen (eds), *Mobile Communications: Renegotiation of the Social Sphere* (335–349), London: Springer.

Livingstone, S. (2002) *Young People and New Media*, London and Thousand Oaks, CA: Sage.

Livingstone, S. (2005) Introduction, in S. Livingstone (ed.), *Audiences and Publics: When Cultural Engagement Matters for the Public Sphere* (9–16), Bristol: Intellect Books.

Livingstone, S. (2010a) Digital learning and participation among youth: Critical reflections on future research priorities, *International Journal of Learning and Media*, 2 (2–3): 1–13.

Livingstone, S. (2010b) Youthful participation: What have we learned, what shall we ask next? Paper presented at the 1st Annual Digital Media and Learning Conference: Diversifying Participation, University of California, San Diego, 18–20 February.

Livingstone, S. and Haddon, L. (2009) *EU Kids Online: Final Report 2009*, London: EU Kids Online.

Lowe, D. (2014) MOOLs: Massive open online laboratories: An analysis of scale and feasibility, in *Proceedings of 11th International Conference on Remote Engineering and Virtual Instrumentation (REV)*: 1–6.

Lukes, S. (1973) *Individualism*, Oxford: Basil Blackwell.

Lyon, D. (2010) Liquid surveillance: The contribution of Zygmunt Bauman to surveillance studies, *International Political Sociology*, 14: 325–338.

Madge, C., Meek, J., Wellens, J. and Hooley, T. (2009) Facebook, social integration and informal learning at university: 'It is more for socialising and talking to friends about work than for actually doing work', *Learning, Media and Technology*, 34 (2): 141–155.

Mark, G., Voida, S. and Cardello. A. (2012) A pace not dictated by electrons: An empirical study of work without email. Paper presented at the 30th Annual SIGCHI Conference on Human Factors in Computing Systems (CHI '12), Austin, TX, 5–10 May.

Markauskaite, L. and Goodyear, P. (2014) Tapping into the mental resources of teachers' working knowledge: Insights into the generative power of intuitive pedagogy, *Learning, Culture and Social Interaction*, 3 (4): 237–251. Online. Available http://dx.doi.org/10.1016/j.lcsi.2014.01.001 (accessed 30 January 2015).

Markauskaite, L., Goodyear, P. and Bachfischer, A. (2014) Epistemic games for knowledgeable action in professional learning. Paper presented at the ICLS 2014 Symposium: Enrollment of Higher Education Students in Professional Knowledge and Practices, Boulder, CO, 23–27 June.

Marton, F. and Säljö, R. (1976a) On qualitative differences in learning, I: Outcome and process, *British Journal of Educational Psychology*, 46: 4–11.

Marton, F. and Säljö, R. (1976b) On qualitative differences in learning, II: Outcome as a function of the learner's conception of the task, *British Journal of Educational Psychology*, 46: 115–127.

Marton, F. and Säljö, R. (1984) Approaches to learning, in F. Marton, D. Hounsell and N.J. Entwistle (eds), *The Experience of Learning* (36–55), Edinburgh: Scottish Academic Press.

Mauss, M. (1934) Les techniques du corps, *Journal de Psychologie*, 32 (3–4): 271–293. Reprinted in M. Mauss (1936), *Sociologie et anthropologie* (366–386), Paris: PUF.

Matsuda, M. (2005) Mobile communication and selective sociality, in M. Ito, D. Okabe and M. Matsuda (eds), *Personal, Portable, Pedestrian: Mobile Phones in Japanese Life* (123–142), Cambridge, MA: MIT Press.

Matthews, R.S. (1996) Collaborative learning: Creating knowledge with students, in R.H. Menges, M. Weimer and associates (eds), *Teaching on Solid Ground: Using Scholarship to Improve Practice* (101–124), San Francisco, CA: Jossey-Bass.

Mercer, N., Dawes, L., Wegerif, R. and Sams, C. (2004) Reasoning as a scientist: Ways of helping children to use language to learn science, *British Educational Research Journal*, 30 (3): 359–378.

Merchant, G. (2012) Mobile practices in everyday life: Popular digital literacies and schools revisited, *British Journal of Educational Technology*, 43 (5): 770–782.

Meyer, J.H.F. and Eley, M.G. (2006) The approaches to teaching inventory: A critique of its development and applicability, *British Journal of Education Psychology*, 76: 633–649.

Meyer, J.H.F. and Land, R. (2003) Threshold concepts and troublesome knowledge: Linkages to ways of thinking and practising, in C. Rust (ed.), *Improving Student Learning: Theory and Practice Ten Years on* (412–424), Oxford: Oxford Centre for Staff and Learning Development.

Meyer, J.H.F. and Land, R. (2006) Threshold concepts and troublesome knowledge: Issues of liminality, in J.H.F. Meyer and R. Land (eds), *Overcoming Barriers to Student Understanding: Threshold Concepts and Troublesome Knowledge* (19–32), Abingdon: RoutledgeFalmer.

Mezirow, J. (1985) A critical theory of self-directed learning, in S. Brookfield (ed.), *Self-Directed Learning: From Theory to Practice* (17–30), San Francisco, CA: Jossey-Bass.

Mezirow, J. (1991) *Transformative Dimensions of Adult Learning*, San Francisco, CA: Jossey-Bass.

Miliszewska, I. and Horwood, J. (2004) Engagement theory: A framework for supporting cultural differences in transnational education, in *Proceedings of the HERDSA Conference, July 4–7, in Miri, Malaysia*: 223–231.

Miller, C. and Bartlett, J. (2012) 'Digital fluency': Towards young people's critical use of the internet, *Journal of Information Literacy*, 6 (2): 35–55.

Minocha, S. (2013) 3D virtual geology field trips. Paper presented at the 2nd Monthly International Workshop on Science Exhibits in Online 3D Environments, Abyss Observatory, Second Life, 20 April. Online. Available http://oro.open.ac.uk/39527/2/Abstract-3D-Virtual-Geology-FieldTrip-ORO.pdf (accessed 2 November 2014).

Morrissey, K. and Kirakowski, J. (2013) 'Realness' in chatbots: Establishing quantifiable criteria, in M. Kurosu (ed.), *Human–Computer Interaction: Interaction Modalities and Techniques* (87–96), Berlin: Springer-Verlag.

Nakamura, L. (2000) *Race in/for Cyberspace: Identity Tourism and Racial Passing on the Internet*. Online. Available www.humanities.uci.edu/mposter/syllabi/readings/nakamura.html. (accessed 2 June 2014).

Nakamura, L. (2010) Race and identity in digital media, in J. Curran (ed.), *Mass Media and Society* (336–347), London: Bloomsbury Academic.

Newman, J. (2004) *Videogames*, London: Routledge.

Nicol, D. and Macfarlane-Dick, D. (2006) Formative assessment and self-regulated learning: A model and seven principles of good feedback practice, *Studies in Higher Education*, 31 (2): 199–218.

Oakeshott, M. (1989) The idea of a university: Michael Oakeshott on education, in T. Fuller (ed.), *The Voice of Liberal Learning* (95–104), New Haven, CT, and London: Yale University Press.

Ofcom (2011) Communications market report: UK. Online. Available http://stakeholders.ofcom.org.uk/market-data-research/market-data/communications-market-reports/cmr11/uk/ (accessed 21 December 2011).

Okri, B. (1997) *A Way of Being Free*, London: Phoenix House.

O'Neill, O. (2002) *A Question of Trust*, BBC Reith Lectures, Cambridge: Cambridge University Press.

Ophira, E., Nass, C. and. Wagner, A.D. (2009) Cognitive control in media multitaskers, *Proceedings of the National Academy of Sciences*, 106 (37): 15583–15587. Online. Available www.ncbi.nlm.nih.gov/pmc/articles/PMC2747164/ (accessed 3 November 2014).

Palen, L. and Dourish, P. (2003) Unpacking 'privacy' for a networked world, in *Proceedings from ACM CHI Conference on Human Factors in Computing System, Fort Lauderdale, FL*: 129–136.

Papadapoulos, C. and Roman, A.S. (2010) Implementing an inverted classroom model in engineering statistics: Initial results, in American Society for Engineering Statistics, *Proceedings of the 40th ASEE/IEEE Frontiers in Education Conference, Washington, DC, October 2010*: F1–F3.

Parry, D. (2011) Mobile perspectives: On teaching mobile literacy, *Educause Review*, March/April. Online. Available http://net.educause.edu/ir/library/pdf/ERM1120.pdf (accessed 12 November 2013).

Pask, G. (1976) Styles and strategies of learning, *British Journal of Educational Psychology*, 46 (2): 128–148.

Pathak-Shelat, M. (2014) Media literacy and well-being of young people, in A. Ben-Arieh, F. Casas, I. Frønes and J.E. Korbin (eds), *Handbook of Child Well-being* (2057–2092), London: Springer.

Pausch, R., Proffitt, D. and Williams, G. (1997) Quantifying immersion in virtual reality, in G.S. Owen, T. Whitted and B. Mones-Hattal (eds), *Proceedings of the 24th International Conference on Computer Graphics and Interactive Techniques*: 13–18.

Pavlik, J.E. (2012) Concept: Media ethics in the digital age, *Media Ethics*, 24 (1). Online. Available www.mediaethicsmagazine.com/index.php/browse-back-issues/144-fall-2012/3998645-concept-media-ethics-in-the-digital-age (accessed 3 June 2014).

Pearson, E. (2009) All the World Wide Web's a stage: The performance of identity in online social networks, *First Monday*, 14 (3). Online. Available http://firstmonday.org/htbin/cgiwrap/bin/ojs/index.php/fm/article/view/2162/2127 (accessed 3 June 2014).

Perkins, D. (1999) The many faces of constructivism, *Educational Leadership*, 57 (3): 6–11.

Perkins, D. (2006) Constructivism and troublesome knowledge, in J.H.F. Meyer and R. Land (eds) *Overcoming Barriers to Student Understanding: Threshold Concepts and Troublesome Knowledge* (33–48), Abingdon: RoutledgeFalmer.

Perry, W.G. (1970) *Forms of Intellectual and Ethical Development during the College Years: A Scheme*, New York: Holt, Rinehart & Winston.

Perry, W.G. (1988) Different worlds in the same classroom, in P. Ramsden (ed.), *Improving Learning: New Perspectives* (145–161), London: Kogan Page.

Petrakou, A. (2010) Interacting through avatars: Virtual worlds as a context for online education, *Computers and Education*, 54 (4): 1020–1027.

Phipps, A.M. (2007) The sound of higher education: Sensuous epistemologies and the mess of knowing, *London Review of Education, 5 (1): 1–13*.

Piaget, J. (1929) The Child's Conception of the World, London: Routledge & Kegan Paul.

Plester, B., Wood, C. and Joshi, P. (2009) Exploring the relationship between children's knowledge of text message abbreviations and school literacy outcomes, *British Journal of Developmental Psychology*, 27: 145–161.

Porter, S. (2006) Institutional structures and student engagement, *Research in Higher Education*, 47 (5): 531–558.

Poster, M. (1990) *The Mode of Information: Poststructuralism and Social Context*, Chicago, IL: University of Chicago Press.

Prensky, M (2001) Digital natives, digital immigrants, *On the Horizon*, 9 (5). Online. Available www.marcprensky.com/writing/Prensky%20-%20Digital%20Natives,%20Digital%20Immigrants%20-%20Part1.pdf (accessed 1 May 2012).

Ravenscroft, A. and Matheson, M.P. (2002) Developing and evaluating dialogue games for collaborative e-learning, *Journal of Computer Assisted Learning*, 18: 93–101.

Raynes-Goldie, K. (2010) Aliases, creeping, and wall cleaning: Understanding privacy in the age of Facebook, *First Monday*, 15 (1–4): 1–8. Online. Available http://firstmonday.org/article/view/2775/2432 (accessed 31 October 2014).

Resnick, M. (2012) Mother's Day, warrior cats, and digital fluency: Stories from the Scratch online community, in *Proceedings of the Constructionism 2012 Conference, Athens, Greece*. Online. Available http://web.media.mit.edu/~mres/papers/mothers-day-warrior-cats.pdf (accessed 6 June 2014).

Richter, T., Tetour, Y. and Boehringer D. (2011) Library of labs: A European project on the dissemination of remote experiments and virtual laboratories, in *Proceedings of SEFI Annual Conference 2011, Lisbon, Portugal, September 28–30*: 555–562.

Rideout, V., Roberts, D.F. and Foehr, U.G. (2010) *Generation M²: Media in the Lives of 8–18 Year Olds*, Menlo Park, CA: Kaiser Family Foundation. Online. Available www.kff.org/

entmedia/upload/Executive-Summary-Generation-M-Media-in-the-Lives-of-8–18-Year-olds.pdf (accessed 2 June 2014).

Ritzer, G. (1993) *The McDonaldization of Society*, London: Sage.

Roberts, D.F. and. Foehr, U.G. (2008) Trends in media use, *The Future of Children*, 18 (1): 11–38.

Roberts, D.F., Foehr, U.G. and Rideout, V.J. (2005) *Generation M: Media in the Lives of 8–18 Year-olds*, Menlo Park, CA: Kaiser Family Foundation.

Robertson, G., Czerwinski, M. and van Dantzich, M. (1997) Immersion in desktop virtual reality, in G. Robertson and C. Schmandt (eds), *Proceedings of the 10th Annual ACM Symposium on User Interface Software and Technology*: 11–19.

Rogers, C. (1969) *Freedom to Learn*, Columbus, OH: Merrill.

Rogers, C. (1983) *Freedom to Learn for the '80s*, Columbus, OH: Merrill.

Royal Liverpool Children's Inquiry Report (The Redfern Report) (2001), London: The Stationery Office.

Rubinstein, J.S., Meyer, D.E. and Evans, J.E. (2001) Executive control of cognitive processes in task switching, *Journal of Experimental Psychology: Human Perception and Performance*, 27 (4): 763–797.

Rust, C. (2001) *A Briefing on the Assessment of Large Groups*, LTSN Assessment Series No. 12, York: Higher Education Academy. Online. Available http://78.158.56.101/archive/palatine/resources/assessment-resources/index.html (accessed 3 November 2014).

Ryberg, T. and Larsen, M.C. (2008) Networked identities: Understanding relationships between strong and weak ties in networked environments, *Journal of Computer Assisted Learning*, 24 (2): 103–115.

Salaway, G., Caruso, J.B. and Nelson, M.R. (2007) *The ECAR Study of Undergraduate Students and Information Technology, 2007*, Boulder, CO: Educause Center for Applied Research. Online. Available www.educause.edu/ecar (accessed 2 November 2014).

Säljö, R. (1979) *Learning in the Learner's Perspective, I: Some Common-sense Assumptions*, Report No. 76, Göteborg: University of Göteborg, Institute of Education.

Salmon, G. and Edirisingha, P. (2008) *Podcasting for Learning in Universities*, Maidenhead: McGraw-Hill.

Savin-Baden, M. (2000) *Problem-based Learning in Higher Education: Untold Stories*, Buckingham: Open University Press/SRHE.

Savin-Baden, M. (2014) Problem-based learning: New constellations for the 21st century, *Journal of Excellence in College Teaching*, 25 (3–4): 197–220.

Savin-Baden, M., Gourlay, L., Mawer, M., Steils, N., Tombs, C. and Tombs, G. (2010) Situating pedagogies, positions and practices in immersive virtual worlds, *Educational Research*, 52 (2): 123–133.

Savin-Baden, M. and Major, C. (2013) *Qualitative Research: The Essential Guide to Theory and Practice*, Abingdon: Routledge.

Savin-Baden, M. and Sinclair, C. (2010) Lurking on the threshold: Being learners in silent spaces, in R. Land and S. Bayne (eds), *Digital Differences* (29–44), Rotterdam: Sense Publishers.

Savin-Baden, M., Tombs, G. and Bahkta, R. (2014) Sharing secrets with robots? Paper presented at the EdMedia Conference, Tampere, Finland, June.

Savin-Baden, M., Tombs, G., Burden, D. and Wood, C. (2013) It's almost like talking to a person, *International Journal of Mobile and Blended Learning*, 5 (2): 78–93.

Savin-Baden, M., Tombs, C., Poulton, T., Conradi, E., Kavia, S., Burden, D. and Beaumont, C. (2011) An evaluation of implementing problem-based learning scenarios in an immersive virtual world, *International Journal of Medical Education*, 2: 116–124.

Schoenfeld, A.H. (1989) Exploration of students' mathematical beliefs and behaviour, *Journal for Research in Mathematics Education*, 20: 338–355.

Schumpeter, J. (1934) *The Theory of Economic Development*, Cambridge, MA: Harvard University Press.

Sefton-Green, J. (2004) *Literature Review in Informal Learning with Technology outside School*, London: UK FutureLab.

Sefton-Green, J. (2013a) *Learning at Not-School*, Cambridge, MA: MIT Press.

Sefton-Green, J. (2013b) *Mapping Digital Makers: A Review Exploring Everyday Creativity, Learning Lives and the Digital*, Nominet Trust State of the Art Reviews, Oxford: Nominet Trust.

Selwyn, N. (2012) Bursting out of the 'ed-tech' bubble, *Learning, Media and Technology*, 37 (4): 331–334.

Selwyn, N. (2013) Digital technologies in universities: Problems posing as solutions?, *Learning, Media and Technology*, 38 (1): 1–3.

Selwyn, N. (2014) Education and 'the digital', *British Journal of Sociology of Education*, 35 (1): 155–164.

Seymour, W. (2001) In the flesh or online? Exploring qualitative research methodologies, *Qualitative Research*, 1: 147–168.

Shaffer, D.W. (2006) Epistemic frames for epistemic games, *Computers and Education*, 46 (3): 223–234.

Shakespeare, W. (1610–1611/2004) *The Tempest*, London Wordsworth Editions.

Sharpe, R., Beetham, H. and de Freitas, S. (eds) (2010) *Listening to Learners in the Digital Age*, Abingdon: Routledge.

Sharples, M., McAndrew, P., Weller, M., Ferguson, R., FitzGerald, E., Hirst, T. and Gaved, M. (2013) *Innovating Pedagogy 2013: Open University Innovation Report 2*, Milton Keynes: Open University.

Sharples, M., Taylor, J. and Vavoula, G. (2005) Towards a theory of mobile learning, in *Proceedings of mLearn2005 – 4th World Conference on mLearning, Cape Town, South Africa, 25–28 October 2005*. Online. Available www.mlearn.org.za/CD/papers/Sharples-%20Theory%20of%20Mobile.pdf (accessed 3 May 2012).

Sheehy, K. (2010) Inclusive education and virtual worlds: The Teacher Embodiment and Learning Affordance Framework (TEALEAF), in S. Kieron, R. Ferguson and G. Clough (eds), *Virtual Worlds: Controversies at the Frontier of Education: Education in a Competitive and Globalizing World* (159–183), Hauppauge, NY: Nova Science Publishers.

Sherwood, C. (1991) Adventure games in the classroom: A far cry from A says Apple, *Computers and Education*, 17 (4): 309–315.

Shulman, L. (1986) Those who understand: Knowledge growth in teaching, *Educational Researcher*, 15 (2): 4–14.

Shulman, L. (1987) Knowledge and teaching: Foundations of the new reform, *Harvard Educational Review*, 57 (1): 1–22.

Shulman, L. (2005) The signature pedagogies of the professions of law, medicine, engineering, and the clergy: Potential lessons for the education of teachers. Paper presented at the Teacher Education for Effective Teaching and Learning Workshop, hosted by the National Research Council's Center for Education, Irvine, CA, 8 February. Online. Available http://hub.mspnet.org/index.cfm/11172 (accessed 16 December 2012).

Shulman, L.S. (2006) Signature pedagogies in the professions, *Daedalus*, Summer: 52–59.

Siemens, G. (2008a) *About: Description of connectivism. Connectivism: A learning theory for today's learner*. Online. Available www.connectivism.ca/about.html (accessed 10 June 2014).

Siemens, G. (2008b) *Learning and Knowing in Networks: Changing Roles for Educators and Designers*. University of Georgia IT Forum, Paper 105. Online. Available http://it.coe.uga.edu/itforum/Paper105/Siemens.pdf (accessed 10 June 2014).

Siemens, G. (2009) *Technologically Externalized Knowledge and Learning*. Online. Available www.connectivism.ca/?p=181 (accessed 9 June 1014).

Simsek, E. and Simsek. A. (2013) New literacies for digital citizenship, *Contemporary Educational Technology*, 4 (2): 126–137.

Skinner, B.F. (1953) *Science and Human Behavior*, New York: Macmillan.

Smith, S. (2011) Narrating lives and contemporary imaginaries, *PMLA*, 126 (3): 564–574.

Squire, K. (2009) Mobile media learning: Multiplicities of place, *On the Horizon*, 17 (1): 70–80.

Squire, K. and Dikkers, S. (2012) Amplifications of learning: Use of mobile media devices among youth, *Convergence: The International Journal of Research into New Media Technologies*, 18: 445–464.

Stald, G. (2008) Mobile identity: Youth, identity, and mobile communication media, in D. Buckingham (ed.), *Youth, Identity, and Digital Media* (143–164), MacArthur Foundation Series on Digital Media and Learning, Cambridge, MA: MIT Press.

Steils, N. (2013) Exploring learner identity in virtual worlds in higher education: Narratives of pursuit, embodiment and resistance, Ph.D. thesis, Coventry University.

Stenhouse, L. (1975) *An Introduction to Curriculum Research and Development*, London: Heinemann.

Strayer, J. (2012) How learning in an inverted classroom influences cooperation, innovation and task orientation, *Learning Environments*, 15 (2): 171.

Tapscott, D. (2008) *Grown up Digital: How the Net Generation is Changing Your World*, Buckingham: McGraw-Hill.

Terkowsky, C., Jahnke, I., Pleul, C. and Tekkaya, A.E. (2011) Platform for e-Learning and Telemetric Experimentation (PeTEX): Tele-operated laboratories for production engineering education, in *Proceedings of the IEEE Global Engineering Education Conference (EDUCON 2011), Amman, Jordan, 4–6 April*: 491–497.

Thrift, N. (2006) Donna Haraway's dreams, *Theory, Culture and Society*, 23, 189–195.

Thurlow, C. (2006) From statistical panic to moral panic: The metadiscursive construction and popular exaggeration of new media language in the print media, *Journal of Computer Mediated Communication*, 11 (3): 667–701.

Thurlow, C. (2007) Fabricating youth: New-media discourse and the technologization of young people, in S. Johnson and A. Ensslin (eds), *Language in the Media: Representations, Identities, and Ideologies* (213–233), London: Continuum.

Thurlow, C. and Bell, K. (2009) Against technologization: Young people's new media discourse as creative cultural practice, *Journal of Computer-Mediated Communication*, 14: 1038–1049.

Tomlinson, J. (2007) *The Culture of Speed*, London: Sage.

Traxler, J. (2011) Mobile learning: Starting in the right place, going in the right direction?, *International Journal of Mobile and Blended Learning*, 3 (1): 57–67.

Trigwell, K., Prosser, M. and Waterhouse, F. (1999) Relations between teachers' approaches to teaching and students' approaches to learning, *Higher Education*, 37: 57–70.Tripp, L.M. and Herr-Stephenson, R. (2009) Making access meaningful: Latino young people using digital media at home and at school, *Journal of Computer-Mediated Communication*, 14 (4): 1190–1207.

Trowler, P. (2014) Depicting and researching disciplines: Strong and moderate essentialist approaches, *Studies in Higher Education*. Online. Available www.research.lancs.ac.uk/

portal/en/publications/depicting-and-researching-disciplines%2828e6d9ab-73f1-45b9-850a-c0d07d4673d9%29.html (accessed 25 October 2014).

Trowler, V. and Trowler, P. (2010) Student engagement literature review, *Higher Education Academy*. Online. Available www.heacademy.ac.uk/resources/detail/evidencenet/Student_engagement_literature_review (accessed 14 July 2011).

Tufekci, Z. (2008) Can you see me now? Audience and disclosure regulation in online social network sites, *Bulletin of Science, Technology and Society*, 28(1): 20–36.

Turan, Z. and Hasan, T. and Yuksel, G. (2013) The reasons for non-use of social networking websites by university students, *Comunicar*, 21 (41): 137–145.

Turing, A. (1950) Computing machinery and intelligence, *Mind*, 49: 433–460.

Turk, T. and Johnson, J. (2012) Toward an ecology of vidding, *Transformative Works and Cultures*, 9. Online. Available http://journal.transformativeworks.org/index.php/twc/article/view/326 (accessed 13 June 2014).

Turkle, S. (1996) *Life on the Screen: Identity in the Age of the Internet*, London: Weidenfeld & Nicolson.

Turkle, S. (1999) Looking toward cyberspace: Beyond grounded sociology, *Contemporary Sociology*, 286: 643–648.

Turkle, S. (2005) *The Second Self: Computers and the Human Spirit*, 2nd edn, Cambridge, MA: MIT Press.

Turkle, S. (2008) Always-on/always-on-you: The tethered self, in J.E. Katz (ed.), *Handbook of Mobile Communication Studies* (121–138), Cambridge, MA: MIT Press.

Turkle, S. (2010) In good company? On the threshold of robotic companions, in Y. Wilks (ed.), *Close Engagements with Artificial Companions: Key Social, Psychological, Ethical and Design Issues* (3–10), Amsterdam and Philadelphia, PA: John Benjamins.

Turkle, S. (2011a) *Alone Together*, New York: Basic Books.

Turkle, S. (2011b) The tethered self: Technology reinvents intimacy and solitude, *Continuing Higher Education Review*, 75: 28–31.

Ulmer, G. (2003) *Web Supplement to Internet Invention*. Online. Available www.clas.ufl.edu/users/glue/longman/pedagogy/electracy.html (accessed 1 May 2013).

Utz, S. and Krämer, N. (2009) The privacy paradox on social network sites revisited: The role of individual characteristics and group norms, *Cyberpsychology: Journal of Psychosocial Research on Cyberspace*, 3 (2). Online. Available http://cyberpsychology.eu/view.php?cisloclanku=2009111001&article=2 (accessed 3 November 2014).

Vecchione, A. (2010) Texting: Leveraging the statistics to your advantage, *The Scoop* (electronic publication of the Idaho Commission for Libraries). Online. Available http://works.bepress.com/cgi/viewcontent.cgi?article=1005andcontext=amy_vecchioneandsei-redir=1#search=%22texting%20class%22 (accessed 4 June 2014).

Virilio, P. (1996) Architecture principe, in P. Johnston (ed.), *Theory of the Oblique* (51–57), London: Architectural Association Documents.

Virilio, P. (1997) *Open Sky*, London: Verso.

Vygotsky, L.S. (1978) *Mind in Society: The Development of Higher Psychological Processes*, Cambridge, MA: Harvard University Press.

Waern, A. (2013) Game analysis as a signature pedagogy of game studies, in M.J. Nelson (ed.), *Foundations of Digital Games*. Online. Available www.fdg2013.org/program/papers/paper36_waern.pdf (accessed 6 June 2014).

Wahl-Jorgensen K (2008) On the public sphere, deliberation, journalism and society: An interview with Seyla Benhabib, *Journalism Studies*, 9 (6): 962–970.

Warburton, S. (2009) Second Life in higher education: Assessing the potential for and the barriers to deploying virtual worlds in learning and teaching, *British Journal of Educational Technology*, 40 (3): 414–426.

Watson, J.B. (1924) *Behaviorism*, New York: People's Institute Publishing Company.

Wellman, B. and Hogan, B. (2004) The immanent internet, in J.R. McKay (ed.), *Netting Citizens: Exploring Citizenship in a Digital Age* (54–80), Edinburgh: St Andrews Press.

Westin, A., Harris, L. and associates (1991) *Harris–Equifax Consumer Privacy Survey*. [No longer available online, but discussed in depth in Kumaraguru, P. and Cranor, L.F. (2005) *Privacy Indexes: A Survey of Westin's Studies*, Pittsburgh, PA: School of Computer Science, Carnegie Mellon University. Online. Available www.cs.cmu.edu/~ponguru/CMU-ISRI-05-138.pdf (accessed 3 November 2014).]

Wheeless, L. and Grotz, J. (1977) The measurement of trust and its relationship to self-disclosure, *Human Communication Research*, 3 (3): 250–257.

Whelan, J. (2008) Metaxis, *After the Future*. Online. Available http://afterthefuture.typepad.com/afterthefuture/2008/12/metaxis.html (accessed 10 November 2013).

White, D., Connaway, L.S, Lanclos, D., Le Cornu, A. and Hood, E. (2012) *Digital Visitors and Residents: Progress Report*, Bristol: JISC.

White, D. and Le Cornu, A. (2011) Visitors and residents: A new typology for online engagement, *First Monday*, 16 (9). Online. Available http://journals.uic.edu/ojs/index.php/fm/rt/printerFriendly/3171/3049 (accessed 2 June 2014).

Whitty, M.T. and Joinson, A.N. (2009) *Truth, Lies, and Trust on Internet*, Abingdon: Routledge.

Wisker, G. and Kiley, M. (2008) Learning to be a researcher: The concepts and crossings, in R. Land, J.H.F. Meyer and J. Smith (eds), *Threshold Concepts within the Disciplines* (399–414), Rotterdam: Sense Publishers.

Wisker, G., Kiley, M. and Aiston, S. (2006) Making the learning leap: Research students crossing conceptual thresholds, in M. Kiley and G. Mullins (eds), *Quality in Postgraduate Research: Knowledge Creation in Testing Times* (195–201), Canberra: Australian National University.

Williamson, B. (2014) Policy networks, database pedagogies, and the new spaces of algorithmic governance in education, in S. Bayne, C. Jones, M. de Laat, T. Ryberg and C. Sinclair (eds), *Proceedings of the 9th International Conference on Networked Learning*: 547–554.

Willig, C. (2001) *Qualitative Research in Psychology: A Practical Guide to Theory and Method*, Buckingham: Open University Press.

Willis, P. (2003) Foot soldiers of modernity: The dialectics of cultural consumption and the twenty-first-century school, *Harvard Educational Review*, 73 (3): 390–415.

Wood, C., Jackson, E., Hart., L., Plester, B. and Wilde, L. (2011a) The effect of text messaging on 9–10 year old children's reading, spelling and phonological awareness, *Journal of Computer Assisted Learning*, 27: 28–36.

Wood, C., Meacham, S., Bowyer, S., Jackson, E., Tarczynski-Bowles, M.L. and Plester, B. (2011b) A longitudinal study of the relationship between children's text messaging and literacy development, *British Journal of Psychology*, 102: 431–442.

Yee, N. (2006) The demographics, motivations and derived experiences of users of massively multi-user online graphical environments, *Presence*, 15 (3): 309–329.

Young, M.S, Robinson, S. and Alberts, P. (2009) Students pay attention! Combating the vigilance decrement to improve learning during lectures, *Active Learning in Higher Education*, 10 (1): 41–55.

Zepke, N. and Leach, L. (2010) Improving student engagement: Ten proposals for action, *Active Learning in Higher Education*, 11 (3): 167–177.

Zimmer, M. (2008) The externalities of Search 2.0: The emerging privacy threats when the drive for the perfect search engine meets Web 2.0, *First Monday*, 13 (3): 1–11. Online. Available http://firstmonday.org/article/view/2136/1944 (accessed 3 November 2014).

Žižek, S. (1998) The cyberspace real. Online. Available www.egs.edu/faculty/slavoj-zizek/articles/the-cyberspace-real/ (accessed 25 October 2014).

Žižek, S. (1999) The matrix, or two sides of perversion, *Philosophy Today*, 43. Online. Available www.nettime.org/Lists-Archives/nettime-l-9912/msg00019.html.

Žižek, S. (2005) *Interrogating the Real*, London: Continuum.

INDEX

academic voice 133
anime music video (AMV) 70
augmented reality 73–4, 88, 109
avatar 49, 57, 106, 109–111

benchmarking 19
Blackboard 41
blogs 12, 34, 60, 89, 106, 108, 111

cartographers on tour 2, 4, 103, 105
chatbots 74, 124–5, 137
Circuit warz 34
class difference 8, 82, 105
commodification 40–41, 43, 63, 94
commodity capitalism 136
conditions of flexibility 20–21
connectivist pedagogy 50, 85–6, 88–9
connectivity 5–7, 131

demographic factors 8, 131
digital capabilities 13, 34, 89, 92;
    connectivity i, 5–7, 49–50, 131; electracy
    3, 90–92; flow 133, 136; fluency 2–6, 21,
    49, 62, 76, 90–102, 131, 133; intervals
    135; knowledge 7, 132; learning i, 2, 5,
    15, 75, 87; literacy 3, 36, 76, 90–93;
    spaces i, 7, 10, 27, 33, 41, 84, 94, 96, 103,
    106
disciplinarity: and digital impact 13;
    learning context 55–6; 68, 80; specific
    content 12, 18–19, 21, 25, 30, 53, 66,
    132
discipline-based pedagogy 16, 19, 33, 45–6,
    52–3, 85, 104

disjunction 14, 25–6, 52–4
Dropbox 114

embodiment 39, 94, 109–110, 112
ethnicity differences 8; presentation 109

Facebook: authentic identity 107–8, 112,
    115; friends 94, 107, 113–14, 116, 119;
    illegal driving 1, 5; participatory culture
    4, 14, 82, 92, 102; posting on 74, 77, 89,
    123, 125; study group 12, 66, 81
flaming 126
friendship-driven genres of participation
    10–12, 14, 63, 66, 82–4, 113, 132
friendship identity 3, 80, 103, 112

gender differences 8, 10, 23, 72, 82, 109,
    131

hyperconnectivity 86, 88
hypersociality 136
hypertexter 131

Instagram 114
interactional stance 81

Kik 11

ladder of opportunity 8–9
league tables 25, 131
learner identity 10, 18, 26, 28, 40, 110,
    131–2
learning context 22, 40, 46, 47, 67, 103, 132;
    trajectories 3, 45, 101

learning spaces 21, 23, 33, 41, 58;
classification of 95; collaborative 3, 62;
new 2, 31, 91, 135–6, 138
liminal 3, 15, 62, 70, 80, 135
LinkedIn 107
liquid: books 47, 59–60; learning 12, 22, 30,
47, 53, 61, 99, 101, 138–9; learning
spaces 6, 8, 30, 44, 47, 102; modernity 30,
121; surveillance 121–2
liquidification 70–72
lurking 26, 41, 126

machinima 102
mixed: messages 78–9, 81; reality 109
mobile: learning 87; literacy 87
MOOCs 21, 41–3, 49–51
MOOLs 51
MySpace 110, 112–113, 119

networked society 1, 77, 108

parent: control 117; education 8, 131;
independence from 82, 84; links 12; skills
8, 66, 137; views/values held by 65, 73,
76–7, 80, 83
pedagogical agents 47–9, 72–4, 107
pirate code 32
podcast 47, 60, 114
political: debates 4, 130; forces 6; goals 67,
91; views 80, 94, 121, 137
politicians 124
politics 67, 73; participatory 137–8
posthumanism 73–4
posting 70, 74, 82, 89, 112, 116–17,
125–6
poststructuralist 73–4
PRISM 127
privacy 115–21, 124, 126–31, 136–7;
social 43, 69, 74, 79, 108
problem-based learning 65, 81, 101
problem-solving learning 9, 26, 80, 87
professional bodies 19

quality 19, 21, 25, 65, 68, 130, 132

race differences 8, 105, 109, 131
robot 49, 137

Search 2.0 121
Second Life 56, 57, 105
security 103, 114, 120, 127, 131; personal
79, 127
social networking sites: for friendship 11,
112–13; and identity 10, 125; learning 2;
media sharing 71, 94–5, 114; posting on
82; privacy issues 79, 115–16, 119,
121–2, 126, 128
student: access 20; autonomy 28; centred
learning 57–9, 62, 65, 68, 83; conceptions
of knowledge 17, 37, 98; criticality 9, 34,
42; and disciplinarity 19, 33–4, 46, 55, 80,
104; disjunction 14, 16; distraction 6, 15,
23, 131; engagement 2, 5–6, 10, 15, 21,
23–4; equipping 69–70, 80, 99;
expectation 15, 23, 25, 30, 32, 81;
feedback 47–8; identity 8, 104, 110–111;
needs 13, 26; retention 19, 24; satisfaction
2, 16, 25; spaces 2, 22, 31, 135; voiceless 26
surveillance 94, 107, 115–129; lateral 121,
123; participatory 121–3; social 117
suspicion 103, 130

tethered liquidity 138
threshold concepts 16, 18, 52
troublesome knowledge 24, 25, 25
Tumblr 71, 91
Twitter 88–9, 108, 110, 112, 120, 125, 127

young people: development of 4, 8–9,
13–15, 29, 63, 77–86; engagement 7–8,
10, 13–15, 28, 76; friendship 12–14, 23,
29, 63, 81–6; negative effect on 1, 5, 8–9,
12, 36, 64, 71; support of 8, 13–14, 52, 86
YouTube 4, 7, 14, 62, 70, 89, 102, 125

virtual learning environment (VLE) 27, 30,
41, 122, 133
virtual reality 56, 104, 139

Whackademia 133
Whatsapp 11, 66, 81, 96
Wikileaks 124–5
Wikipedia 13, 136
wikis 60
wizardry 129, 139